Lecture Notes in Computer Science   8846

Commenced Publication in 1973
Founding and Former Series Editors:
Gerhard Goos, Juris Hartmanis, and Jan van Leeuwen

Yvon Kermarrec (Ed.)

Advances in Communication Networking

20th EUNICE/IFIP EG 6.2, 6.6
International Workshop
Rennes, France, September 1–5, 2014
Revised Selected Papers

 Springer

Editor
Yvon Kermarrec
Institut Mines Telecom
École National Supérieure des
    Télécommunications
Brest Cedex
France

ISSN 0302-9743   ISSN 1611-3349   (electronic)
Lecture Notes in Computer Science
ISBN 978-3-319-13487-1   ISBN 978-3-319-13488-8   (eBook)
DOI 10.1007/978-3-319-13488-8

Library of Congress Control Number: 2014956528

LNCS Sublibrary: SL3 – Information Systems and Applications, incl. Internet/Web, and HCI

Springer Cham Heidelberg New York Dordrecht London

Printed on acid-free paper

Springer International Publishing AG Switzerland is part of Springer Science+Business Media
(www.springer.com)

Preface

The 20th edition of the EUNICE summer school and conference is part of a series of annual international conferences devoted to the promotion and advancement of all aspects of Information and Communication Technologies. The main objective of these events is to provide a forum to promote educational and research cooperation between its member institutions and foster the mobility of students, faculty members, and research scientists working in the field of information and communication technologies.

This edition marked a return to France by selecting the splendid venue of Brittany, a region marked by its history with a strong Celtic tradition and a remote location at the western tip of the EU continent that was the initiator of many innovations and disruptive technologies in the telecommunication and network domains. Télécom Bretagne was the location of the very first edition of the events back in 1994 and we are proud to celebrate the 20th edition.

Following its usual style, the conference included a three-day technical program, where the papers contained in these proceedings were presented. Papers were received from various parts of Europe and the EUNICE community. The technical program was then followed by two tutorial days where attendants had the opportunity to catch up on issues related to new trends in software engineering for telecommunication and big data.

The conference features three distinguished keynote speakers, who delivered state-of-the-art information on related topics of great importance, both for the present and future of telecommunication systems:

- Prosper Chemouil, from Orange Labs, delivered a talk on "Network management trends for future networks."
- Nora and Frédéric Cuppens, from Institut Mines Télécom, delivered a talk on "Multilevel response systems to maintain information in optimal security Conditions."

We would like to express our sincere gratitude to these distinguished speakers for sharing their insights and views with the conference participants.

The conference also included an interesting selection of tutorials, featuring well-known experts, who presented introductory and advanced material in the scope of the conference and summer school:

- Vanea Chiprianov, from Université de Pau, France, gave a tutorial on "How modeling techniques can address new service creation and deal with complexity."
- Emmanuel Bertin, from Orange Labs in Caen, France, continued this previous tutorial with "New services: an IT and operator view."
- Erwan Le Merrer, from Technicolor, Rennes, France gave a tutorial on big data issues: "Storage + processing: data crunching at the big data age."

We wish to extend our gratitude to these experts, for the work they put in preparing and presenting these contents during the summer school, and for their dedication to train PhD students to these challenging domains.

The 20th edition of the EUNICE conference and summer school was made possible through the generous support of "Conseil Régional de Bretagne" and "Institut Mines Télécom." Their names and logos appear on the conference web site.

We would like to thank the effort and contribution of the Technical Program Committee for their careful and precise reviews of the submitted papers, and for the insightful comments they provided to the authors, guidance for their future work, and suggestion to improve their research. EasyChair was used throughout the various phases of the conference calls and proceedings and we did appreciate this great support environment.

The organization committee was led by Mrs. Ghislaine Le Gall, who coordinated and worked very hard to make the conference a success and in helping us with the intricate and complex details of the organization.

Finally, we also thank the authors of the contributions submitted to the conference, and all the participants who helped in achieving the goal of the conference: to provide a forum for young researchers for the exchange of information and ideas about ICT. We hope they all enjoyed the program as well as the social events of the 20th edition of the EUNICE conference and summer school.

August 2014   Yvon Kermarrec

Organization

Program Committee

Finn Arve Aagesen	Norwegian University of Science and Technology, Norway
Thomas Bauschert	TU Chemnitz, Germany
Alberto Blanc	Télécom Bretagne, France
Jean Marie Bonnin	Télécom Bretagne, France
Rolv Braek	Norwegian University of Science and Technology, Norway
Ana Cavalli	GET/INT, France
Vanea Chiprianov	Université de Pau, France
Joerg Eberspaecher	Technische Universität München, Germany
Annie Gravey	Télécom Bretagne, France
Martin Heusse	ENSIMAG, France
Yvon Kermarrec	GET/ENST Bretagne, France
Thomas Knoll	TU Chemnitz, Germany
Paul J. Kuehn	University of Stuttgart/IKR, Germany
Ralf Lehnert	TU Dresden, Germany
Miquel Oliver	Universitat Pompeu Fabra, Spain
Laurent Pautet	Télécom ParisTech, France
Aiko Pras	University of Twente, The Netherlands
Peter Reichl	Universität Wien, Austria
Sebastia Sallent	Universitat Politècnica de Catalunya, Spain
Robert Szabo	Budapest University of Technology and Economics, Hungary

Additional Reviewers

Domingo, Mari Carmen	Radeke, Rico	Robles, Jorge
Landmark, Lars	Remondo, David	Santanna, Jair
Metzger, Florian	Richter, Volker	Schmidt, Ricardo
Nguyen, Huu Nghia	Rincon, David	Toumi, Khalifa
Øverby, Harald	Rivera, Diego	

Contents

An Orchestrator-Based SDN Framework with Its Northbound Interface

Amin Aflatoonian[1,2](✉), Ahmed Bouabdallah[2], Vincent Catros[1],
Karine Guillouard[1], and Jean-Marie Bonnin[2]

[1] Orange Labs, Rennes, France
{amin.aflatoonian,vincent.catros,karine.guillouard}@orange.com
[2] TELECOM Bretagne, Cesson Sévigné, France
{amin.aflatoonian,ahmed.bouabdallah,jm.bonnin}@telecom-bretagne.eu

Abstract. Software Defined Networking (SDN) is deemed to empower next generation network and cloud services in several aspects. The authors argue that its high flexibility can be exploited not only in retrieving services efficiently but also in yielding new ones by introducing programming capabilities on its top. This however requires to structure its northbound interface (NBI) with an abstract application programming interface (API), the definition of which is actually one of the SDN challenges.

We propose in this paper a global analysis of the capabilities of the NBI of the SDN articulated to a generic but simple double sided model of service lifecycle. Its analysis determines interesting properties of the NBI leading to precisely identify the associated API. We derive from this service lifecycle a general framework structuring the internal architecture of the SDN in two orchestrators dedicated respectively to the management of services and resources. Our approach which provides a firm foundation for the implementation of the NBI is illustrated with an example.

Keywords: Software Defined Networking (SDN) · Service orchestrator · Northbound Interface (NBI) · SDN framework

1 Introduction

Nowadays Internet whose number of users approaches 2,7 billions [20], is massively used in all human activities from the professional part to the private ones via academical ones, administrative ones, etc. The infrastructure supporting the Internet services rests on various interconnected communication networks managed by network operators. This continuously growing infrastructure evolves very dynamically and becomes quite huge, complex, and sometimes locally ossified. To configure and maintain their communication networks and provide high-level services, network operators have therefore to deal with a large number of routers, firewalls, switches and various heterogeneous devices with a progressively reduced lifecycle due to the fast hardware and software changes. This growing complexity makes the introduction of a new service or a new protocol together

© Springer International Publishing Switzerland 2014
Y. Kermarrec (Ed.): EUNICE 2014, LNCS 8846, pp. 1–13, 2014.
DOI: 10.1007/978-3-319-13488-8_1

with its configuration, an exceptionally difficult task, because network operators have to translate a high-level service specification to low-level distributed device configurations and next to configure these ones through their command line interface (CLI). This introduction have non trivial side effects leading to frequent network state changes for which operators have to adapt manually the existing network configuration to integrate the new services or protocols. As a result, this manual configuration may lead to frequent misconfigurations [16]. Last but not least, all these may have an adverse effect on the management cost of the operator (OPEX).

One of the main origins of the problem comes from the heterogeneous, decentralized and proprietary based control plane of the network. Indeed, each network device usually merges the control and the data plane in a proprietary box. Moving the control function out of the data plane element leads to an interesting two layer-based architecture. The potential benefits of such a separation have been explored in many previous studies. The 4D architecture [13], for example, separates completely an Autonomous System (AS) decision logic from the protocols governing the interactions among network elements. In this approach the routers and switches simply forward packets. This principle of decorrelating the control plane from the data one has indeed many advantages: it allows each one to evolve independently and with a high flexibility, moreover the vendor-agnostic control plane is programmable and provides a centralized network view. This approach leads to the development of a new promising network paradigm called Software Defined Networking (SDN) exploiting such a separation [17].

The main benefits brought by SDN rest on the centralized implementation of the entity managing the control plane which is usually called network controller [21]. Its interacting capabilities with the controlled network devices are done through the southbound interface (SBI) and have several advantages. Firstly, the programmability of the network straightforwardly follows from its centralized nature. It is clear that the introduction of new changes in the network through a program is easier than manually modifying the network using proprietary CLI of heterogeneous network devices. Secondly, observing the global network state, in a centralized way, allows the setting-up of precious knowledge exploited by the management program to optimize network traffic forwarding decisions. Nowadays, numerous commercial and non-commercial communities are developing SDN controllers, e.g. Controllers such as NOX [14], Beacon [12], Maestro [9], Floodlight [4], OpenDayLight [6]. It is worth noting that OpenFlow [19], proposed by Open Networking Foundation (ONF) [1], is the only standardized protocol implementing the SBI. Another interesting feature of the SDN concerns the capability to provide to third party applications an abstract view of the forwarding plane and of the network state. By interacting with different network devices, the controller may extract information and present through the northbound interface (NBI) an abstract view to network applications, such as load balancing and VLAN provisioning. This interface permits a rich synergy between the network and its applications. Network applications may conversely use the network abstraction to achieve the desired network behavior without knowledge of detailed physical network configuration. Supplying network information to the application, in order to reduce transition costs while improving applications performance, was proposed by the P4P framework [22]. In order to provide a network abstraction view, the IETF standardized a protocol for Application Layer Traffic Optimization (ALTO) [3]. The abstracted view is provided by the map of network regions and a ranking for connections between them. The work [15], also proposes the use of ALTO as a source of network topology and information to manipulate network state.

It is clear that, on one hand, an SDN based network management by significantly reducing the workload of network configurations, directly improves the operator's OPEX and CAPEX (Capital expenditure). On the other hand, we argue that the full potential of SDN is far from being reached specially when considering the actually unexploited capabilities associated to the NBI. Indeed, in all the existing SDN controllers implementation [4,6,9,12,14] in order to make some modifications in the underlying network, an application (e.g. clients, orchestrators, admin, etc.) pushes some parameters via a REpresentational State Transfer (REST) interface into the NBI of the SDN controller. In order to govern the underlying network, existing controllers benefit a set of application blocks implementing basic network functions such as topology manager, switch manager, etc. To implement a service on an SDN based network, operators face a large number of controllers each one using a specific configuration work flow. This diversity of accesses to controllers through NBI prevents pooling processes which are fundamentally the same management tasks, if we consider them with the correct abstraction. It means that we finally moved from heterogeneous proprietary network devices to a miscellaneous SDN controllers world. It appears that providing a service abstraction on the top of the SDN controller may directly improve the network management. Nowadays, developing the right abstractions is one of the SDN challenges. This problematic has at our knowledge been once addressed by Tail-F who proposes a partial proprietary solution [10]. In order to reduce the Operation Support System (OSS) cost and also the time-to-market of services, Tail-F Network Control System (NCS) [2] introduces an abstraction layer on the top of the NBI in order to implement different services, including layer 2 or layer 3 VPN. It addresses an automated chain from the service request, on one hand, to the device configuration deployment in the network, on the other hand. This solution uses the YANG data model [8] in order to transform the informal service model to a formal one. The service model is mapped into device configurations as a data model transformation. The proposed work doesn't however cover all management phases of the service lifecycle, specially service monitoring, maintenance, etc. Due to the proprietary nature of this product it is not possible to precisely analyze its internal structure.

We present in this paper a comprehensive solution to this problematic by identifying a reasonable set of capabilities of the NBI of the SDN together with the associated Application Programming Interfaces (API). Our first contribution rests on a global analysis of an abstract model of the operator platform articulated to a generic but simple service lifecycle, described in Sect. 2, which takes into account the view of the user together with that of the operator. Tackling the service lifecycle following these two sides simplifies the service abstraction design. The first viewpoint allows us to identify the APIs structuring the NBI and shared by both actors (operator and service consumer). By analyzing the second viewpoint we determine a model of the operator platform based on SDN which constitutes our second contribution. This platform model is abstracted through a framework involving a minimal set of functions required to manage any network service. We organize this set of functions in two orchestrators, one dedicated exclusively to the management of the resources: the resource orchestrator, and the other one grouping the remaining functions: the service orchestrator. The general framework structuring the internal architecture of SDN is presented in Sect. 3 and illustrated with an example. This framework is externally limited by NBI and SBI and internally clarifies the border between the two orchestrators by identifying an internal interface between them, called the middle interface. Finally, in the Sect. 4 we conclude the paper and outline some future works.

2   SDN Service LifeCycle Analysis

The ability of managing the lifecycle of a service is essential to implement it in an operator platform. Existing service lifecycle frameworks are oriented on human-driven services. For example, if a client needs to introduce or change an existing service, the operator has to configure the service manually. This manual config-uration may take hours or sometimes days. It may therefore significantly affect the operators OPEX. It clearly appears that the operator has to re-think about its service implementation in order to provision dynamically and also to develop on-demand services. There are proposals in order to enhance new on-demand net-work resource provisioning. For instance, the GYESERS project [11], proposed a complex service lifecycle model for on-demand service provisioning. This model includes five typical stages, namely service requests/Service Level Agreement (SLA) negotiation, composition/reservation, deployment/register and synchro-nization, operation (monitoring), decommissioning. The main drawback of this model rests on its inherent complexity. We argue this one may be reduced by splitting the global service lifecycle in two complementary and manageable view points: client and operator view. Each one of both views captures only the infor-mation useful for the associated actor. The global view may however be obtained by composing the two partial views. We present below a detailed description of these two views together with the associated global view.

2.1   The Client View

Client-Side Service Lifecycle. The client-side service lifecycle is illustrated in Fig. 1. This service lifecycle consists of four main steps:

– Service creation: The client specifies the service characteristics she needs, she negotiates the associated SLA which will be available for limited duration and finally she requests a new service creation.

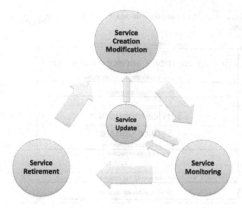

Fig. 1. Client-side service lifecycle

- Service monitoring: Once created, the service may be used by the client for the negotiated duration. The service consummation which concerns the client's work-flow induces it's monitoring with statistics production in order to control its exploitation.
- Service modification: The client may request the modification of some parts of the existing service because of a new need. Its treatment is globally similar to the service creation request.
- Service update: The management of the operator's network may lead to the update of the service which can be issued because of a problem occurring during the service consummation or a modification of the network infrastructure. This update may be minimal or it may impact the previous steps, with consequences on the service creation and/or on the service consummation.
- Service retirement: The client retires the service at the end of the negotiated duration. This step defines the end of the service life.

The Northbound Interface. The client-side service lifecycle is carried with interactions between the client's service portal and the operator platform through the northbound interface (NBI). Our approach generalizes the classical SDN one where the NBI defines the interface which interconnects the client-side application with the SDN controller [17,21].

Figure 2 gives an overview of the communication between the service portal and the operator system through the NBI. This communication is divided in two main types: top-down and bottom-up, each one composed of requests acknowledged by responses or of notifications.

- Top-down communication rests on a set of messages initiated from the service portal to the operator system. This message family includes service creation, modification, retirement and monitoring requests.
- Bottom-up communication consists of a set of update notifications and update request messages initiated from the operator system to the service portal. An

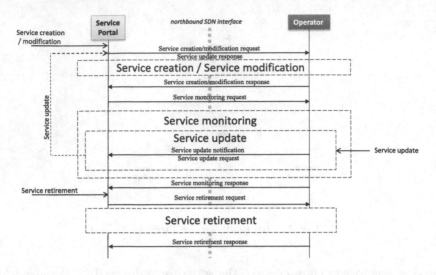

Fig. 2. Client-side service control

update notification allows to inform the client while an update request message should alter the current behavior of the service.

Figure 2 presents detailed steps of a generic call flow involving all the client-side service lifecycle.

1. In the first step the client requests a new service creation or a modification of an existing one. This step will ended with a response occurring when the service is implemented in the operator's platform.
2. During the service consummation phase, the client may request the monitoring of the service. A service update initiated by the operator may also happen. If this update is minor it just leads to a service update notification. Otherwise, it may trigger a service update request sent to the client, as for example for an update of the operator's network (software, hardware, etc.). The client acknowledges it with a service update response and initiates the service lifecycle from the beginning.
3. Finally, in the end of the service life, the client requests the service retirement.

The NBI will be implemented with help of an API distributed between the service portal and the operator system. The operator one's is structured into two packages implementing service management control functions:

– One package dedicated to implement service creation, modification and retirement functions and,
– One package focusing on service monitoring functions.

The API located at the service portal consists of a single package that manages the service update functions. The analysis of this API is currently under

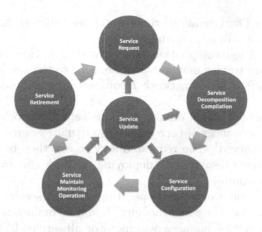

Fig. 3. Operator-side Service lifecycle

progress. We will publish in a subsequent paper [7] an original and comprehensive specification of this API not resting on the REST paradigm.

2.2 The Operator View

Operator-Side Service Lifecycle. Figure 3 shows the operator-side service lifecycle which is composed in six main processes:

– Service request: Once a service creation or modification request arrives from the user's service portal, the request manager negotiates the SLA and service specification in order to implement it. It is worth noting that before agreeing the SLA the operator should ensure that the existing resources can cope

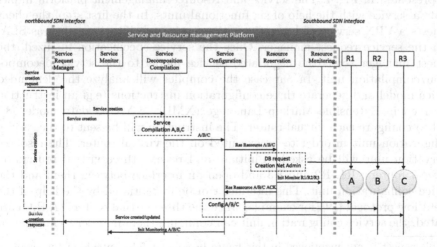

Fig. 4. Operator-side Service Creation Call Flow

with the requested service at the time it will be deployed. In case of unavailability, the request will be enqueued.

- Service decomposition, compilation: The requested service is decomposed into several elementary service models which are sent to the service compiler. The compiler generates a set of network resource configurations which compose that service.
- Service configuration: Based on the previous set of network resource configurations, several instances of corresponding virtual resources will be created, initialized and reserved[1]. The requested service can then be implemented on these created virtual resources by deploying network resource configurations generated by the compiler.
- Service maintain, monitoring and operation: Once a service is implemented, its availability, performance and capacity should be maintained automatically. In parallel, a service log manager will monitor all service lifecycle.
- Service update: During the service exploitation the network infrastructure may necessitate changes due to some execution problems or technical evolution requirements, etc. It leads to update which may impact the service in different way. The update may be transparent to the service or it may require to re-initiate a part of the first steps of the service lifecycle.
- Service retirement: The service configuration will be retired from the infrastructure as soon as a retirement request arrives to the system. The service retirement issued by the operator is out of the scope of this paper.

Illustrating Example. We describe the main processes through the example of a Virtual Private Network (VPN) service connecting three remote sites (assured by virtual routers: A, B and C) of a client connected to physical routers: R1, R2 and R3. The first step of the service lifecycle which consists in the "Service Creation" gives rise in the nominal case to a call flow the details of which are presented in Fig. 4. The service and resource management platform implements a service with the help of six functional units. In the first step, the client requests a VPN service and negotiates the service specifications, such as SLA, with the service request manager. Once the service specification finalized, the request manager sends the negotiated service model to the service decomposition/compilation unit. In our case the compiler will analyze the demanded service model and generate three configuration instructions (e.g. an instruction described in Extensible Markup Language (XML) or YANG data model [8]) used to configure each virtual router. The instruction will be sent to the service configuration unit in order to be executed on the virtual router. The resource reservation unit will be asked to initiate and reserve three virtual routers on physical routers: R1, R2 and R3 and open an interface between them and the service configuration unit. This interface can be instantiated by the help of the OpenFlow protocol [19], for example. Once the three virtual routers (A,B,C) are created, the service configuration unit can configure them in order to implement

---

[1] This aspect is not mentioned in this figure because it falls outside of the scope of the service lifecycle.

the demanded service. This unit can manage the virtual routers by the help of a remote configuration and management protocol (e.g. OF-Config [5]). Once the service is implemented, the service monitoring unit will be informed to monitor the service in its lifecycle. Finally the client will be informed about the service implementation through the request manager. As is mentioned previously the service portal will interact with the operator's system through the northbound interface. The resource monitoring and resource reservation units manage the underlying physical resources via the southbound interface.

2.3 The Global View

The global service lifecycle is the combination of two service lifecycles explained in Sects. 2.1 and 2.2. Figure 5 illustrates the interactions between these two service lifecycles. During the service run-time the client and the operator interact with each other using the NBI. This interface interconnects different phases of each part, as described below:

- Service creation and Modification ↔ Service request, decomposition, compilation and configuration: the client-side service creation and specification phase leads to three first phases of the service lifecycle in the operator side; service request, decomposition, compilation and configuration.
- Service monitoring ↔ Service maintain, monitoring and operating: client-side service monitoring, which is executed during the service consummation, is in parallel with operator-side service maintain, monitoring and operation.
- Service update ↔ Service update: operator-side service maintain, monitoring and operation phase may lead to the service update phase in the client-side service lifecycle.

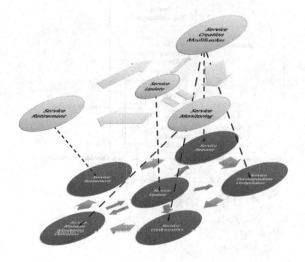

Fig. 5. Global service lifecycle

– Service retirement ↔ Service retirement: In the end of the service life, the client-side service retirement phase will be executed in parallel with the operator-side service retirement.

3   Proposed Framework

In this section we propose to implement the operator-side lifecycle through two orchestration units. The "service orchestrator" will be dedicated to the service part (request, compilation/composition, configuration, maintain, monitoring, operation and retirement), while the "resource orchestrator" will manage resource reservation and resource monitor. The proposed framework is illustrated in Fig. 6. The model is composed of two main orchestration layers:

– Service Orchestration
– Resource Orchestration

Service Orchestrator (SO): This orchestrator has to receive service orders and initiate their establishment by decomposing complex service requests to elementary service models. These ones allow it to derive the type and the size of resources needed in order to implement that service. The SO will demand the virtual resource reservation from the lower layer and deploy the service configuration on the virtual resources.

Resource Orchestrator (RO): This orchestrator which manages physical resources, will reserve and initiate virtual resources on-demand. It maintains and

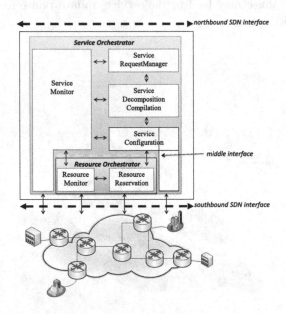

Fig. 6. Proposed SDN framework

monitors physical resources using southbound interface. The interface can be implemented by existing protocols/drivers, such as: onePK [18] and OpenFlow protocol.

The first orchestrator, SO, consists of four main functions as mentioned in Fig. 6. The request manager handles client's service request and negotiates the service specifications, such as Service Level Agreement (SLA). A service can be an elementary service known by the orchestrator or a composition of several elementary services. The orchestrator will break-down all received service demands to one or several elementary service models. Once the elementary service model is produced, the service compiler will extract resource configurations needed to deploy that service. For example, in our case, described in Sect. 2.2, the compiler receives the VPN configuration, discovers virtual routers needed to implement that service and finally generates some configuration instructions (e.g. an instruction described in XML or YANG data model) used to configure the virtual routers. The service configuration unit is used in order to configure resources using these instructions. It may use a location database to find the appropriate router concerning the configuration. If a resource is missing the RO will be requested to initiate it by creating a virtual instance on the physical infrastructure. In the service run-time, the RO monitors and maintains the physical equipments that are hosting several virtual resources. It doesn't have any perspective of running configuration of each virtual resource and it just keeps in mind the physical configuration to ensure the resource performance. If the RO faces an issue it will inform the problem to the SO that is consuming the resource. The service run-time lifecycle and performance is monitored by the SO. When it faces an upcoming alarm sent by the RO or a service run-time problem occurring on virtual resources, it will either perform some task to resolve the problem autonomously or send an alarm to the service consumer application.

Generally this framework contains three interfaces, one is the southbound interface which interconnects the RO to the physical infrastructure and the SO to it's virtual resources. The second is the northbound interface which is used for service request and monitoring phases of service lifecycle. Inter-orchestrator (middle) interfaces which interconnect one SO to several ROs and vice versa may be used to implement a distributed orchestration architecture.

4   Conclusion

In this paper, we proposed a model of the NBI together with the associated API. The model is issued from a double sided service lifecycle which has been also used to define a SDN framework. This one structures in a modular way the internal architecture of the SDN in two orchestrators dedicated respectively to the management of services and resources. The proposed framework is externally limited by NBI and SDI and internally clarifies the border between the two orchestrators by identifying an internal interface between them, called the middle interface, which provides a virtual resource abstraction layer on the top the resource orchestrator. Our approach gives the foundation for the rigorous definition of the SDN architecture. It will be used to implement in a future work the NBI and the middle interface. It will help us to explore the distribution of the resource orchestrator.

References

1. ONF Open Networking Foundation. https://www.opennetworking.org/
2. Tail-f network control system (ncs) datasheet (2012). http://www.tail-f.com/wordpress/wp-content/uploads/2014/01/Tail-f-Datasheet-NCS.pdf
3. Application-layer traffic optimization (alto), ietf (2014). http://datatracker.ietf.org/wg/alto/charter/
4. Floodlight openflow controller (2014). http://www.projectfloodlight.org/floodlight
5. ONF Open Networking Foundation: OpenFlow management and configuration protocol (Octobre 2014), OF-Config 1.2
6. Opendaylight — a linux foundation collaborative project, technical overview (2014). http://www.opendaylight.org/project/technical-overview
7. Aflatoonian, A., Bouabdallah, A., Catros, V., Guillouard, K., Bonnin, J.M.: An asynchronous push/pull solution for Northbound Interface of SDN based on XMPP - Work on progress (2014)
8. Bjorklund, M.: YANG - a data modeling language for the network configuration protocol (NETCONF) (October 2010), RFC 6020
9. Cai, Z., Cox, A.L., Ng, T.S.E.: Maestro: a system for scalable openflow control. Technical report TR10-08, Rice University (2010)
10. Caroline, C.: Creating the programmable network, the business case for netconf/yang in network devices, October 2011. http://www.tail-f.com/wordpress/wp-content/uploads/2013/10/HR-Tail-f-NETCONF-WP-10-08-13.pdf
11. Demchenko, Y., Chen, X.: Gyesers project, service delivery framework and services lifecycle management in on-demand services/resources provisioning. wp2/wp3 technical document, version 0.2, March 2012
12. Erickson, D.: The beacon openflow controller. In: Proceedings of the Second ACM SIGCOMM Workshop on Hot Topics in Software Defined Networking. HotSDN '13, pp. 13–18. ACM, New York (2013). http://doi.acm.org/10.1145/2491185.2491189
13. Greenberg, A., Hjalmtysson, G., Maltz, D.A., Myers, A., Rexford, J., Xie, G., Yan, H., Zhan, J., Zhang, H.: A clean slate 4d approach to network control and management. SIGCOMM Comput. Commun. Rev. **35**(5), 41–54 (2005). http://doi.acm.org/10.1145/1096536.1096541
14. Gude, N., Koponen, T., Pettit, J., Pfaff, B., Casado, M., McKeown, N., Shenker, S.: NOX: towards an operating system for networks. SIGCOMM Comput. Commun. Rev. **38**(3), 105–110 (2008). http://doi.acm.org/10.1145/1384609.1384625
15. Gurbani, V., Scharf, M., Lakshman, T.V., Hilt, V., Marocco, E.: Abstracting network state in software defined networks (sdn) for rendezvous services. In: 2012 IEEE International Conference on Communications (ICC), pp. 6627–6632, June 2012
16. Joseph, D.A., Tavakoli, A., Stoica, I.: A policy-aware switching layer for data centers. In: Proceedings of the ACM SIGCOMM 2008 Conference on Data Communication. SIGCOMM '08, pp. 51–62. ACM, New York (2008). http://doi.acm.org/10.1145/1402958.1402966

17. Lantz, B., Heller, B., McKeown, N.: A network in a laptop: rapid prototyping for software-defined networks. In: Proceedings of the 9th ACM SIGCOMM Workshop on Hot Topics in Networks. Hotnets-IX, pp. 19:1–19:6. ACM, New York (2010). http://doi.acm.org/10.1145/1868447.1868466

18. McKeown, N., et al.: Cisco open network environment: bring the network closer to applications, white paper, July 2013

19. McKeown, N., Anderson, T., Balakrishnan, H., Parulkar, G., Peterson, L., Rexford, J., Shenker, S., Turner, J.: Openflow: enabling innovation in campus networks. SIGCOMM Comput. Commun. Rev. **38**(2), 69–74 (2008). http://doi.acm.org/10.1145/1355734.1355746

20. Sanou, B.: ICT facts and figures, the world in 2013. http://www.itu.int/en/ITU-D/Statistics/Documents/facts/ICTFactsFigures2013-e.pdf

21. Shin, M.K., Nam, K.H., Kim, H.J.: Software-defined networking (sdn): a reference architecture and open apis. In: 2012 International Conference on ICT Convergence (ICTC), pp. 360–361, October 2012

22. Xie, H., Krishnamurthy, A., Silberschatz, A., Yang, R.Y.: P4P: explicit communications for cooperative control between P2P and network providers. http://www.dcia.info/documents/P4P_Overview.pdf

A Tabu Search Optimization for Multicast Provisioning in Mixed-Line-Rate Optical Networks

Mohamed Amine Ait-Ouahmed[✉] and Fen Zhou

CERI-LIA, University of Avignon, Agroparc, BP 1228, Avignon, France
amine_aitouahmed@hotmail.com, fen.zhou@univ-avignon.fr

Abstract. Mixed-Line-Rate (MLR) optical networks provide the flexibility for satisfying heterogeneous traffic demands. However, the existence of multiple line rates makes the network planning problem more complicated. In this paper, we aim at minimizing the network cost (the joint cost of transponder, wavelength channel usage and the number of used wavelengths) for provisioning multiple multicast sessions simultaneously in MLR optical networks. Two distinct methods are proposed to optimize the network cost: A novel path-based integer linear program (ILP) and a tabu search based heuristic algorithm. Simulation results validate our proposed methods and demonstrate that our tabu search based method is able to compute a near-optimal multicast provision strategy.

Keywords: Optical networks · Mixed Line Rate (MLR) · Multicast provisioning · Tabu search · Integer Linear Programming (ILP) · Light-tree · Lightpath

1 Introduction

In mixed-line-rate optical networks, multiple line rates are available for carrying network traffic with the help of different modulation techniques, for instance 10, 40, and 100 Gbps [1]. As transponder costs and maximum reaches are different for each line rate, using the combination of different line rates for establishing optical communications may help to greatly reduce the network cost. This is why optical networks with mixed line rates are more attractive compared to that of single line rate, especially for satisfying heterogeneous network traffics. All-optical multicasting is an ideal technique for carrying bandwidth-harvest traffic in core networks (e.g. aggregated video traffic or huge data center migration traffic [5]), since it is able to provide a huge bandwidth and achieve the lowest delay [7] by keeping the signal in the optical domain along a light-path or a light-tree [3,10,11]. However, supporting all-optical multicasting is a challenging work in optical networks with mixed line rates. The co-existence of multiple line rates adds a third dimension for network optimization (i.e. line rate selection for each lightpath or a light-tree) in addition to the traditional two dimensions (i.e. routing and wavelength assignment) [9]. Thus, Multicast Routing and Wavelength

© Springer International Publishing Switzerland 2014
Y. Kermarrec (Ed.): EUNICE 2014, LNCS 8846, pp. 14–25, 2014.
DOI: 10.1007/978-3-319-13488-8_2

Assignment with the presence of Mixed Line Rates (MRWA-MLR) becomes a new critical optimization problem for optical network planning.

The multicast routing and wavelength assignment problem for single line rate optical networks has been deeply studied [3,10,11]. Their objective is to find a set of light-trees for satisfying all multicast requests while minimizing the wavelength channel cost or cutting energy consumption. Since these works did not consider the fact that a wavelength can operate at different line rates with different maximum reaches, they can not be reused for solving the MRWA-MLR problem. To the best of our knowledge, [4,9] are the only two papers dealing with the MRWA-MLR problem. Paper [4] proposed a heuristic algorithm to provision static multicast communications in mixed-line-rate Ethernet-Over-WDM networks. As the proposal is only for Ethernet, it is not suitable for WDM core networks. This is because the maximum reach constraint is not considered. Recently, we just propose an ILP model to formulate the MRWA-MLR problem in [9]. However, this model is time consuming and not able to give a solution for networks with up to 11 nodes. Thus, a time-efficient and effective heuristic algorithm is required for provisioning multicast communications with mixed line rates. This motivates our current work.

In this paper, we aim at minimizing the joint network cost while satisfying multiple multicast sessions simultaneously in MLR optical networks. The considered joint network cost involves the transponder cost, wavelength channel usage and the number of used wavelengths. To this end, two distinct methods are proposed: a novel path-based ILP formulation and a tabu search based meta-heuristic algorithm. The proposed new ILP model adopts the concept of using a set of light-paths to form light-trees, while the ILP model [9] constructs directly light-trees. However, both models do not scale with the network size. Thus, a tabu search based method is proposed to optimize the network cost in a reasonable time. Simulation results demonstrate that our tabu search based method is able to compute a near optimal solution for provisioning multicast communications in mixed line rate optical networks. It is also scalable with the network size.

We organize the rest of the paper as follows. The multicast routing and wavelength assignment problem considering multiple line rates is presented in Sect. 2. Then, we propose a novel path-based ILP model to formulate the problem in Sect. 3. A tabu search based meta-heuristic algorithm is proposed to solve the problem for big optical networks in Sect. 4. Simulations are conducted in Sect. 5 to compare the exact solution and the approximated solutions. Finally, the paper is concluded in Sect. 6.

2   Multicast Provisioning in Optical Networks with Mixed Line Rates

All-optical multicasting is an efficient technique for satisfying bandwidth-harvest and delay-critical traffic (e.g. the aggregated traffic of high definition IPTV, or Video conference and etc.). Dimensioning optical networks with multicast traffic is a hard work, especially for optical networks with mixed line rates, what needs to be investigated. In this section, we first give the optical network model and then present the multicast provisioning problem with mixed line rates.

2.1   MLR Optical Network Model

We consider a transparent optical network with mixed line rates. Thus, no regenerator is assumed. We model the studied optical network as a symmetric digraph $G(V, E)$, where V denotes the set of optical cross-connects (OXCs) and E represents the set of links between them. Two links are deployed between two adjacent OXCs with each one for an opposite direction communication. We use d_{uv} to denote the length of a directed link from OXC u to v. All optical links support the same set of wavelengths (noted W) and the same set of line rates (noted R), e.g., $R = \{10, 40, 100\,\text{Gbps}\}$. A transponder working at one line rate $r \in R$ is required to enable a source-to-destination communication in a lightpath or a light-tree. We dispose different line rates, but their maximum reaches are different and so are their costs. The *maximum reach* of a line rate r is denoted by H_r. As reported in [1], the maximum reaches are $H_{10} = 1750\,\text{km}$, $H_{40} = 1800\,\text{km}$ and $H_{100} = 900\,\text{km}$ for line rate $10/40/100\,\text{Gbps}$ respectively, when the MLR optical network is dispersion-minimized for 10 Gbps. We should note that higher maximum reach is achieved by 40 Gbps line rate than 10 Gbps in the considered networks [1,8]. In [6], they also define the normalized transponder cost C_r as follows: $\{C_{10} = 1, C_{40} = 2.5, C_{100} = 3.75\}$. Furthermore, we consider huge traffic demand in optical networks. Let S be the set of multicast source OXCs. We assume that multiple multicast communications $\{(s, D_s, B_s) : s \in S, D_s \subset V\}$ arrive at the same time. For a multicast communication originated from source s, D_s is the set of involved destination OXCs, and B_s is the required bandwidth, which is generally bigger than the bandwidth of the highest line rate. Thus a multicast communication may need to use multiple line rates at the same time to satisfy the bandwidth requirement.

2.2   MRWA-MLR Optimization Problem

We study the problem of provisioning multiple multicast sessions simultaneously in optical networks with mixed line rates. Our objective is to minimize the joint network cost, which can be a linear combination of transponder cost for supporting different line rates, the wavelength channel usage, and the number of used wavelengths. The co-efficiency of different costs may be defined the network operator to reduce the real network deployment cost. The advantage of using mixed line rates is that it enables us to satisfy heterogeneous traffic demands efficiently. But, it also increases the network optimization complexity. Thus, when solving the MRWA-MLR problem, one should take into account the following three subproblems:

- (a) Multicast Routing with light-trees or lightpaths.
- (b) Line rate Assignment for light-trees or lightpaths.
- (c) Wavelength Assignment for light-trees or lightpaths

We suppose that light-splitters are available on all OXCs in the network. This enables any OXC to support all-optical multicasting. The wavelength conversion is not considered due to its high cost and hardware complexity. In subproblem (a), several light-trees may be required to satisfy the bandwidth requirement. A light-tree should use the same wavelength and operate at the same line rate over all links. In subproblem (b), the depth of a light-tree, or the length of a lightpath should be bounded to support a certain line rate. Finally, the distinct wavelength constraint (i.e. two light-trees should be allocated with distinct wavelengths unless they are link-disjoint) should be taken into account when solving subproblem (c).

In what follows, two distinct solutions are proposed to solve the MRWA-MLR problem: Path-based ILP formulation and tabu search based meta-heuristic algorithm.

3   A Path-Based ILP Formulation

A light-tree can be viewed as a set of light-paths from the source to each leaf destination who may share a common part with the same wavelength. Based on this concept, we propose a novel path-based ILP formulation in this section, which is different from our previously proposed tree-structure based ILP [9]. We defined four vectors of variables $x_{uv\lambda r}^{nd}$, $h_{v\lambda r}^{nd}$, $y_{uv\lambda}$ and z_λ as follows:

$x_{uv\lambda r}^{sd} \in \{0,1\}$: Equals 1 if arc (u,v) belongs to the path used between the source node s and the destination node d with the line rate r on wavelength λ.

$h_{v\lambda r}^{sd} \in [0,M]$: The distance of the path used between the source node s and the destination node d with the line rate r on wavelength λ.

$y_{uv\lambda} \in \{0,1\}$: Equals 1 if wavelength λ is used on arc (u,v), otherwise 0.

$z_\lambda \in \{0,1\}$: Equals 1 if wavelength λ is used in the final solution, otherwise 0.

We define V_s as the set of OXCs except the source node, i.e., $V_s = V \setminus \{s\}$. We use $N(v)$ to represent the neighbor OXCs of v in the optical network. For a transponder of line rate r, its cost is noted by c_r. Let C_t be total transponder cost, C_l be the total wavelength channel usage cost, and C_z be the number of used wavelengths, i.e.,

$C_t = \sum_{s\in S}\sum_{d\in D_s}\sum_{\lambda\in W}\sum_{v\in N(s)}\sum_{r\in R} c_r \cdot x_{sv\lambda r}^{sd}$

$C_l = \sum_{(u,v)\in E}\sum_{\lambda\in W} y_{uv\lambda}$

$C_z = \sum_{\lambda\in W} z_\lambda$.

Our objective is to minimize the total joint cost, which can thus be expressed as

$$\min\ \alpha \cdot C_t + \beta \cdot C_l + \gamma \cdot C_z \tag{1}$$

The objective function is subject to the following constraints:

$$\sum_{u \in N(v)} x^{sd}_{uv\lambda r} = \sum_{u \in N(v)} x^{sd}_{vu\lambda r} \quad \forall s \in S, \forall d \in D_s, \forall v \in V - \{s,d\},$$

$$\forall \lambda \in W, \forall r \in R \qquad (2)$$

$$h^{sd}_{d\lambda r} \leq H_r \cdot \sum_{v \in N(d)} x^{sd}_{vd\lambda r} \quad \forall s \in S, \forall d \in D_s, \forall \lambda \in W, \forall r \in R \qquad (3)$$

$$h^{sd}_{v\lambda r} \geq h^{sd}_{u\lambda r} + d_{uv} - M \cdot (1 - x^{sd}_{uv\lambda r}) \quad \forall s \in S, \forall d \in D_s,$$

$$\forall \lambda \in W, \forall r \in R, \forall (u,v) \in E \qquad (4)$$

$$\sum_{r \in R} \sum_{\lambda \in W} \sum_{v \in N(d)} r \cdot x^{sd}_{vd\lambda r} \geq B_s \quad \forall s \in S, \forall d \in D_s \qquad (5)$$

$$\sum_{r \in R} x^{sd}_{uv\lambda r} + \sum_{r \in R} x^{s'd'}_{uv\lambda r} \leq y_{uv\lambda} \quad \forall s, s' \in S, s' > s, \forall d \in D_s, \forall d' \in D_{s'},$$

$$\forall \lambda \in W, \forall (u,v) \in E \qquad (6)$$

$$x^{sd}_{uv\lambda r} + x^{sd'}_{uv\lambda r'} \leq y_{uv\lambda} \quad \forall s \in S, \forall d, d' \in D_s, d' \neq d, \forall r, r' \in R,$$

$$r' > r, \forall \lambda \in W, \forall (u,v) \in E \qquad (7)$$

$$z_\lambda \geq y_{uv\lambda} \quad \forall (u,v) \in E, \forall \lambda \in W \qquad (8)$$

$$z_\lambda \geq z_{\lambda+1} \quad \forall \lambda \in W \qquad (9)$$

Constraint (2) ensures that for a rate r and a wavelength λ, the number of incoming arcs in a vertex v is equal to the number of outgoing arcs. The constraint (3) makes sure that the length of a path is no bigger than the maximum reach H_r of the line rate chosen for this path. Constraint (4) prohibits cycles and gives a lower height bound to $h^{sd}_{v\lambda r}$. Constraint (5) ensures that traffic received by each destination $d \in D_s$ is at least equal to the traffic required by the multicast session with source s. Constraint (6) prohibits two paths to have the same wavelength if they have a common arc and but start from different sources. Constraint (7) makes sure that two paths starting from the same source can not use the same wavelength if they share a common arc but use different line rates. Constraints (8) and (9) allow us to count the number of used wavelengths and assign them in ascending order.

As we will see in Sect. 5, it is time consuming to compute the optimal solution using this ILP model. Thus, next we present a tabu search based heuristic algorithm for provisioning multicast communications.

4   A Tabu Search Based Multicast Provisioning Algorithm

The tabu search is based on the concepts of neighborhood solution and allowed movements. The neighborhood of a solution is a set of solutions that can be achieved from the first by performing a predefined movement. Each movement is added to a list with fixed size (tabu list) that contains the banned movements. Adequate adaptation of the tabu search metaheuristic is proposed, the general functioning is introduced in Algorithm 1 and its different steps are detailed in the remainder of this section.

Algorithm 1. Tabu search based multicast provisioning

CALCULATION INITIAL SOLUTION
- Generate a set of line rates for each source-destination pair (s, d) of each multicast session. We use the dynamic programming to assure that initial solution satisfy the demand B_s. The selected set of rates represents the modeling of the initial solution.
- Calculate a feasible paths solution corresponding to the selected rates and make the assignment of the wavelengths using a heuristic method.

MOVEMENT SEARCH
- Search the best move (the best switch of line rates) to get the best neighbor solution, except the set of line rates already placed in the tabu list.
- Compute a feasible path solution corresponding to the newly selected line rates and assign wavelengths using a heuristic method (Algorithm 2 introduced later).

UPDATING THE TABU LIST
- Store the newly selected set of line rates in the tabu list.

STOP CONDITION
- Restart the search for a solution until a stop condition is verified (limited movement or computation time).

4.1 Solution Modeling

Any instance of an MRWA-MLR problem is associated with a finite set of feasible solutions; each of which is characterized by a formulation which allows the distinction between different solutions. A solution to the MRWA-MLR problem involves the selection of line rates and the allocation of wavelengths.

Selection of Line Rates. Due to the structure complexity, we consider only the set of selected line rates in the modeling of a solution, the allocation of wavelengths is obtained by a method presented below. Let $Rates_{Sol}$ be the selected line rates for a solution Sol of an instance of the problem, in our tabu search a solution Sol is defined with $Rates_{Sol} = \{Rates_{sd} : \forall s \in S, \forall d \in D_s\}$, where $Rates_{sd} = \{r_1, r_2, ...r_n : r_i \in R, \sum_i r_i \geq B_s\}$ is the set of line rates assigned to each source-destination pair (s, d) that can satisfy the demand B_s and respect the constraints of the maximum transmission reach. More formally, for all $r \in Rates_{sd}$ must exist at least a path between s and d with a length shorter than H_r.

Wavelengths Assignment. Suppose that $Rates_{Sol} = \{Rates_{sd} : \forall s \in Sa, \forall d \in D_s\}$ is the set of selected line rates which define a feasible solution Sol for an instance of the MRWA-MLR problem. We propose a greedy heuristic that is used to calculate the paths of the solution Sol from the selected line rates $Rates_{Sol}$ and make the assignment of the wavelengths. The heuristic proceeds in several iterations, each of which we calculate the best path that could be added to the partial solution.

Before presenting the main contribution of this work, i.e., the wavelengths allocation heuristic algorithm, we introduce the Elementary Shortest Path with Constraints Resources algorithm (ESPPRC) presented in [2]. ESPPRC algorithm permits to calculate the shortest path between a source and a destination under the resource constraint in a network. It will be used several times in our tabu search based multicast provisioning. Let us consider a network $G(V, E, W)$ and the associated arc length d_{uv} for each arc $(u, v) \in E$. In order to calculate the elementary shortest path from a given source $s \in V \cap S$ to one destination $d \in V \cap D_s$ with a given line rate $r \in R$, we adapt the ESPPRC algorithm by considering resources as the total length of the path, which should not be beyond the maximum transmission reach of the selected line rate.

The main idea of the proposed greedy heuristic algorithm is to search in each iteration for the best path that can be added to the partial solution without violating wavelengths allocation constraints. Given a partial solution, we calculate the best path form a given source node s to a given destination node d using a given line rate r on a given wavelength λ using the ESPPRC procedure applied on a graph $G'(V, E, W)$ obtained by deleting from $G(V, E, W)$ each arc (u, v) that satisfies at least one of these three cases:

- The arc (u, v) is crossed by a path p belonging to the partial solution on λ wavelength and the node source of the path p is different from s.
- The arc (u, v) is crossed by a path p belonging to the partial solution on λ wavelength and the line rate used by the path p is different from r.
- The arc (u, v) is crossed by a path p belonging to the partial solution on λ wavelength and the path p provision the session (s, d).

The wavelengths allocation heuristic algorithm is described in Algorithm 2.

4.2   Neighborhood Function

The neighborhood function is an application such that for all Sol associates Sol' if and only if exist at least a session (s, d) such as $Rates_{sd} \neq Rates'_{sd}$ and $Rates_{sd} \in Rates_{Sol}$ and $Rates'_{sd} \in Rates_{Sol'}$. A neighborhood solution Sol' of Sol can be obtained by simple exchange of a line rate $r_i \in Rates_{sd}$ for any session (s, d) but with taking into consideration that the new sets of line rates $Rates'_{sd}$ must satisfy the demand of the session (s, d) and exist at least a path using the line rate r_i that satisfies the constraint of the maximum transmission reach between s and d. It is very clear that the size of the neighborhood depends on the number of sessions and the demand of each session.

4.3   Tabu List

A fundamental element of the tabu search is the use of memory, which is used to keep track of past operations. We can store information relevant to certain stages

---

Algorithm 2. Wavelengths Allocation Heuristic Algorithm

Data: $G(V, E, W)$ /*The graph modeling the optical network */
1   $Rates_{sd} = \{r_1, r_2, ...r_n : r_i \in R\}$ /*Set of line rates for each (s, d) */
2   $Rates_{Sol} = \{Rates_{sd} : \forall s \in S, \forall d \in D_s\}$ /*All used line rates in the solution */
  Result: $Paths_{Sol}$ /* A set of paths that constitute the solution. */
3   initialization;
4   $Paths_{Sol} \leftarrow \emptyset$;
5   **forall** $Rates_{sd} \in Rates_{sol}$ **do**
6   **forall** $r_i \in Rates_{sd}$ **do**
7         $AllPaths_{sd}^{r_i} \leftarrow \emptyset$;
8   **forall** $\lambda \in W$ **do**
9   /* $G'(V, E, W)$: a graph used in each iteration of the algorithm to model the partial solution. */
10            $G'(V, E, W) \leftarrow G(V, E, W)$;
11   /* $Cost$:a matrix that contains the costs of arcs in the graph. */
12   **forall** $(u, v) \in W$ **do**
13               $Cost[u, v] \leftarrow 1$;
14   **forall** $(s', d', r', \lambda') : Path_{s'd'}^{r'\lambda'} \in Paths_{Sol}$ **do**
15   /* affect the cost 0 to each arc already used and remove each arc which can violate the wavelength constraint. */
16   **forall** $(u, v) \in Path_{s'd'}^{r'\lambda'}$ **do**
17   **if** $\lambda' = \lambda$ **then**
18                     $Cost[u, v] \leftarrow 0$;
19   **if** $s' \neq s$ & $\lambda' = \lambda$ **then**
20                     $G'(V, E, W) \leftarrow G'(V, E, W \setminus (u, v))$;
21   **if** $r' \neq r_i$ & $\lambda' = \lambda$ **then**
22                     $G'(V, E, W) \leftarrow G'(V, E, W \setminus (u, v))$;
23   **if** $s' = s$ & $d' = d$ & $\lambda' = \lambda$ **then**
24                     $G'(V, E, W) \leftarrow G'(V, E, W \setminus (u, v))$;
25   /* calculate with the ESPPRC procedure, the shortest path from s to d using the line rate r_i, wavelength λ, the graph $G'(V, E, W)$ and the matrix $Cost$. */
26            $AllPaths_{sd}^{r_i} \leftarrow$ $AllPaths_{sd}^{r_i} \cup \{ESPPRC(s, d, r_i, \lambda, G'(V, E, W), Cost)\}$;
27   /* chose the path with the minimal cost. */
28         $Paths_{Sol} \leftarrow Paths_{Sol} \cup \{\min(AllPaths_{sd}^{r_i})\}$;

---

of research. This list helps to prevent blockages in the local minima by preventing switching to solution previously visited. The exploration of one neighbor solution is expensive in terms of computation time because of the use of wavelengths allocation heuristic, so in our tabu search method we explore a small number of solutions. This allows us to use a static tabu List which contains all configuration line rates $Rates_{Sol}$ for each solution Sol already visited.

4.4   Initial Solution

We choose to start the tabu search with a solution that minimizes total transponder cost without taking into account the number of used wavelengths. We resolve the problem of minimizing the cost of line rates for each (s, d) with $s \in S$ and $d \in D_s$. The problem can be formulated as a knapsack problem for each (s, d) where $M_{sd} = \{r_i : \sum_{i, r_i = r} r_i \geq B_s \quad \forall r \in R\}$ is the set of all lines rates that can be selected to salsify the demand B_s, C_{r_i} the cost of the transponder operating at line rate r_i and $x_i^{sd} \in \{0, 1\}$ a decision variable that equals 1 if the line rate $r_i \in M_{sd}$ is used for provisioning (s, d). The objective is to minimize total transponder cost used for each (s, d) pair.

$$\max \sum_{r_i \in M_{sd}} (1 - x_i^{sd}) \cdot C_{r_i} \tag{10}$$

Subject to constraint:

$$\sum_{r_i \in M_{sd}} r_i \cdot (1 - x_i^{sd}) < (\sum_{r_i \in M_{sd}} r_i) - B_s \tag{11}$$

For each (s, d) pair of a multicast session, we resolve the Knapsack with dynamic programming. Once all line rates are selected for each (s, d), we use the

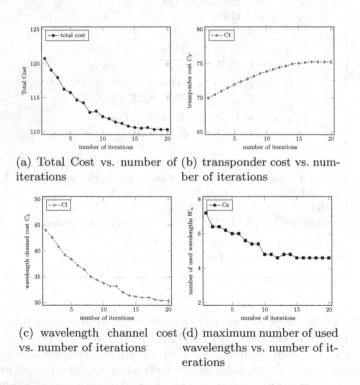

(a) Total Cost vs. number of iterations

(b) transponder cost vs. number of iterations

(c) wavelength channel cost vs. number of iterations

(d) maximum number of used wavelengths vs. number of iterations

Fig. 1. Evolution of costs versus the number of iteration of the tabu search on the 6-node transparent MLR topology [9]

wavelength allocation heuristic algorithm to find the set of lightpaths and assign the wavelengths for the initial solution.

5   Simulation and Numerical Results

We evaluate our tabu Search based multicast provisioning heuristic algorithm on three different topologies: 6-node sample network [9], the cost-239 network (11 nodes and 52 directed links) [1], and European Optical Network (EON, 28 nodes and 88 directed links) [8]. Simulations were conducted using IBM ILOG CPLEX version 12.5 on an Intel Core PC equipped with a 3.3 GHz CPU and 4G Bytes RAM. The Total Cost in the set of tests is given by the objective function (Eq. (1)), where the coefficients α, β and γ are equal to 1 but our algorithm is valid for any coefficients. To validate the proposed tabu search based heuristic algorithm, we consider two metrics: the convergence speed (the number of iterations for convergence) and the gap to the optimal solution.

Figure 1 presents the evolution of different costs for the 6-node optical network versus the number of iteration of the proposed tabu search based heuristic algorithm. We can observe at the end of 15 iterations, our approach is about to obtain the best total cost. It is shown that our approach starts with the best possible transponder cost by using dynamic programming. The tabu search tries

Table 1. Simulation Results

Instances				MILP model			Tabu search				
Name	Session	$|D_s|$	B_s	Total cost	Gap (%)	Time (s)	Total cost	Ct	Cl	Cz	Time
6-MLR	2	3	120	53.5	0	9.55	54.5	37.5	14	3	40.793
	3	3	120	80.5	0	2163.8	81.25	56.25	22	3	80.852
	4	3	120	107	11.43	9760	110	75	30	5	124.437
	5	3	120	132.75	14.2	11048.5	135.75	92.75	37	6	198.594
	6	3	120	164.75	15.3	10126.3	167.75	113.75	48	6	261.866
Cost-239 MLR	2	3	100	58.5	40.93	6910.03	58.5	37.5	18	3	26.292
	4	3	100	–	–	7200	104.5	67.5	33	4	53.396
	6	3	100	–	–	7200	158.25	101.25	53	4	146.245
	8	3	100	–	–	7200	221.75	138.75	76	7	362.446
	10	3	100	–	–	7200	279.5	172.5	100	7	802.142
Cost-239 MLR	2	5	300	–	–	7200	216.5	147.5	61	8	32.879
	4	5	300	–	–	7200	428.25	286.25	129	13	133.931
	6	5	300	–	–	7200	656.75	432.75	211	13	638.075
	8	5	300	–	–	7200	930.5	607.5	299	24	4157.52
	10	5	300	–	–	7200	1180.75	761.75	396	23	3868.7
28 EON	2	5	300	–	–	7200	309.5	182.5	112	15	231.889
	4	5	000			7200	589.5	332.5	235	22	803.447
	6	5	300	–	–	7200	859.25	501.25	336	22	2604.55
	8	5	300	–	–	7200	1221.75	673.75	523	25	2938.78
	10	5	300	–	–	7200	1397.5	794.5	579	24	4287.12

to decrease the wavelength channel cost and the number of used wavelengths progressively in each iteration so that the total cost can be improved. In other words, the tabu search deteriorates the transponder cost to cut down the used wavelengths and the wavelength channel usage. We can observe also that total cost is reduced by 8.28 % on average.

Table 1 summarizes our empirical results for the aforementioned three topologies. As we find that computation time mainly depends on the network size, the number of sessions, the number of destinations of a multicast session, and the traffic demand, we report test results mainly based on these factors. We can see that the ILP is still too time-consuming to compute the optimal solution in median and big optical networks. Our tabu search based algorithm obtains almost the same results as the optimal solution computed by the ILP model (with a gap of 1.84 % on average) in the 6-node optical network. The tabu search method also permits to get approximated solutions for big instances in Cost-239 network and 28-node EON in a reasonable time while the ILP based counterpart can not. Thus, we can say our tabu search based heuristic algorithm is able to find the near-optimal solution and it is scalable for large networks.

6   Conclusion

An efficient tabu search based heuristic algorithm is proposed to provision multiple multicast communications in Mixed-Line-Rate optical networks. Our objective is to minimize the joint network cost. In our approach, we use dynamic programming to find the suitable set of line rates, and use a new wavelength allocation heuristic to solve the lightpath computation and wavelength assignment. For comparison, a path-based ILP formulation is also proposed to search the optimal solution for small networks. Simulation results confirm that our proposed tabu search based algorithm allows to get a near-optimal strategy for multicast provision, and this method is scalable for large optical networks with mixed line rates.

Acknowledgments. This work is supported by the internal grant of the Computer Science Lab (LIA), University of Avignon, France and the open project (2013GZKF031 309) of the State Key Laboratory of Advanced Optical Communication Systems and Networks, Shanghai Jiao Tong University, China. The authors would like to thank Dr. Boris Detienne (IMB, University of Bordeaux 1) for his valuable discussions and suggestions.

References

1. Chowdhury, P., Tornatore, M., Nag, A., Ip, E., Wang, T., Mukherjee, B.: On the design of energy-efficient mixed-line-rate (MLR) optical networks. IEEE J. Lightwave Technol. **30**(1), 130–139 (2012)
2. Feillet, D., Dejax, P., Gendreau, M., Gueguen, C.: An exact algorithm for the elementary shortest path problem with resource constraints: application to some vehicle routing problems. Networks **44**(3), 216–229 (2004)

3. Hamad, A.M., Kamal, A.E.: Power-aware connection provisioning for all-optical multicast traffic in WDM networks. IEEE/OSA J. Opt. Commun. Netw. 2(7), 481–495 (2010)

4. Harve, S.K., Batayneh, M., Mukherjee, B.: Optimal multicasting in a multi-line-rate ethernet-over-WDM network. In: IEEE Asia Communications and Photonics Conference and Exhibition, pp. 1–4 (2009)

5. Malacarne, A., Meloni, G., Berrettini, G., Sambo, N., Poti, L., Bogoni, A.: Optical multicasting of 16QAM signals in periodically-poled lithium niobate waveguide. IEEE J. Lightwave Technol. 31(11), 1797–1803 (2013)

6. Nag, A., Tornatore, M., Mukherjee, B.: Optical network design with mixed line rates and multiple modulation formats. IEEE J. Lightwave Technol. 28(4), 466–475 (2010)

7. Xu, L., Zhang, S., Yaman, F., Wang, T., Liao, G., Chen, K., Singla, A., Singh, A., Ramachandran, K., Zhang, Y.: All-optical switching data center network supporting 100gbps upgrade and mixed-line-rate interoperability. In: Optical Fiber Communication Conference and Exposition (OFC/NFOEC), pp. 1–3 (2011)

8. Zhao, J., Subramaniam, S., Brandt-Pearce, M.: QoT-aware grooming, routing, and wavelength assignment (GRWA) for Mixed-Line-Rate translucent optical networks. In: Proceedings of the 1st IEEE International Conference on Communications in China, pp. 318–323, August 2012

9. Zhou, F.: Multicast provision in transparent optical networks with mixed line rates. In: Proceedings of the 17th IEEE International Conference on Optical Networking Design and Modeling, pp. 125–130 (2013)

10. Zhou, F., Molnar, M., Cousin, B., Qiao, C.: Cost bounds and approximation ratios of multicast light-trees in WDM networks. IEEE/OSA J. Opt. Commun. Netw. 3(4), 323–334 (2011)

11. Zhou, F., Molnar, M., Cousin, B., Simon, G.: Power optimal design of multicast light-trees in WDM networks. IEEE Commun. Lett. 15(11), 1240–1242 (2011)

Consensus Based Report-Back Protocol for Improving the Network Lifetime in Underwater Sensor Networks

Ameen Chilwan[1]([⊠]), Natalia Amelina[2], Zhifei Mao[1], Yuming Jiang[1], and Dimitrios J. Vergados[1]

[1] Department of Telematics, NTNU, Trondheim, Norway
{chilwan,zhifei.mao,jiang,dimitrios.vergados}@item.ntnu.no
[2] St. Petersburg State University, St. Petersburg, Russia
ngranichina@gmail.com

Abstract. One of the main objectives of wireless sensor network design is to prolong the network lifetime. In underwater sensor networks, this problem is even more critical due to the difficulty in battery replacement and/or recharging. In this paper, we study the problem of extending the network lifetime for underwater sensor networks. We consider a clustered network, that consists of two types of nodes: the cluster heads ("supernodes") that send the information to the sink, and the ordinary sensor nodes that collect the information about the environment. The nodes are considered to have dynamic stochastic topology, and noisy measurements about their own and their neighbors' current battery levels. A differentiated consensus based report-back protocol is introduced for determining the workload distribution throughout the network with different algorithms for cluster heads and monitoring sensors. To analyze the original stochastic system, an averaged deterministic model is introduced. In addition, the protocol is also implemented in software to study the performance of the proposed protocol. Results from the implementation show that the proposed protocol achieves consensus among the respective nodes and also has a positive impact on lifetime of the network without any compromise on power efficiency.

Keywords: Acoustic sensors · Consensus · Underwater sensor networks

1 Introduction

Recently, sensor networks for monitoring environmental indicators are gaining popularity. Each of these sensors collects information about some environmental indicator and sends it to the processing sites. Sensor networks have also been deployed under the water; in seas, oceans, and lakes for monitoring physical and/or biological indicators. Underwater sensors have been in deployment since the development of SONAR (SOund Navigation And Ranging) technology and have been used to navigate submarines and detect bodies under the water.

© Springer International Publishing Switzerland 2014
Y. Kermarrec (Ed.): EUNICE 2014, LNCS 8846, pp. 26–37, 2014.
DOI: 10.1007/978-3-319-13488-8_3

In addition to the legacy of using SONAR, there are other reasons also for choosing acoustic waves over radio and optical waves for underwater sensing, as in [12].

Some limitations of Underwater Sensor Networks (UWSN) are inherited from the nature of acoustic signals, while the others arise due to limitations of sensor hardware. The weaknesses of acoustic signals compared to radio signals are; narrower frequency bands, higher propagation delay, and larger transmission loss due to medium absorption and geometric spreading [8]. The bottlenecks due to sensor hardware are; limited processing, storing capacity, and fixed and constrained power available for processing and transmitting. The former two factors are not vital as they are sufficient enough for the amount of task sensors have to perform but the latter imposes challenge for maintaining a UWSN.

It is this problem of sensors running out of battery independently, and hence incurring high maintenance cost, that is addressed in the current study. A method is proposed which will cause all the sensors in a UWSN to completely exhaust their batteries almost at the same time. This is provided by implementing the proposed distributed consensus based report-back protocol on each node. In addition, the proposed algorithm maximizes the network lifetime by selecting the nodes that are required to transmit in each iteration, an idea introduced in [4]. This causes all the nodes to run out of batteries at the same time and hence it ensures that all the available energy in the network is utilized, efficiently.

The approach presented in this paper also leverages upon the selective and aggregated transmission of collected data from sensors in a clustered network. Hence the network studied in this paper is **clustered**, with **stochastic topology**, and uses a **distributed algorithm** to find which nodes shall transmit in a data collection iteration. This is coupled with the idea that the sensors and cluster heads should reach consensus, on the battery level, among themselves so that they drain off almost at the same time.

2   Related Work and Contributions

There are a number of methods proposed that suggest how to reduce the number of times a sensor battery is replaced or recharged. Some of them try to estimate and optimize battery lifetime of a single sensor in order to get maximum benefit before it runs out [9]. While, the others try to optimize the network to ensure that all the sensors will run out of battery almost at the same time [3,10].

Consensus algorithms are widely used for control of distributed network systems [13,15]. The consensus problem is to find a control protocol that drives all states of agents to some constant steady-state values. The consensus approach has been used for various problems in sensor networks. The greatest advantage of this approach is that it is entirely distributed, i.e., it does not require a central node that discovers the topology of the whole network to function.

In [3,10], the authors focus on the sensors life-time increasing problem by optimizing the network topology. In [5], it is shown that there exists an optimal transmit power, depending upon the network topology, that minimizes the overall energy consumption. In [6], the problem of minimization of the number of iterations needed to achieve consensus is considered. In [11], the authors consider the effect of uncertainties on the consensus method in sensor networks.

The contributions of this paper are many-fold. First, the paper proposes a consensus based report-back protocol for prolonging network lifetime by ensuring that all sensor nodes run out of batteries at the same time. This causes that all the collective energy present in the network is utilized efficiently. Also, UWSNs with inter-dependent differentiated nodes, sensor nodes and cluster heads, are studied and different protocol is developed for each. In addition, a UWSN is studied with stochastic network topology that changes dynamically at every iteration to emulate the nodes that are floating randomly underwater. The paper studies a scenario of UWSN with sensor nodes deployed on the sea-floor. This is very practical in case of, e.g., seismic imaging for underwater oil-fields and tactical surveillance.

3   System Model

3.1   System Under Study

In this paper, we consider an underwater sensor network for water bottom monitoring. As depicted in Fig. 1, a large number of nodes are anchored to the bottom of the water and a base station or sink is fixed on the water surface. The basic elements of the system to be identified for this study are: the nodes, their deployment, the network topology, and the underwater environment.

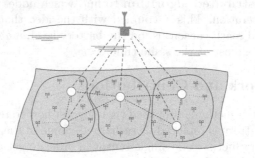

Fig. 1. Model of underwater sensor network

There are two types of nodes deployed, sensor nodes and cluster heads. The sensors, shown as dumbbell-like nodes in Fig. 1, are responsible for observing the environment and collecting data, while the cluster heads, shown as round nodes in Fig. 1, are used to relay the sensors' collected data to the sink. Each sensor is equipped with a short-range acoustic modem, and a battery of limited power. Cluster heads, however, have more powerful battery and higher communication capabilities. The sensors, cluster heads, and the sink communicate with one another through acoustic modems. Since the sensors' transmission range is short, they cannot communicate with the sink directly. Thus, they first send the collected data to a nearby cluster head which will relay the data to the sink. Thus, the studied system is termed as **deep-sea network with vertical topology**.

Multiple sensors are deployed in same spot of which just a subset is required to transmit at each iteration, for a couple of reasons. The first reason is that it provides reliable measurements even in the case of incidental node failures. Secondly, it gives an opportunity to choose just a few sensors to transmit at an instant and in this way utilize the collective sensor energy efficiently.

Topologically speaking, the network is divided into clusters since the number of sensors covering the area is large. It keeps the control distributed and data handling load fairly balanced across the network, among other benefits. A cluster consists of a cluster head(s) and affiliated sensor nodes. The sensors within the same cluster can communicate directly with each other as long as they fall within the transmission range. The cluster head has an access to all the sensors within its boundaries. The overall network topology changes with time as the sensors float around and get connected to their nearest cluster heads.

In addition to the nodes and their topology, another feature of the system is its environment, the deep-sea. It tends to be harsh to the sensor nodes, especially due to interference of underwater creatures, fast-flowing current, high water pressure, and fail of waterproofing. A number of limitations in UWSNs exist because of this harsh environment of which the noise introduced in the communication channel and the increasing attenuation of signals are worth-mentioning.

3.2 Model Description

The model derived from the above explained system has four basic elements; the nodes (sensors and cluster heads), their deployment (multiple sensors with selective transmission), network topology (clustered vertical topology) and environment (deep-sea) which form the basis of this model. Figure 1 also represents the model that is analyzed and implemented in this study. But there are some assumptions made in order to come up with a simplified yet realistic model.

First, it is helpful to understand the working of the system model. Initially, it should be noticed that the sensors perform their sensing tasks periodically, and send the measurement data to their respective cluster heads. Moreover, cluster heads relay the sensors' collected data to the sink over a certain schedule. Therefore, the functionality of the whole network is actually triggered after a lapse of certain period of time, and hence can be considered as iterations. The time period between two iterations is considered to be constant with the value 20 min. This value is obtained by rigorous reasoning in [9].

In terms of topology, it is known to be vertical topology and the maximum cluster diameter is fixed at 100 m, that means that the maximum distance between a sensor and its farthest neighbor is 100 m. On a similar note, the maximum distance between a cluster head and its neighbor cluster head is 200 m. Another very salient feature of this study is that it considers a stochastic dynamic topology. This means that the sensors, which are constantly moving, connect to the nearest cluster head at each iteration. Although there exist some patterns in sensor movements, we have considered a topology that changes with every iteration randomly to keep the study conservative.

Next aspect of this model is that it identifies the parameters that affect the data transmission and consequently power consumption. These parameters are chosen by considering specific communication technology, i.e. acoustic communication, and specific deployment environment, i.e. deep-sea with a depth of around 4 km. In most relative works, e.g. [9,14], these parameters are found to be; **the channel frequency, the inter-node distance, frequency of data updates and noise level**. The values chosen for each of them are based on conservative assumptions to study worst case behavior.

To this end, the conservative assumptions made for the four basic parameters are as follows. For the channel frequency, 1 kHz is chosen as the constant value that is used in this model. The reason for such a selection out of the range of available frequencies upto as high as 50 kHz is that, because the attenuation is very high in the deep-sea environment, it is prescribed to have very low frequencies to experience minimum attenuation. But still, just tens of Hz is not practical frequency for sending measurement data, as it will be too slow, thus a fair value of 1 kHz is chosen. Which, in turn, implies the data rate of 1 kbps. If a measurement packet sent by a sensor in an iteration is considered to be of fixed size at 1 kbit, then it can be noticed that the time given between two iterations of sending data, 20 min, is very safe value. This is because considering the speed of sound in water, which is 1500 m/s, one packet will require only ~4 s for its transmission and propagation till the sink. An additional remark about the data packets is that the sensors also feature 200 bit long acknowledgement packets, that may trigger re-transmission of the packet. For the second parameter, the frequency of sending data updates, it is already argued to be kept constant at 20 min. Similarly, the proposed value for maximum inter-node distance is kept constant at 100 m as previously mentioned.

Table 1. Amount of energy required for transmitting/receiving a single packet

Interface	Transmission energy (E_{Tx}) [J]	Reception energy (E_{Rx}) [J]
Sensor-sensor	0.08	0.02
Sensor-cluster head	0.8	0.3
Cluster head-cluster head	1.6	0.6
Cluster head-sink	5.0	N/A

Finally, the noise level in deep-sea communication is found by the model proposed in [7,14]. According to these models, the deep-sea propagation model is considered to be a sphere and the passive SONAR equation can be used to find the amount of energy required to transmit one packet, by considering all the noises. Thus, with the values assumptions made in the preceding paragraphs, the amount of energy required for transmission and for reception of a single measurement packet are summarized in Table 1.

4   Model Analysis

In this section, an analytical treatment of the proposed differentiated consensus based report-back protocol is presented. This forms the theoretical basis of the implementation of the proposed protocol on UWSNs.

Consider an underwater sensor network of n nodes and m clusters. Assume, that each node belongs to a particular cluster. Denote $N = \{1, \ldots, n\}$ as a set of nodes, and $M = \{1, \ldots, m\}$ as a set of clusters, $M \subset 2^N$. Let the elements of M be clusters g_k, $g_k \subset N$. Suppose, they do not intersect. We define the adjacency matrix A of the network by clusters. Let A_t^k denote the adjacency matrix of cluster g_k at time instant t. The sink is also considered as a cluster of one node. Let N_t^i stand for the neighbors set of node i at time t. We introduce three characteristics of node i, $i = 1, \ldots, n$ at any time t; amount of packages with information in the queue q_t^i, rate of discharge p_t^i, and energy level r_t^i. We suppose that supernodes relay the sensors' collected data to the sink every τ_1 time instant. Moreover, sensor nodes perform sensing tasks every τ_2 time instant.

We assume that, to form the control strategy, each sensor $i \in N$ at time t has information about; noisy observations about its own energy level (1), noisy observations about its neighbors' energy levels (2), and the information about its rate of discharge p_t^i and about its neighbors' rates of discharge p_t^j, $j \in N_t^i$.

$$y_t^{i,i} = r_t^i + w_t^{i,i}, \tag{1}$$

$$y_t^{i,j} = r_t^j + w_t^{i,j}, \ j \in N_t^i, \tag{2}$$

where $w_t^{i,j}$ are noises and $N_t^i \neq \emptyset$.

We introduce the protocol for supernodes (cluster heads) **(Protocol 1)**:

- For each node i, if $N_t^i \neq \emptyset$, we compare $y_t^{i,i}$ and $y_t^{i,j}$ where $j \in N_t^i$, i.e. compare the observations about it's own energy level and it's neighbors' energy levels.
- We choose throughout set $N_t^i \cup \{i\}$ the node with maximum energy level. If it is not node i, then node i sends all its amount of packages to that node. Else u_t^i equals to the sum of packages that sensor i gets from it's neighbors.

Note that this is a greedy algorithm, in which we make the locally optimal choice at each step.

Let symbol s_t^i indicates whether sensor i is switched on or switched off at time t (equals 1 or 0 respectively). The dynamics of each node is described by

$$q_{t+1}^i = q_t^i + z_t^i s_t^i + u_t^i; \ i \in N, \ t = 0, 1, \ldots, T, \tag{3}$$

where z_t^i are new packages collected or received by node i at time t (for supernodes z_t^i are new packages that received from sensor nodes; for sensor nodes z_t^i are new data collected by sensor i at time t); s_t^i is control action which equals 1 for supernodes, and s_t^i equals 0 or 1 for sensor nodes according to the **Protocol 2** which will be described below; u_t^i are other control actions. For supernodes control actions u_t^i are defined by **Protocol 1**. Also

$$p_{t+1}^i = p_t^i - c^i \ln(t); \ i \in N, \ t = 0, 1, \ldots, T, \tag{4}$$

where c^i is some coefficient of the battery discharge. Note that this coefficient includes communication overhead (energy that is spent on observations about sensor energy level and its neighbors' energy levels) as well.

$$r^i_{t+1} = r^i_t - s^i_t \mathbf{1}_{\{|u^i_t|)>0\}} h^i p^i_t; \quad i \in N, \; t = k\tau_l, \tag{5}$$

where u^i_t are control actions, h^i is the coefficient of energy loss in the communication session, and $\mathbf{1}_{\{\cdot\}}$ is the characteristic function such as

$$\mathbf{1}_{\{A\}} = \begin{cases} 1, & \text{if } A \text{ is true,} \\ 0, & \text{otherwise.} \end{cases}$$

We assume, that if $t \neq k\tau_l, l = 1, 2$ then $r^i_{t+1} = r^i_t$.

In this work the consensus goal differs for different types of nodes. Specifically, for supernodes the goal is to maintain the maximum energy level since the task of sending the information to the sink has the highest priority. For sensor nodes the goal is to retain the average energy level. This is a new consensus problem, termed *differentiated consensuses* in [2].

Assume, that there are multiple sensor nodes in a cluster and all are collecting the same type of information (doing the same job). Usually, at the beginning most of sensors have equal energy level. If we do not need all sensor nodes work at the same time, then, to save the energy, we can introduce the probability with which sensor i switches off (sleeps, does not collect the information) v^i_t.

We introduce the following protocol for sensor nodes (**Protocol 2**):

- For each node i, if $N^i_t \neq \emptyset$, we compare $y^{i,i}_t$ and $y^{i,j}_t$ where $j \in N^i_t$, i.e. compare its energy level with its neighbor's.
- If observed energy levels are equal, then u^i_t equals 0 or 1 with probability v^i_t.
- If the neighbor's observed energy level $y^{i,j}_t, j \in N^i_t$ is greater than it's own observed energy level $y^{i,i}_t$, then u^i_t equals to 0 or 1 with probability $v = \frac{N^i_t v^i_t}{n^i_t}$, where v is the proportion of the minimum number of sensors in a cluster, which should work at the same time, n^i_t is the number of neighbors of sensor i with greater energy level, v^i_t is the probability with which sensor i switches off.

Thus, $s^i_t = \mathbf{1}_{\{\sum_{j \in \tilde{N}^i_t} (y^{i,j}_t - y^{i,i}_t) > 0\}}$.

5   Consensus in Heterogeneous Sensor Networks

Basically, the lifetime of supernodes is sufficiently acceptable to transmit the data that have been collected in the system. This will be characterized by simulations in Sect. 7. To introduce some properties of the network topology, the following definitions from the graph theory will be used. Consider a graph $G = (N, E)$ with a set of nodes $N = \{1, 2, \ldots, n\}$ and a set of edges E. Symbol $E_{\max} = \{(j, i) : \sup_{t \geq 0} a^{i,j}_t > 0\}$ stands for the maximal set of communication links.

We associate a weight $a_t^{i,j} > 0$ at time t with each edge $(j,i) \in E$. Matrix $A_t = [a_t^{i,j}]$ is an adjacency matrix of the graph at time t. Denote $\mathcal{G}_{A_t}$ as the corresponding graph. Generally, we can introduce the averaged deterministic model, corresponding to initial stochastic model. This deterministic model could be obtained by averaging over all possible input actions:

$$\bar{r}_{t+1}^i = \bar{r}_t^i - \mathbf{1}_{\{\sum_{N_{\max}} \sum_{k=1}^d a_{\max}^{i,j} \bar{r}_{t-k}^i - \bar{r}_t^i\}} \mathbf{1}_{\{|u_t^i|)>0\}} h^i p_t^i \tag{6}$$

$$i \in N, \ t = 0, 1, \ldots, T.$$

Let $A_{\max}$ denote the adjacency matrix of the averaged system. $N_{\max}^i$ is defined by the matrix $A_{\max}$. Let $(\Omega, \mathcal{F}, P)$ be the underlying probability space corresponding to the sample space, the collection of all events, and the probability measure respectively and assume that the following conditions are satisfied:

A1. $\forall i \in N, j \in N_{\max}^i$ the noises $w_t^{i,j}$ are centered, independent and have bounded variance $E(w_t^{i,j})^2 \leq \sigma_w^2$.

A2. $\forall i \in N, j \in N_{\max}^i$ appearances of variable edges (j,i) in graph $\mathcal{G}_{A_t}$ are independent random events. Moreover, all these random variables and matrices are mutually independent.

A3. Graph $\mathcal{G}_{A_{\max}}$ is spanning tree, and for any edge $(j,i) \in E_{\max}$ $a_{\max}^{i,j} > 0$.

Theorem 1. *If conditions* **A1–A3** *are satisfied then the solutions of trajectories of the initial stochastic system (5) are close in the mean square sense to the average trajectories of the averaged system (6).*

The proof can be carried out by analogy with the corresponding result form [1] as consequence of the usage of a slightly modified protocol. Eventually, since the trajectories of solutions of the averaged system are close to the original stochastic system we can use averaged system to study initial stochastic system. For averaged system other common techniques could be applied similar to [3,5,6,10] to study the system.

6   Software Implementation

In order to have an insight in the functionality of the proposed protocol and evaluate it, it is implemented in software using Simula. The advantages that the results obtained from implementing the protocol include; verification of the strength of the protocol in networks with stochastic topology, and relaxed assumption to make it more realistic. In the software implementation each sensor and cluster head has local implementation of protocol. Thus the decision of which cluster should the sensor be allocated to is taken by the sensor itself. Since, it is done by independent random selections, the network topology remains purely stochastic. Therefore, each sensor explores the nearest cluster head in every iteration (memoryless property), and uses some amount of energy In the course of exploration and gets associated to a cluster head. Also, a high limit and a low limit is given to each cluster. So, in the present implementation, there must be at least 3 sensors in a cluster and a cluster can't have more than 5 sensors.

The next step in the protocol for sensors is to discover their neighbors. In the current implementation, all sensors connected to a single cluster head are considered to be neighbors. Also, a cluster is assumed to have single cluster head. Thus, sensors request IDs of all the sensors connected to their respective cluster heads and in the process they consume some energy. Then each sensor can run the proposed protocol, details in Sect. 4, and find out whether it will transmit the collected data or not. On the same course, the cluster heads also discover their neighbors at every iteration randomly, thus completing the stochastic property of the network topology. In the current implementation, the number of neighbors to a cluster head are limited to *two*. This implies that each cluster head has two clusters on each side which seems simplified but enough. After discovering the neighbors and receiving and buffering the measurements from subsequent sensors, a cluster head simply finds which is the cluster head with highest energy remaining in the triplet, and all packets are forwarded to that cluster head to be sent to the sink. Finally, the values in Table 1 are used as the energy discharge values in the implementation.

7 Result Discussion

7.1 Consensus Validation

In this section of results, the proposed differentiated protocol is evaluated by plotting battery discharge curves that help in noticing discharge behavior and possible alignment. In order to conduct the study, the protocol-running sensors are compared with the case in which sensors are randomly chosen for transmitting their measurements. This is because both of them select sensors to transmit from the pool and not all sensors transmit at an iteration. But this comes at the cost that the sensors start dying randomly for the latter. Nevertheless, the case in which sensors are randomly selected for transmitting measurements makes it logically closer to the goals of our study, and hence logical comparison scenario.

To begin with the algorithm implemented on the environmental monitoring sensors, the energy level plot is depicted in Fig. 2 for both the cases when the protocol is implemented on the sensors and when the sensors are randomly chosen. The results show only a subset of all the sensors deployed in the simulator in order to exhibit their discharge pattern. It is safely noted that similar characteristics are shown by all the sensors across the network. Similarly, another aspect that has been scaled down in these plots is the total battery life of a sensor. The actual value of a common sensor battery life is 35 kJ (1 cell × 9 V × 1.2 Amp-h) but it is taken to be only 100 J in the plots in Fig. 2.

It can clearly be seen from the figure that the case with the protocol implemented performs better than the case when sensors are randomly chosen. This means that all the sensors discharge at approximately equal rates and hence the chances of majority of them dying together is large. On the contrary, the randomly chosen sensors run out of battery independently and hence no guarantee can be given on the expected value of network lifetime. Thus, it can safely

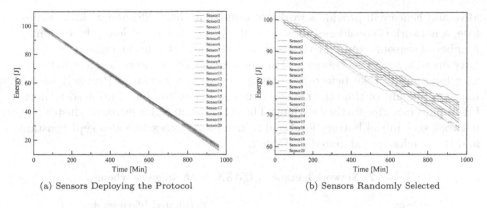

(a) Sensors Deploying the Protocol

(b) Sensors Randomly Selected

Fig. 2. Energy Plot of a sample of environmental sensors

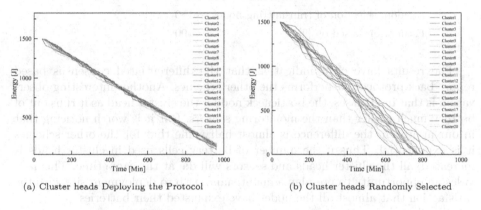

(a) Cluster heads Deploying the Protocol

(b) Cluster heads Randomly Selected

Fig. 3. Energy plot of the cluster heads

be said that consensus in terms of remaining battery life is reached among the sensors that deploy the protocol.

Similar considerations as in Fig. 2 are taken when displaying the effect of implementing the second algorithm on cluster heads. The plots in Fig. 3 are scaled down to the total battery life of 1500 J instead of the actual 225 kJ (5 cells). The plots show all the cluster heads implemented and it reflects an obvious advantage that the protocol-driven cluster heads have over the randomly chosen-to-transmit cluster heads. The alignment in the decay of battery life of cluster heads is achieved, as required, by the proposed protocol and it brings with it the underlying benefits as already mentioned.

7.2   Better Network Lifetime

The results presented in this section show a comparison among different methods and schemes which can be used to enhance network lifetime in order to signify the performance of the proposed method in this regard. In order to perform the comparison, a unified criterion is selected that will define whether a network is alive and hence will provide a workable value of network lifetime in days. There-fore, a network is considered to be alive if, for all clusters, at least the minimum number of sensors required to transmit in a cluster, three in the current case, still have enough energy to transmit. This means that the network lifetime indicates how long will it take before the network needs maintenance. Precisely speak-ing, it is amount of time the network will run before the batteries need recharg-ing/replacement for further working. The other settings, for example cluster size, network size, initial battery level and transmission losses, are also kept constant and the results are tabulated in Table 2.

Table 2. Network lifetime of UWSNs with different schemes

Scheme	Estimated lifetime [days]
Consensus based report-back protocol	∼200
Random selection of transmitting nodes	∼150
Estimation based on [9]	<100

The results have clear indication that the differentiated consensus based report-back protocol outperforms the other schemes. Another interesting obser-vation is that in all cases, the bottleneck node is the cluster head as it runs out of battery much earlier than the monitoring sensors. But it is worth noticing that in our approach, the difference is almost half while that for the other schemes it is exponential. Thus if the number of battery cells used in cluster heads is increased, all the cluster heads and sensors will die at the same time. This pro-vides an opportunity to pre-plan a maintenance trip to deployment site with the satisfaction that almost all the nodes have exhausted their batteries.

8   Future Work and Conclusion

To extend the current work, a more extensive study can be conducted on the protocol itself and its vulnerability and sensitivity can be checked in even more dynamic frame. Also, the protocol can be implemented on test-bed and its per-formance optimized. In this way, the algorithm can be refined for optimal actual implementation as well. In addition, the analytical model presented in this paper can be enhanced and a more general mathematical model can be developed.

Conclusively, it can be stated that consensus can be applied in UWSNs to scribe a report-back protocol that can ensure that nearly all sensors in the net-work run out of their batteries at the same time. By achieving this, the logistic costs for maintaining UWSNs will be minimized and easily planned. Another feature of the proposed protocol is that it differentiates between different types of nodes in a network and behaves differently with them. Also, by applying this protocol, a positive impact on the network lifetime is observed.[1]

---

[1] The authors acknowledge the support of SPbSU for a research grant 6.50.1554.2013, RFBR (project 13-07-00250, 14-08-01015) and the Russian Ministry of Education (unique app.no. RFMEFI60414X0035).

References

1. Amelina, N., Fradkov, A., Jiang, Y., Vergados, D.: Approximate consensus multi-agent control under stochastic environment with application to load balancing (June 2013). arXiv:1306.3378, http://arxiv.org/abs/1306.3378
2. Amelina, N., Granichin, O., Jiang, Y.: Differentiated consensuses in decentralized load balancing problem with randomized topology, noise, and delays. In: 53rd IEEE Conference on Decision and Control (CDC2014). IEEE (2014)
3. Asensio-Marco, C., Beferull-Lozano, B.: Network topology optimization for accelerating consensus algorithms under power constraints. In: IEEE 8th International Conference on Distributed Computing in Sensor Systems (DCOSS). IEEE (2012)
4. Avrachenkov, K., El Chamie, M., Neglia, G.: A local average consensus algorithm for wireless sensor networks. In: 2011 International Conference on Distributed Computing in Sensor Systems and Workshops (DCOSS), pp. 1–6. IEEE (2011)
5. Barbarossa, S., Scutari, G., Swami, A.: Achieving consensus in self-organizing wireless sensor networks: The impact of network topology on energy consumption. In: IEEE International Conference on Acoustics, Speech and Signal Processing. ICASSP 2007, vol. 2. IEEE (2007)
6. Chen, L., Carpenter, G., Greenberg, S., Frolik, J., Wang, X.: An implementation of decentralized consensus building in sensor networks. IEEE Sens. J. **11**, 667–675 (2011)
7. Domingo, M.C., Prior, R.: Energy analysis of routing protocols for underwater wireless sensor networks. Comput. Commun. **31**(6), 1227–1238 (2008)
8. Heidemann, J., Ye, W., Wills, J., Syed, A., Li, Y.: Research challenges and applications for underwater sensor networking. In: Wireless Communications and Networking Conference, 2006. WCNC 2006, vol. 1, pp. 228–235. IEEE (2006)
9. Jurdak, R., Lopes, C.V., Baldi, P.: Battery lifetime estimation and optimization for underwater sensor networks. IEEE Sensor Network Operations (2004)
10. Kar, S., Moura, J.M.: Sensor networks with random links: topology design for distributed consensus. IEEE Trans. Signal Process. **56**(7), 3315–3326 (2008)
11. Kar, S., Moura, J.M.: Distributed consensus algorithms in sensor networks with imperfect communication: link failures and channel noise. IEEE Trans. Signal Process. **57**(1), 355–369 (2009)
12. Lanbo, L., Shengli, Z., Jun-Hong, C.: Prospects and problems of wireless communication for underwater sensor networks. Wireless Commun. Mobile Comput. **8**(8), 977–994 (2008)
13. Ren, W., Beard, R.: Consensus seeking in multiagent systems under dynamically changing interaction topologies. IEEE Trans. Autom. Control **50**(5), 655–661 (2005)
14. Sehgal, A., David, C., Schonwalder, J.: Energy consumption analysis of underwater acoustic sensor networks. In: OCEANS 2011 (2011)
15. Tsitsiklis, J., Bertsekas, D., Athans, M.: Distributed asynchronous deterministic and stochastic gradient optimization algorithms. IEEE Trans. Autom. Control **31**(9), 803–812 (1986)

Merging IEC CIM and DMTF CIM – A Step Towards an Improved Smart Grid Information Model

Kornschnok Dittawit[(✉)] and Finn Arve Aagesen

Department of Telematics, Norwegian University of Science
and Technology, Trondheim, Norway
{kornschd,finnarve}@item.ntnu.no

Abstract. In the envisioned future Smart Grid, ICT will be incorporated into the power system at all domains in order to improve the operation and management. The incorporation of ICT must be systematic and incremental. One enabler of this is a well-designed and shared information model. IEC61970-301 Common Information Model (CIM) standard exists for the power system. However, it has some drawbacks that decrease the potential adoption benefits and create the barrier of adoption. We explore this standard along with the DMTF CIM standard used in network management and discusses how the principles in the DMTF CIM can be used to extend the IEC CIM in order to address the aforementioned drawbacks.

Keywords: Smart grid · Common information model · IEC61970 · Interoperability

1 Introduction

One possible definition of the Smart Grid is *a next generation power system that incorporates the use of ICT in the generation, transmission, distribution, and end-use of electricity in order to improve the operation and management of the power grid, which can further lead to greater grid reliability, efficiency, and interoperability* [1,2]. Incorporating ICT into the current power grid is not straightforward. The present power system is a highly complex system built over a hundred year using mainly electrical signals to automate power grid operations. At the same time, many management tasks are still done by human operators at the control centers using mainly heuristics with some help of computerized systems for visualization. The transformation of the current power grid into the ideal envisioned ICT-integrated Smart Grid will most likely be a very long process spanning over decades. However, the grid operators can already obtain great benefits from partial incorporation of ICT, as the automation of some management tasks can increase the efficiency in problem detection and diagnosis which could save time and money. The most important notion is that the change must be systematic, incremental, and will contribute towards a fully ICT-integrated

© Springer International Publishing Switzerland 2014
Y. Kermarrec (Ed.): EUNICE 2014, LNCS 8846, pp. 38–47, 2014.
DOI: 10.1007/978-3-319-13488-8_4

Smart Grid. One enabler of this change is a *structured and shared information model*. Having a well-defined and shared information model will, apart from accelerating the integration of ICT, improve the interoperability in the power system across all domains, from the generation down to the end-use domain.

Discussion on a shared power grid information model is not new. In fact, there exists IEC61970-301 Common Information Model (CIM) standard [3] developed by the International Electrotechnical Committee (IEC), that aims to enable integration among different applications and power utilities. The standard is also well-known to the power engineering community. However, the majority of power utilities do not use the IEC CIM. The potential barriers that prevent a widespread adoption are the required migration time, the intimidating size of the standard, and the uncertainty of expected benefits. In addition, the standard itself does not provide an exact specification on the implementation approach. This promotes flexibility but at the same time creates an integration barrier in conflict with its intended aim.

In this paper, we will be introducing industry standards from another domain, network management, which have been benefiting from various established standards. The purpose of this introduction is to briefly describe the evolution of management standards from a different domain and discuss what the power engineering community can learn from them. Then, we will be exploring the IEC CIM and the DMTF CIM [4] developed by the Distributed Management Task Force (DMTF) as used in network management. The DMTF CIM is similar to the IEC CIM in many ways but with some advantages that the IEC CIM lacks. Their similarities and differences will be discussed along with their weaknesses and strengths. Then, suggestions will be made on how the principles from DMTF CIM can be applied to extend IEC CIM. Finally, an IEC CIM integration plan is suggested.

The remaining part of this paper is organized as follows. Section 2 introduces and discusses network management standards. Sections 3 and 4 briefly describe the IEC CIM and DMTF CIM respectively. The two standards are compared in Sect. 5. Section 6 proposes an approach to merge the two CIMs. Then, Sect. 7 suggests an IEC CIM integration plan. Finally, Sect. 8 concludes.

2   Shared Information Models in Network Management

The power system can be compared to an IP-based networked system. For example, a power system is highly autonomous—the direction of power flow is governed by electrical signals and the voltage regulation under normal circumstances occurs in real-time without human intervention. An IP-based networked system works in a similar fashion. The routing of packets and transmission control are done without human intervention. The shared similarities are likely to exist also in their management approach. The lessons learned by the network management community will provide interesting insights to the power engineering community.

The development of network management standards dated back to the 1980s. Many standards have emerged since then. Some of the well-known standards are Simple Network Management Protocol (SNMP) [5], Web-based Enterprise Management (WBEM) [7], and Network Configuration Protocol (NETCONF) [6]. From the start, SNMP has always been the most prominent network management standard due to its simplicity. However, although SNMP features are implemented in almost all mainstream network equipment, SNMP is mainly used only for network monitoring. Network administrators mostly turn to proprietary Command Line Interface (CLI) for the configuration of network devices. This led to the development of WBEM, a suite of network management technology consisting of the DMTF CIM as the information model standard, that aimed at unifying the management of distributed computing environments. Although still not as widely used as SNMP and CLI, WBEM gained a lot of attention. Variants of WBEM are implemented in major operating systems and there exist many WBEM-compliant applications. Later, IETF began the development of NETCONF that aimed to replace CLI for network configuration task. Unfortunately, the aim has not been achieved; potentially because it uses a less popular remote procedure call and less known information modeling language.

In the power system, there are many proprietary applications for the management of different parts of the system. Most of these applications provide monitoring and diagnostic capability. They can be compared to CLI but possibly with a graphical interface and with functions leaning towards monitoring instead of configuration. The IEC CIM standard is also used by some power utilities for the purpose of exchanging information with other utilities or for monitoring purpose. The IEC CIM and other related standards in the same series (to be explained in Sect. 3) are most similar to WBEM in network management. For example, the information model is object-oriented and the communication between devices is done over HTTP. The success of WBEM indicates that the power engineering community is going in the right direction. However, WBEM has some advantages over IEC CIM. With proper extension to IEC CIM, the standard could become more powerful and serve as the one standard that, as WBEM, unifies all management tasks in the power system at different subdomains.

3   IEC61970-301: Common Information Model

IEC61970-301 is a part of the IEC61970 series. The main purposes of the series are (1) to enable integration of different energy management system applications as well as the integration with legacy systems and (2) to facilitate data exchange between power utilities or between the control center and external systems.

3.1   Model Structure

IEC CIM is object-oriented. It is broken down into packages of related classes, with each class consisting of several attributes. The classes, however, do not have any class-specific methods as the possible set of operations depends on the interface type exposed by the application.

3.2   Application Program Interface

IEC has specified a set of interfaces an application can provide. They are specified in the platform-independent Component Interface Specification (CIS) in IEC61970-4xx where xx is a number representing a specific interface type. The interface types are 402 common services [8], 403 generic data access [9], 404 high speed data access [10], 405 generic eventing and subscription [11], and 407 time series data access [12]. Part 402 serves as the basis for all interface types. Services for each interface type is valid for all implemented classes. For example, the read and update services defined in part 403 can be invoked on objects of any class that is implemented by an application exposing generic data access interface.

3.3   Model Exchange Language

It is up to the application developers to decide on a specific language used to exchange CIM models. IEC so far has provided one recommended encoding language in IEC61970-501 [13]. The language is a semantic web language, RDF/XML [14]—Resource Description Framework (RDF) [15] represented using XML syntax. The mapping from a CIM model to RDF model is often done by means of generation from CIM UML model file automatically by a script.

3.4   IEC CIM-Compliant Component Architecture

Based on the guidelines from the IEC, a possible component architecture for IEC CIM-compliant entities is depicted in Fig. 1. The processes involved in the interactions between the client and server are numbered and explained below.

1. The UML model representing the CIM is exported as a model file.
2. The model file is converted to an RDF schema file using an automated script.
3. The RDF schema is used to initialize the RDF store (RDF database).
4. Power data could be recorded during the systems operating state.

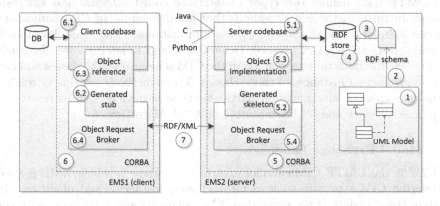

Fig. 1. Possible component architecture for IEC CIM-compliant entities

5. EMS2 employs CORBA to host the application interfaces.
   5.1. The codebase can contain program code in any programming language.
   5.2. A language-specific skeleton is generated from an Interface Definition Language (IDL) file specifying the interface to be exposed to clients
   5.3. The implementation of the skeleton resides in the codebase. These objects extend the skeleton to provide the logic for the defined methods.
   5.4. An Object Request Broker (ORB) is used as a medium for the server and client to communicate
6. The client, in this case, has the same architecture as the server
   6.1. The client codebase may contain code in a different programming language from the servers
   6.2. A language-specific stub is generated using the same IDL file as in the servers case
   6.3. An object reference, as the name suggests, acts as the reference to the remote object on the server. The client uses the object reference as if it resides locally on the client itself.
   6.4. An ORB is used to communicate with the server.
7. The requested power data is returned in RDF/XML format.

4 DMTF CIM: Common Information Model

4.1 Model Structure

There are two ways to represent the CIM: Managed Object Format (MOF) is used as a written form of representation while UML class diagram is used as a visual form. The model is divided into three conceptual layers: Core Model, Common Models, and Extended Models. The Core Model includes information applied to all network management domains. The Common Models include information applied to specific areas although independent of implemented technology. Information that is technology-specific is modeled in the Extended Models.

4.2 Application Program Interface

The DMTF CIM defines two types of interface called *intrinsic* and *extrinsic* method. Intrinsic methods are methods that are defined in the CIM namespace and can be used to manipulate all classes and instances. The examples of such methods are GetClass, GetInstance, DeleteClass, and DeleteInstance. Extrinsic methods are methods that are defined in the CIM schema on CIM classes and can only be invoked on instances of those classes. These methods are closely related to the management functions of a particular type of devices such as reset() on CIM_LogicalDevice and setAlarmState() on CIM_AlarmDevice.

4.3 Model Exchange Language

xmlCIM is the DMTF CIM's model exchange language in which XML is used to describe CIM structure such as CIM classes, instances, and qualifiers. To regulate how the data is represented as XML elements and attributes, both the Document Type Definition (DTD) and XML Schema Definition (XSD) are used.

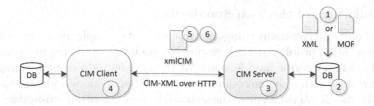

Fig. 2. Possible component architecture for DMTF CIM-compliant entities

4.4   DMTF CIM-Compliant Component Architecture

The DMTF has defined an exact approach for two CIM-compliant entities to interact with each other. *CIM-XML* is a protocol for exchanging CIM data and manipulating CIM object instances or classes. It uses xmlCIM as the payload over HTTP transport protocol. See Fig. 2 for the component architecture of DMTF CIM-compliant entities and their interactions. The processes involved in the interactions are numbered in the figure and explained below.

1. An XML or MOF file encoding a CIM model is used to populate the database
2. The database can be a relational database; the structure depends on the implementation of the server
3. The server must be able to send and receive HTTP requests and responses; it must also be able to query from and manipulate the database
4. CIM client must possess the same communication capabilities as the server
5. The xmlCIM request is sent as a payload in an HTTP request from the CIM client to the CIM server
6. The server sends an HTTP response with an xmlCIM response as a payload

5   Comparison of IEC CIM and DMTF CIM

5.1   Comparing Technical Specifications
(See Table 1).

Table 1. Summary of IEC CIM and DMTF CIM technical specifications

	IEC CIM	DMTF CIM
Model representation	UML, RDF/XML	UML, MOF
Schema language	RDF/XML	XML, MOF
Application interface	CIS (IEC61970-4xx)	Intrinsic/extrinsic method
Communication protocol	IIOP (CORBA) over HTTP/SSL	CIM-XML over HTTP
Transfer encoding	RDF/XML	xmlCIM

5.2   Similarities of the Two Standards

The two standards have many things in common. For example, both aim at solving system integration problem in their respective disciplines and are object-oriented. They both define intermediate formats for exchanging data or performing operations. In addition, they define common services for operations and data exchange that apply to all object types; these include basic create-read-update-delete operations on classes and properties such as get_values(), create_resource(), delete_resource() defined as part of the CIS for generic data access in IEC CIM [9] and GetInstance, GetClass, DeleteClass in DMTF CIM [16].

5.3   Differences Between the Two Standards

Despite the same aim to solve integration problem in their respective disciplines, the DMTF CIM was created as a result of a more ambitious goal which is to faciliate network management tasks. On the other hand, the IEC CIM was intended to be used as a standard for data exchange or public access of power system data. This led to the different levels of operations that can be done on their class instances.

In the IEC CIMs case, a limited number of operations were defined as part of its common interface specifications; each operation is closely-related to the type of interface and applies to all classes and instances in the associated CIM models. Such operations were also defined in the DMTF CIM in the form of intrinsic methods. However, DMTF CIM also defines extrinsic methods for specific classes. This is missing from the IEC CIM because it was not intended that the operations and management in the power system will be done by means of manipulating CIM instances. In other words, it was not considered necessary in the design of the IEC CIM. As a result, the IEC CIM has a simpler schema. In contrast, the DMTF CIM has a more complex schema with each CIM class having a specific set of defined methods.

6   Merging IEC CIM and DMTF CIM

The strength of the IEC CIM is the comprehensiveness of the standard. Most of the power entities in the generation and transmission, and some in the distribution domain, have been included in the model. This provides a taxonomy for the power system that will improve the interoperability between power utilities and applications. Unfortunately, the size of the standard and the open-ended implementation method can create uncertainty in adopting it for practical use. In other words, much of the job is left in the hands of the application developers to decide on the necessary classes, platform, and programming language. Moreover, the benefits may seem limited to obtaining data on specific power components without the ability to actually manipulate them programmatically. In order to fully reap the benefits from the standard, extensions are required. Due to the similarity between IEC CIM and DMTF CIM coupled with the success of DMTF CIM, we propose that some principles in DMTF CIM are applied to IEC CIM as the needed extensions. The applied principles are listed in this section.

6.1   Defining Device-Specific Operations for IEC CIM Classes

The lack of defined device-specific operations in IEC CIM standard prevents full integration of third-party applications that can directly manipulate power components. For example, it may be possible for an application to import a list of relevant power components, perform calculations, and suggest the actions to be done on specific components. However, the instructed actions must be carried out manually by personnels interacting directly with the targeted components or using a separate mediating application. It will be much more efficient if a third-party application can directly invoke operations on targeted components. However, device-specific operations must be standardized in order to ensure compatibility between the application and affected devices. As a result, we propose that the IEC CIM be extended to include device-specific operations equivalent to extrinsic methods in the DMTF CIM. This could be done incrementally for certain power components that are normally maintained by control centers.

6.2   DMTF-CIM-Like Component Architecture for IEC CIM-Compliant Entities

The implementation approach for IEC CIM-compliant entities is not a part of the IEC CIM standard. This is not a problem for IEC CIM-compatible applications implemented and used within a single power utility. However, it can create a problem with third-party applications that use IEC CIM but take a different approach to implement the exposing application program interfaces or use a different language to encode exchanged data. To address this issue, the IEC CIM standard must provide a specific implementation instruction.

One can deduct from the CIS documents that one possible implementation approach is to use CORBA for the communication between two entities exchanging CIM data. However, remote procedure call-based implementation is no longer a popular choice as evident from the unsuccessful push of IETF for NETCONF. We suggest an alternative component architecture that makes use of the approach used by the DMTF CIM in which CIM data is sent as an HTTP payload. The payload for the IEC CIM data requests and responses can be in RDF/XML as suggested in IEC61970-501. In case the IEC CIM is extended to include more complex device-specific operations, the invocation of operations can still be done using this alternative approach. The extension necessary is only to define shared RDF vocabularies to support operation invocation. Figure 3 illustrates the proposed alternative component architecture. The numbering is explained below.

1. A UML model file describing an IEC CIM model gets converted into an RDF schema file using a script.
2. The database can either be a relational database or an RDF store; using a relational database is simpler but requires program code to construct RDF/XML messages while using an RDF store complicates the query but RDF/XML messages can be constructed easily from the query results.

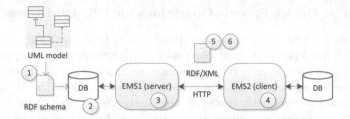

Fig. 3. Alternative component architecture for IEC CIM-compliant entities

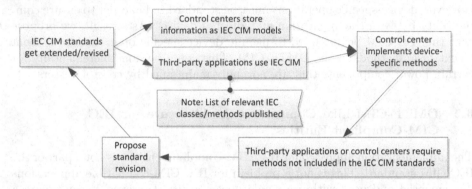

Fig. 4. IEC CIM integration plan

3. EMS1 can operate on any platform as long as it possesses the capabilities to send and receive HTTP requests and responses, parse RDF/XML messages, and manipulate the database.
4. EMS2 must possess the same capabilities as EMS1.
5. EMS2 sends an RDF/XML message requesting for CIM data or invoke operations as an HTTP request's payload.
6. EMS1 sends an RDF/XML message containing the requested CIM data or acknowledgement as an HTTP response's payload.

7 IEC CIM Integration Plan: What Must Happen?

It can be expected that a widespread adoption of IEC CIM will span over decades. Figure 4 depicts a likely integration cycle. First, the IEC CIM standard series are extended as proposed in Sect. 6. Then, both the utility-operating control centers and third-party applications start adopting the IEC CIM as necessary. The control centers have to also implement device-specific methods required by in-house or third-party applications. In case a method not included by the standards is needed, a proposal should be submitted to the IEC to be considered for future revision of the standards. The process then repeats.

8 Conclusions

Present power grid management relies largely on human operators and heuristics. This is envisioned to change in the future Smart Grid where ICT is more tightly integrated into the power system to increase management efficiency which could save time and money for grid operators. A step that will contribute to this change is the establishment of a shared information model that can be used across all domains in the power system. In this paper, we discuss a known standard in the power engineering community, IEC61970-301: CIM, and propose extensions using principles adopted by another successful standard used in network management domain—DMTF CIM. The extensions include the incorporation of device-specific operations and a simpler component architecture. Extending the IEC CIM with device-specific operations will make possible the direct control of power components from third-party applications, while a simpler component architecture can speed up the adoption rate of IEC CIM.

References

1. National Institute of Standards and Technology: NIST Framework and Roadmap for Smart Grid Interoperability Standards. Technical report (2012)
2. CEN-CENELEC-ETSI Smart Grid Coordination Group: Smart Grid Reference Architecture. Technical report, European Standards Organizations (2006)
3. IEC: IEC 61970–301 ed3.0 Energy management system application program interface (EMS-API)—Part 301: Common information model (CIM) base (2011)
4. Distributed Management Task Force: DSP0110: CIM Concepts White Paper v0.9. Technical report (2003)
5. Internet Engineering Task Force: A Simple Network Management Protocol (SNMP) (1990). http://tools.ietf.org/html/rfc1157
6. Internet Engineering Task Force: Network Configuration Protocol (NETCONF) (2011). http://tools.ietf.org/html/rfc6241
7. Distributed Management Task Force: Web-Based Enterprise Management (2014). http://dmtf.org/standards/wbem
8. IEC: IEC 61970–402 ed1.0 Energy management system application program interface (EMS-API)—Part 402: Common services (2008)
9. IEC: IEC 61970–403 ed1.0 Energy management system application program interface (EMS-API)—Part 403: Generic data access (2008)
10. IEC: IEC 61970–404 ed1.0 Energy management system application program interface (EMS-API)—Part 404: High Speed Data Access (HSDA) (2007)
11. IEC: IEC 61970–405 ed1.0 Energy management system application program interface (EMS-API)—Part 405: Generic Eventing and Subscription (GES) (2007)
12. IEC: IEC 61970–407 ed5.0 Energy management system application program interface (EMS-API)—Part 407: Time Series Data Access (TSDA) (2007)
13. IEC: IEC 61970–501 ed1.0 Energy management system application program interface (EMS-API)—Part 501: CIM RDF schema (2006)
14. W3C: RDF 1.1 XML Syntax (2014). http://www.w3.org/TR/rdf-syntax-grammar/
15. W3C: Resource Description Framework (RDF) (2014). http://www.w3.org/RDF/
16. Distributed Management Task Force: DSP0200: CIM Operations over HTTP v1.3.1. Technical report (2009)

How Much LTE Traffic Can Be Offloaded?

Souheir Eido[1,2] and Annie Gravey[1,2(✉)]

[1] Telecom Bretagne, Plouzané, France
{souheir.eido,annie.gravey}@telecom-bretagne.eu
[2] IRISA, Rennes, France

Abstract. In this paper, we propose different offloading scenarios, which help operators controlling the ever increasing of mobile data volumes over the femto and the macro cellular networks. We consider the Selected IP traffic offload (SIPTO) approach in order to selectively offload mobile IP traffic in order to use servers deployed within the metro network "at/above the RAN". A quantitative study is carried out to estimate the potential gains of bandwidth due to mobile traffic offload, both in the core and the metro networks, depending on the location of the servers accessed thanks to the offloading strategy.

Keywords: Mobile data offloading · SIPTO · LIPA

1 Introduction

In the last few years, many fixed network operators have deployed multiple caches close to the end-users in order to limit the bandwidth requirements related to video streaming distribution in the downlink. Moreover, many cloud services can also rely on data centers that are distributed within the network in order to serve demands as close as possible to the users.

In the present paper, we assess whether similar gains can be obtained for mobile traffic carried over an LTE access network. This is not obvious, since using distributed servers in LTE is not as simple as using distributed servers for fixed services, due to the mobile network specific architecture.

Carrying on the same momentum that we have witnessed since the late of the 20th century, the mobile data traffic is expected to grow rapidly during the next decade. The compounded Annual Growth Rate (CAGR) will be close to 75 % [1]. This is due to the increasing number of internet-based services such as online games and video services (streaming, conferencing, etc.).

LTE routing is currently based on tunneling the traffic between the user equipment (UE) and the Packet-data-network Gateway (PGW) in both directions. The PGW is the gateway towards the IP backbone and the Internet. More precisely, the tunneling starts from the user equipment (UE) to the radio base station (eNodeB), then from the eNodeB to the Evolved Packed Core network (EPC), and thus to a Serving Gateway (SGW) which forwards it to a Packet-data-network Gateway (PGW). In particular, even if a video server or a datacenter is geographically close to a UE, the requested content has to go through the EPC in order to enter the tunnel existing between the UE and the PGW.

Y. Kermarrec (Ed.): EUNICE 2014, LNCS 8846, pp. 48–58, 2014.
DOI: 10.1007/978-3-319-13488-8_5

Mobile data offloading potentially allows a telecom operator to dynamically control the delivery of data originally targeted for mobile network using different available technologies such as: WiFi and Femtocells [2]. Each of these technologies proposes both EPC-routed and Non-EPC-routed traffic offloading solutions.

- EPC-routed Traffic offload is based on the network triggering the UE to use either femtocells (home base stations) or WiFi access instead of the macrocells. The traffic is then forwarded towards the EPC network. This solution allows alleviating the load on eNodeBs.
- Non-EPC-routed Traffic offload allows to alleviate the loads on SGW and PGW, and to balance load between available gateways. This is achieved by dynamically controlling routes used by the mobile traffic in the aggregation and core networks regardless of the technology used at the access network. Local IP Access (LIPA) and Selected IP Traffic Offload (SIPTO) are two 3GPP solutions that can be used for traffic offloading in the aggregation/core network.

Assuming that these offloading techniques are actually implemented, what is the gain, in terms of offloaded traffic, that can be expected?

The remainder of this paper is organized as follows. Section 2 presents the state of the art of different mobile data offloading techniques. Section 3 derives estimates of the amounts of offloaded traffic for each network portion and thus quantifies the potential bandwidth gains. Finally, Sect. 4 concludes the paper.

2 Evaluation of the Amount

Over the long term, telecom operators have noticed that with the dramatic increase of the mobile data traffic, the demand for bandwidth will continue to increase at every segment of the network (access, metro and backbone). Offloading mobile data is thus considered as one of the most promising technologies that help reducing the bandwidth demand on both aggregation and core networks. The present section reviews popular offloading approaches relying on femtocells. We first point out the benefits of the deployment of femtocells for telecom operators and its consequences. Next, we present the LIPA and SIPTO approaches that have been introduced by 3GPP. Finally, we outline the importance of mobile data offloading for the end-users as well as the operators.

2.1 Access Network Offloading

Femtocells, also called Home eNodeBs (HeNB), are low power cellular base stations. They were first defined by 3GPP in order to offload the mobile traffic from the standard base stations (macro-cells) and thus improve the indoor voice and data coverage of mobile networks [3]. HeNBs transmit the mobile traffic using the same spectrum than macrocells [4]. Femtocells are connected to the cellular core network by the means of an IP home router, which uses a direct broadband connection such as: Fiber To The Home (FTTH) or Digital Subscriber Line (DSL). This connection replaces the backhaul infrastructure currently used for the macrocells.

Wi-Fi access points located in Home Gateways can be used similarly.

Besides the capacity, coverage and network performance's improvement, the deployment of femtocells helps operators reducing a significant part of capital expenditure (CAPEX) as well as operational expense (OPEX). According to Cisco [1], "33 % of global mobile data traffic (GMDT) was offloaded onto the fixed network using femtocells and Wi-Fi in 2012". By 2017, the offloaded mobile data traffic is expected to reach 46 % of the GMDT and thus, the use of femtocells and WiFi technologies to access the mobile core network will help saving 13 % of CAPEX costs dedicated for macrocells deployment. Furthermore, considering the ongoing costs for running macro base stations, deploying and monitoring their backhaul as well as additional electricity, OPEX is reduced to only 200$ per year per femtocell down from 60,000 $ per year per macrocell [5].

However, due the fact that femtocells transmit on the same spectrum as macrocells, the following problems are still under study:

- Radio interferences
- Femtocell location detection

Moreover, access network offloading does not help in solving the issue raised in Sect. 1, namely mobile traffic routing through the EPC.

2.2   Mobile Aggregation/Core Network Offloading

3GPP has extended the use of femtocells in order to limit the loads of both aggregation and core networks. Indeed, femtocells potentially allow a direct access to the public IP network via the fixed network. Hence, by adding local PDN gateway (L-PGW) which is either co-located with the femtocell or a standalone entity connected to the femtocell via a separate interface, mobile data traffic will bypass the mobile core network and thus reduce the load of the standard gateways (SGW and PGW) used in 3G/4G networks.

The use of the local PDN gateways with the femtocells was initially proposed by 3GPP in Rel-10 [6]. LIPA and SIPTO, two solutions of traffic offloading, were also introduced in order to offload selected IP traffics from the mobile core network. LIPA and SIPTO both offer a direct connection between mobile users and the Home/ Enterprise Local Access Network (LAN) devices. At the same time, a UE shall be able to have simultaneous access to the local IP network (using LIPA/SIPTO) and to the operator's core network through the normal path.

These solutions were improved in 3GPP Rel-12 [7] by solving some of the mobility issues raised in their first version. Figure 1 illustrates the 3GPP regular data path as well as offloading architectures for both LIPA and SIPTO solutions.

LIPA is an offloading technique allowing a direct connection between the UE and the local IP network using a femtocell (HeNB) with a co-located or a standalone Local Gateway (LGW). The LGW must support limited PGW as well as SGW functionalities such as interconnecting with the external IP networks, UE's IP address allocation functionality, DL packet buffering, etc. [8]. However, LIPA is only intended to allow the UEs to access their own Private Local Access Network via a femtocell. Thus, UEs

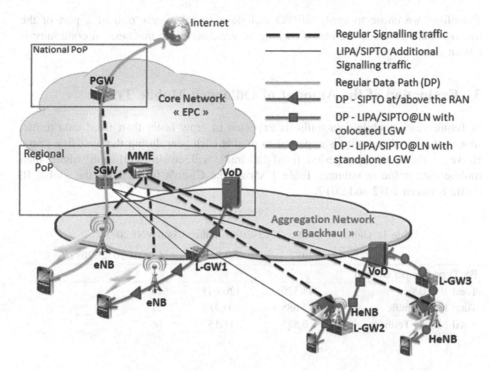

Fig. 1. LIPA and SIPTO solutions for mobile data offloading

may not apply LIPA when connected through a macrocell. In particular, no service continuity is supported in case of mobility (e.g. whenever a UE moves away from the femtocell, all his sessions are terminated).

SIPTO is an offloading mechanism defined by 3GPP to allow mobile operators to selectively breakout some of the user's IP data traffic:

1. "At the local network" using a femtocell with a co-located or a standalone LGW "Similar to LIPA";
2. "At or above the RAN" using a macrocell by selecting an SGW and PGW that are topologically/geographically closer to the radio network [9].

Unlike LIPA, SIPTO can be used in both macrocells and femtocells. However, in SIPTO (as in LIPA) service continuity in case of mobility is not ensured although partial solutions have already been proposed to solve this issue (see for example [10] and [11]). Once this issue solved, the use of LIPA and SIPTO's offloading techniques is expected to allow significant benefits for both mobile operators (in terms of OPEX) as well as for the end-users (in terms of QoS) [12, 13].

In the present paper, we do not address potential enhancements to LIPA/SIPTO, which could solve the issue of session continuity in case of mobility. On the other hand, we want to assess the potential gain in terms of bandwidth, due to offloading the major part of mobile data into the metropolitan network "at/above the RAN".

Therefore, we chose to apply SIPTO technique to selectively offload a part of the mobile data traffic into the metro caching servers, assuming that session continuity is not an issue.

3 Evaluation of the Amount of Offloaded Mobile Traffic

In future years, mobile data traffic is expected to grow faster than fixed data traffic. Indeed, mobile data traffic is expected to double each year during the next five years. However, during the same period, fixed data traffic will remain significantly higher than mobile data traffic in volume. Table 1 shows the Cisco's forecast for the global IP traffic between 2012 and 2017.

Table 1. Global IP Traffic, 2012–2017. Source Cisco VNI 2013 [14]

	2012	2017	CAGR 2012−2017 (%)
By Type (EB per Month)			
Total IP Traffic	43,570	120,643	23
Total Fixed Traffic	42,685	109,486	21
Total Mobile Traffic	0,885	11,157	66

We see that during the time period, mobile data traffic will still remain significantly lower than fixed data traffic in absolute terms, growing from 2 % in 2012 to slightly more than 9 % in 2017.

Considering the continuous growth of IP based traffic, telecom operators must increase the capacity of their networks. In that aim, actual deployments are based on distributing video servers and datacenters as close to the end-users as possible.

3.1 Distribution of Services from the Metro Network

There are currently two different video distribution architectures: "IPTV" and "Internet Video".

In the first one, the Internet Service Provider (ISP) also distributes video; this service is known as "IPTV". As the content provider controls the Digital Rights Management (DRM), and the access of the users to the various content, it is aware of all demands and can dynamically select the server, which shall serve each demand. In particular, IPTV operators distribute servers within the metro network in order to improve user's experience and network performance. There are a few main video servers (large servers) that contain the complete set of offered video content, and several smaller, secondary servers, operating often as caches, which only store the more popular content. A recent publication [15] shows that the file hit ratio in such secondary servers can be relatively small (less than 35 %) while the byte hit ratio in those servers is quite large (75 %), as popular content are requested very often compared to the mean request rate.

In "Internet Video", the Content Provider (CP) distributes the content over the Internet. Content distribution over the Internet relies on an overlay network linking multiple servers located at peering points. Popular content are present at multiple locations, while less popular are pulled on demand from central video servers. The Content Provider may directly distribute its own content (e.g. Google directly distributes YouTube content) or delegate content distribution to Content Distribution Networks (CDNs) such as Akamai and Limelight. CDN servers are located close to the peering points with the ISP and are controlled by the CP or the CDN. The ISP has a role neither in controlling the DRMs, nor in controlling the access to the content. As the ISP usually does not accept another provider to control servers within its own domain, there are no video caches in the metro network and the traffic cannot be offloaded. However, the video distribution ecosystem is constantly evolving, and strategic partnerships such as the one signed in 2012 between Akamai and Orange [16] may lead in the future to locating video caches used by Internet video services within ISPs' domains.

Although video is expected to be dominant in future traffic mixes, other services can also benefit from distributed servers. This is true for all cloud-based services such as on-line gaming and business services.

3.2 Gain of Bandwidth at the Core Network

Let us consider services offered to mobile users. These services can be achieved either in a centralized manner (relying on a central server located in the backbone), or in a distributed manner (relying on distributed servers located in the metro network). We now compare the respective amounts of traffic, generated by mobile services, over specific portions of the network, under different assumptions regarding the location of the distributed servers.

A centralized LTE architecture relies on a very small number of PGWs, located high in the IP backbone, whereas a distributed LTE architecture relies on a larger number of PGWs (which we call LGWs in order to differentiate them from the standard PGWs). LGWs are located closer to the user, typically within the metro network.

Assuming that distributed servers and LGWs are conveniently co-located, the load reduction in the core network (CN) for the years 2012 and 2017 is now computed.

Let X, Y, Z respectively represent the volumes in Total IP traffic, Total traffic generated by fixed services and Total traffic generated by the mobile services. Let also X_c, Y_c and Z_c respectively represent the volumes in Total IP traffic that crosses the CN, Total fixed network's traffic that crosses the CN and Total mobile network's traffic that crosses the CN.

G_{cm} quantifies the potential gain of bandwidth in the core network due to mobile traffic offloading. G_{cm} is the percentage of traffic crossing the CN that can be diverted from the CN if mobile offloading is applied. The demands corresponding to this traffic are served from servers located in the metro network.

Obviously:

$$Xc = Yc + Zc \tag{1}$$

According to [17] we have

$$Xc = \alpha * X \tag{2}$$

with $\alpha = 0.43$ in 2012 and $\alpha = 0.25$ in 2017.

In a centralized LTE architecture, none of the mobile traffic is offloaded, which yields $Zc = Z$ and $Yc = Xc\text{-}Z$.

The amount of fixed traffic, which is not offloaded from the CN, is then

$$Yc = \alpha * X - Z \tag{3}$$

In a distributed LTE architecture, mobile traffic can be offloaded. We also assume that the proportions of traffic generated respectively by fixed services and mobile services, which can be served in the metro network, are identical:

$$Zc/Z = Yc/Y \tag{4}$$

The amount of traffic crossing the CN, generated by mobile services and that can be offloaded is equal to $Z*(1-Yc/Y)$ which finally yields Gcm

$$Gcm = 100 * (1 - Yc/Y) * Z/Xc \tag{5}$$

Table 2 applies the above derivation to the data given in Table 1 in order to assess the impact on the CN of distributing the LTE architecture. The obtained results imply that:

Table 2. Quantifying bandwidth gain in core network due to mobile traffic offloading

	2012		2017	
X	43.570		120.643	
Y	42.685		109.486	
Z	0.885		11.157	
Xc	18.735		30.160	
Yc	17.850		19.010	
	Centralized LTE	**Distributed LTE**	**Centralized LTE**	**Distributed LTE**
Zc	0.885	0.370	11.157	1.941
Gcm	0	**2.75 %**	0	**30.55 %**

- In 2012, mobile traffic offloading allows to reduce the volume of traffic supported by the CN by less than **3 %**. This gain can be considered as negligible compared to the investment (in terms of LGW deployment) required to achieve it.

- In 2017, more than **30 %** of CN bandwidth can be offloaded if a distributed mobile LTE architecture is implemented. This significant gain can potentially justify the CAPEX increase due a distributed LTE architecture.

3.3 Gain of Bandwidth at the Metropolitan Network

As the gain in distributing the LTE architecture is not significant in 2012, we focus the following study to predictions relative to 2017.

Regarding the traffic growth study presented in [17], two distribution models have been introduced:

1. *Metro Centralized Caching:* In this model, servers are centralized at the edge of the backbone network (Fig. 2, servers P3).
2. *Metro Distributed Caching:* In this model, servers are distributed within the metro network at the edges of the access/metro segment of the network (Fig. 2, servers P1) and at the edge of the metro/core segment of the network (Fig. 2, servers P2).

Depending on the bandwidth demand statistics, operators may choose to implement either the first model or the second one. Moreover, operators can also implement a combination of both models.

In order to estimate the gain of bandwidth in the metro network for 2017, we proposed three different scenarios. The first one assumes that a limited number of servers are located in the metro network (typically, at the edge of the CN). We also consider (arbitrary) distribution architectures, where servers are located deeper in the metro network.

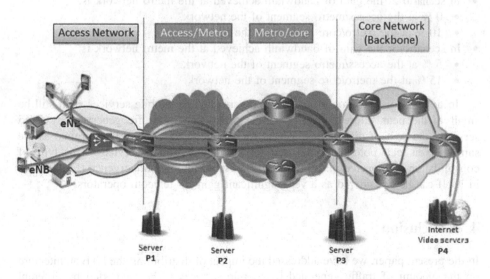

Fig. 2. Locating servers in the metro and core networks

Scenario 1: All the traffic that terminates in the metro network is offloaded at the centralized cache (Fig. 2, servers P3) at the edge of the backbone.

Scenario 2:

- 50 % of the total IP traffic is offloaded at the distributed cache (Fig. 2, servers P2) at the edge of the metro/core segment of the network.
- 25 % of the total IP traffic is offloaded at the centralized cache (Fig. 2, servers P3) at the edge of the backbone.
- 25 % of the total IP traffic traverses the backbone to the national IP server (Fig. 2, servers P4).

Scenario 3:

- 30 % of the total IP traffic is offloaded at the distributed cache (Fig. 2, servers P1) at the edge of the access/metro segment of the network.
- 25 % of the total IP traffic is offloaded at the distributed cache (Fig. 2, servers P2) at the edge of the metro/core segment of the network.
- 20 % of the total IP traffic is offloaded at the centralized cache (Fig. 2, servers P3) at the edge of the backbone.
- 25 % of the total IP traffic traverses the backbone to the national IP server (Fig. 2, servers P4).

We can now apply similar methods as in the previous subsection to derive the gain on various portions of the metro network due to using different distributions of servers in the metro network.

- In scenario 1: the only gain of bandwidth is achieved at the CN (Sect. 3.2). Thus, the gain of bandwidth at the metro network is 0 % for the first scenario.
- In scenario 2: the gain of bandwidth achieved at the metro network is:
  - 0 % at the access/metro segment of the network.
  - 10 % at the metro/core segment of the network.
- In scenario 3: the gain of bandwidth achieved at the metro network is:
  - 5 % at the access/metro segment of the network.
  - 15 % at the metro/core segment of the network.

In addition, as the proportion of traffic generated by mobile services shall still be small in the near future compared to the proportion of traffic generated by fixed services, the cost of distributing servers for mobile services may be marginal as the same servers can potentially be used for fixed and mobile services. This type of consolidation is expected in the framework of fixed-mobile convergence (FMC). This in itself can be considered as a very significant gain for telecom operators.

4   Conclusion

In the present paper, we have addressed the impact of distributing the LTE architecture on the amount of traffic generated by mobile services to be supported by different portions of the network. First, we briefly surveyed the various tools specified in the

LTE architecture to offload mobile generated traffic. We then assumed that these tools were actually implemented (distributed LTE architecture), or not (centralized LTE architecture). Using well-accepted traffic prediction assumptions, we assessed the traffic reduction on the CN and on various portions of the metro network, due to mobile traffic offloading, under different server distribution assumptions.

We have shown that the gain to be expected from server distribution for mobile traffic in the near future is small, but that in 5 year time, as much as 30 % of backbone traffic can thus be offloaded. Smaller but significant gains can also be obtained in the metro network if servers are implemented deeper in the metro network, closer to the users.

In the future, we intend to evaluate the anticipated costs due to offloading the mobile IP traffic. We shall also study SIPTO improved implementations that support session continuity in case of mobility.

Acknowledgment. The research leading to these results has received funding from the European Community Seventh Framework Program FP7/2013- 2015 under grant agreement n° 317762 COMBO project.

References

1. Cisco Visual Networking Index: Global Mobile Data Traffic Forecast Update, 2012–2017, White Paper, CISCO (2013)
2. 3GPP "Service requirements for Home Node B (HNB) and Home eNode B (HeNB)", TS 22.220 (2011)
3. Knisely, D.N., Yoshizawa, T., Favichia, F.: Standardization of Femtocells in 3GPP. IEEE Communications Magazine (2009)
4. Cisco 3G Femtocell: CISCO Public Information document (2010)
5. Chandrasekhar, V., Andrews, J., Gatherer, A.: Femtocell networks: a survey. IEEE Commun. Mag. **46**, 59−67 (2008)
6. 3GPP Local IP Access and Selected IP Traffic Offload (LIPA-SIPTO), TS 23.829 (2011)
7. 3GPP LIPA Mobility and SIPTO at Local Network (LIMONET), TR 23.859 (2013)
8. 3GPP Evolved Universal Terrestrial Radio Access (E-UTRA) and Evolved Universal Terrestrial Radio Access Network (E-UTRAN), Stage 2, TS 36.300 (2014)
9. Sankaran, C.: Data offloading techniques in 3 gpp rel-10 networks: a tutorial. IEEE Commun. Mag. **50**, 46−53 (2012)
10. Taleb, T., Samdanis, K., Schmid, S.: Dns-based solution for operator control of selected ip traffic offload. In: IEEE ICC (2011)
11. Taleb, T., Hadjadj-Aoul, Y., Samdanis, K.: Efficient solutions for enhancing data traffic management in 3GPP networks. IEEE Syst. J. (2011)
12. NEC's Femtocell Solutions. http://uk.nec.com/en_GB/global/solutions/nsp/3g/products_ and_solutions/prod_femtocell/benefits/
13. Mobile Traffic Offload: NEC's Cloud Centric Approach to Future Mobile Networks, White Paper, NEC (2013)
14. Cisco Visual Networking Index: Forecast and Methodology, 2012–2017, White Paper, CISCO (2013)

15. Gravey, A., Guillemin, F., Moteau, S.: Last Mile Caching of Video Content by an ISP, ETS 2013: 2nd European Teletraffic Seminar (2013)
16. Young, J., Wright, T., Temple, N.: Orange and Akamai form Content Delivery Strategic Alliance (2012)
17. Bell Labs Metro Network Traffic Growth: An architecture impact study, White Paper, Alcatel-Lucent (2013)

Approaches for Offering QoS and Specialized Traffic Treatment for WebRTC

Ewa Janczukowicz[1,2](✉), Stéphane Tuffin[1], Arnaud Braud[1],
Ahmed Bouabdallah[2], Gaël Fromentoux[1], and Jean-Marie Bonnin[2]

[1] Orange Labs, Lannion, France
{ewa.janczukowicz,stephane.tuffin,arnaud.braud,
gael.fromentoux}@orange.com
[2] Institut Mines-Telecom, Telecom Bretagne, Cesson Sévigné, France
{ahmed.bouabdallah,jm.bonnin}@telecom-bretagne.eu

Abstract. Real-time communications are much more than only traditional voice services. They have become interactive, transversal and are expected to be integrated as a feature of other applications. More and more communications services are offered by web companies that have been taking advantage of Internet flat rate charges and mostly use best-effort capabilities. Simultaneously, many efforts are currently devoted to improve the quality of experience of clients using communication services. The paper analyses current implementations of managed VoIP and emerging WebRTC technology in order to assess the possibility of offering specialized media flow treatments to real-time web communications. It proposes two research approaches: "in-network" and "over-the-network" and several elements that could contribute to an overall solution allowing web communication services to benefit from specialized network services.

1 Introduction

Nowadays, communication services are much more than only traditional voice services as they have become multimedia, unified with other communication means and are expected to be integrated as a feature of other applications. More and more communication services are offered not by carriers but by web companies. There is a growing interest in web technology based solutions as proven by the success of WhatsApp and WeChat as well as the continuous effort of Google in this field with Google Voice, Hangouts and WebRTC (Web Real Time Communication). New actors that have entered the market have had a major influence on traffic characteristics and relations between different players. Additionally separation of network and communication services may be observed.

The major actors in this ecosystem are:

- Network service provider (NSP) that can also act as communication service provider (Telco-CSP).
- 3rd party communication service provider (OTT-CSP), where Over The Top (OTT) means that services are provided without the NSP's involvement.

© Springer International Publishing Switzerland 2014
Y. Kermarrec (Ed.): EUNICE 2014, LNCS 8846, pp. 59–69, 2014.
DOI: 10.1007/978-3-319-13488-8_6

Telco-CSPs are constantly challenged by OTT-CSPs. However, OTT-CSPs have not had to deal with deploying network and service infrastructure nor with maintaining the continuity of the public telephone service. They take advantage of the Internet access flat rate based charging model and use connection with best-effort capabilities. To achieve a satisfactory quality they rather adapt the applications. However, supporting reliable service and end-to-end transmission is a common problem for access networks and also core routers and links [1].

There are several technical and economic aspects that make it difficult to exactly predict at what rhythm changes to the traffic will be done and at what point new investments into networks should be anticipated.

Firstly, the speed of growing demands concerning network capacity is not the same as the actual speed of increasing network resources. This is true especially for access networks. DSL and FTTx use a dedicated link for each home whose capacity can be easily congested especially as the number of connected screens increase. On cellular access, the radio resources are shared by the users in a cell. The capacity may be increased by using e.g. spectrum sharing or small cell technologies. However it is more uncertain that it will allow keeping-up with the future demand.

Secondly, there are certain implementations that cause the unpredictability of the traffic. Especially it is caused by Content Delivery Service providers that assure routing management at the application layer and based on their own criteria. So NSPs do not have a clear visibility on the traffic and may not always predict how the flows will behave. Additionally, peer to peer (P2P) traffic is not easy to predict as it causes unexpected congestion points [2].

Last but not least, there are difficulties when creating commercial agreements, as NSPs need their investments to be justified and refunded [1]. The interconnection between Internet Service Providers (ISPs) may be a congestion point. In order to assure capacity management connected ISPs need to agree. It is not trivial since there is a strong competition between different NSPs (or ISPs) and their interests are not always in line, especially when traffic becomes too asymmetric, e.g. for video content delivery. Thus they may not be always willing to invest into enhancing the network.

OTT-CSPs constantly offer challenging services to customers. As a result they need a reliable network infrastructure supporting the increasing number of applications [1]. Real time communications need network to support mechanisms for protecting a certain delay for sensitive traffic and controlling congestion problems. Some mechanisms are built into OTT-CSPs applications to adapt to uncertain best-effort quality, however these mechanisms imply trade-offs in the user experience (e.g. switching to lower quality codecs) and can only adapt to limited best-effort network issues. Thus it is important to invest in deploying network services specialized for real-time web communications [3].

The aim of this paper is to analyse Telco-CSPs and OTT-CSPs (based on emerging WebRTC) solutions in order to evaluate the possibility of applying managed VoIP principles to WebRTC.

The paper is structured as follows. Section 2 focuses on WebRTC that is currently under standardization, which is not common for OTT-CSPs work, and as a result has a big potential. Section 3 gives an overview of currently used managed VoIP solutions. In Sect. 4 the reasons of why managed VoIP principles cannot be directly applied to

WebRTC are given. Section 5 highlights two possible research approaches and pro-poses a multi-criteria analysis as an evaluation method for chosen solutions. In Sect. 6 conclusion and future research works are discussed.

2 WebRTC

2.1 Simplicity and Availability of WebRTC Technology

Web Real Time Communication (WebRTC) [4] is a new technology that allows browser to browser communications, i.e. audio and video communications, screen sharing, data transfer. It simplifies not only developers' but also users' tasks. Since provided native browser tools are based on HTML5 and JavaScript, a certain level of web technology knowledge would be enough to implement a web page with a real-time communication service. There is no major cost when integrating WebRTC into the existing web infrastructure. Also interoperability between devices does not cause problems since everything is integrated into the browsers. Web users do not need to install plugins to use these capabilities. As a result this technology makes significant changes in real-time communication by lowering barriers to entry. Thus there is a large spectrum of actors that will be willing to use it.

2.2 Proprietary Control Planes and Endpoint Based Media Plane

In WebRTC the media plane is separated from the signalling one as it is in managed VoIP. The difference is that WebRTC standardizes only the media plane and the APIs in the browsers but does not impose anything for signalling. Three standardisation bodies include major companies, i.e. Google, Mozilla, Skype-Microsoft, Cisco, Al-catel-Lucent and Ericsson:

- IETF working on the media plane [5];
- W3C working on Application Programming Interfaces (APIs) for browsers [6];
- 3GPP working on WebRTC access to IMS (IP Multimedia Subsystem) [7].

The signalling plane is not meant to be standardized and its choice is up to the OTT-CSP. The communication is established thanks to exchanging signalling mes-sages by using a web server. Since each OTT-CSP wants to have its own base of users, all communicating parts need to be connected via the same OTT-CSP, so proprietary "bubbles" are created [8].

The media plane is different from the one used by NSPs. As for web services it is important to choose codecs that can adapt to best-effort conditions by using the information on the quality of the network. As a result the quality of communication is managed at the device level. Also the congestion management is assured at the browser level for example by using Real-time Transport Control Protocol (RTCP) feedback and local measurements. For example Receiver-side Real-time Congestion Control (RRTCC) is implemented in WebRTC-capable browsers. However it works well only for low delay networks [13]. In order to assure the confidentiality and integrity media encryption at the browser level is mandatory on the contrary to NSPs solutions where it is assured beneath the IP level [8].

2.3 Media Relay as a Last Resort

In WebRTC ideally, there should be no application intermediary in the media plane, thus the security must be provided by the devices. Avoiding media relays is not always possible because of certain architecture implementations (mostly for enterprises). Also media relays are needed when using access networks not compatible with P2P traffic, e.g. mobile networks disabled P2P traffic that prevented applying appropriate charging, because the charging gateway is situated behind the edge router. However, sending media through a media relay is done only when other connections are not possible. In order to choose an appropriate connection type Interactive Connectivity Establishment (ICE) is used [9]. ICE enables endpoints to discover possible media addresses that can be used in order to receive the media. When discovered, they are sent to the remote endpoint via the signalling channel.

Three major connection modes are presented in the Fig. 1.

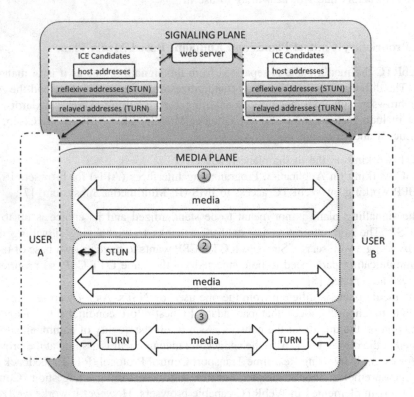

Fig. 1. WebRTC possible media connections

1. Direct media connection is possible when endpoints' host addresses can be used.
2. STUN server is used when at least one of the endpoints is behind a NAT. It allows it to learn its public address. When one endpoint sends a STUN binding requests to the STUN server, it gets in return the public transport address—a reflexive address. As a result a NAT binding is created and the reflexive address is used by the remote endpoint to send the media data [10].
3. The TURN protocol is defined as an extension of the STUN protocol. TURN servers act as media relays and are directly placed in the media path. TURN server gets all the media packets from an endpoint and sends them towards the remote one or to another TURN server, if it is also used by the remote endpoint [11].

3 Managed VoIP

Telco-CSPs have used traditional telephony approach when designing new services. Thus, the ecosystem of conversational services for carrier relies mostly on IMS. Each NSP provides its services for its network and to its own subscribers, and then it interconnects with other NSPs to assure the end-to-end service with managed quality. NSPs' principle was to have a control over all elements, i.e. user devices, services, network. However given the need of offering competitive communication services on the global scale and the large variety of currently used devices it is unrealistic for IMS provider to have a control of the whole ecosystem [8].

In this section a quick overview of managed voice mechanisms is given, but the scope is limited to mass market VoIP solutions. The standardization does not describe the full implementation of these solutions so a common practice among the network providers will be presented.

3.1 Access Network

Media flows are prioritized at the access level. There are two main cases: fixed access network (i.e. Digital Subscriber Line, DSL or Fiber to the x, FTTx) and mobile access network (i.e. LTE). Economic and technological differences between the wireline and mobile solutions lead to different network access architectures and as a result a different quality of service (QoS) mechanisms.

In fixed networks there are two traffic differentiation mechanisms.

- Mechanism based on DiffServ IP uses DSCP (Differentiated Services Code Point). In this solution, when packets are generated by the VoIP software running on the home gateway, they get an appropriate DSCP tag and are treated with a priority.
- Mechanism based on ATM multiVC solution. In this implementation there are multiple local IP interfaces on the home gateway, so there is one virtual circuit (VC) for Internet and another one for conversational traffic. When packets are generated by the VoIP software the conversational VC is used.

In the DSL technology both traffic differentiation mechanisms are used for historical and technical reasons. In the FTTx technology, only the mechanism based on DiffServ IP is used.

In LTE access network the traffic differentiation mechanism is connection oriented. At the session establishment, EPS bearers are set up between the end point and Packet Data Network Gateway. Each bearer is configured with a QoS Class Identifier (QCI), e.g. voice specific. How the end point applies local differentiated treatment and how upstream VoIP traffic is steered within the dedicated QCI is implementation specific inside the device but standardized on the interface device-network. Based on QoS parameters like QCI, the radio scheduler is configured in order to allocate radio resources to different bearers [12].

As it was shown above, packet prioritization is fully controlled by NSPs that do not take into account any 3rd party prioritization attempts. Any packet markings set by an untrusted end point will not be taken into consideration.

3.2   IP Backbone

The IP backbone uses the same technologies for wireline and mobile networks. IP-VPNs are created in order to sort and separate the traffic (e.g. VPN MPLS). Session Border Controllers (SBCs) are currently used to transfer the traffic and to control dedicated IP-VPNs, i.e. only the flows that have crossed these SBCs can access these VPNs. The SBCs are implemented at the access and Interco level. This approach simplifies the implementations of security solutions including the Access Control List (ACL) management and makes routing and traffic management easier.

The separation of VoIP media from the other traffic is not primarily used for prioritisation, since IP backbone is more easily overprovisioned than other network segments, but in order to protect VoIP media plane equipment, e.g. devices, media servers, gateways. The dedicated media VPN are also useful in case of connection failures as it assures fast rerouting.

3.3   Interco

The managed VoIP interconnections also use the same technologies for wireline and mobile networks. As seen previously, Internet interconnection is best-effort. For managed VoIP, Telco-CSPs use dedicated interconnections that allow them managing capacity and quality of the traffic. These interconnections make use of Interco SBCs. There are two possible implementations: direct interconnection between two Telco-CSPs or connection hubs such as an IPX where traffic is carried across private IP networks that respect SLA (Service Level Agreement) and ensures QoS.

3.4   Service Fulfillment

In order to assure the efficiency of operational infrastructure each NSP/Telco-CSP has to monitor the quality of experience and be proactive to restore the service quality in case of issues and coordinated network operations impacting the managed service. It is done by using internal procedures and cooperation between NSP/Telco-CSP's teams that manage the end-to-end managed VoIP service, the IMS platform and the involved network segments.

4 Managed VoIP Approach for WebRTC?

There are several issues with directly applying managed VoIP design principles to WebRTC technology as it does not correspond to technical choices previously made by NSPs when designing VoIP in continuity with the PSTN design.

Each Telco-NSP has interfaces with its own network resources and federates with the other NSPs to provide a global VoIP service. Many aspects of the coupling between the application layer and the network layer are inapplicable to OTT-CSPs. The device-side APIs that would allow using specialized network services are left unspecified. The network-side APIs raise a currently unsolved brokering issue since there are hundreds of NSPs worldwide. OTT-CSP that would desire to access such an API would firstly need to determine NSPs which are used by the communicating endpoints. However interfacing many NSPs would require a single API design but business relationship covering many NSPs. Until now, the few existing network APIs initiatives, such as the 3GPP PCC API address only some access network types. Moreover these APIs are not globally available.

In managed VoIP approach, the use of a standard call control signalling plays a key role as it allows the network to get the knowledge about media flows authorized to benefit from specialized treatment. As described previously, this is used both at the user-network interface (e.g. with access SBC and with the coupling between P-CSCF/PCRF/PCEF) and at the network-network interface. In case of WebRTC, the signalling is not standardised. As a result each OTT-CSP creates a proprietary "bubble", thus the previous managed VoIP principles do not apply.

SBC based media steering plays a key role in the coupling of the network layer and the application layer at access and interconnection level. Each NSP needs to distinguish the flows that should benefit from specialized treatments. Also when a call is admitted by a next-hop NSP it is simultaneously entitled to use specialized network services of the next-hop NSP. However, in WebRTC, TURN servers are used as last resort partly because of the cost of operating a media relay. Also OTT-CSPs tend to privilege peer-to-peer media that is currently subject to best-effort routing, whereas the interconnection of VoIP is distinct from Internet interconnection, with a different capacity management due to different business incentives.

In managed VoIP approach some network capacity management aspects directly depend on forecast and observations regarding the managed VoIP service demand, e.g. at interconnection. OTT-CSPs forecast would be less accessible and predictable by NSPs. Thus a more elastic capacity management for OTT-CSPs would be needed.

Additionally, service fulfilment solutions are proprietary to each NSP/Telco-CSP. Giving OTT-CSPs the possibility to provide a full troubleshooting and supervision service to their customers would require standard and open troubleshooting and supervision interfaces avoiding the previously mentioned brokering issue.

To summarize it is important to point out that in WebRTC everything is managed at the application level, whereas NSPs use coupling of application and network layers. As a result the service intelligence and logic are not in the same place.

5 Survey of Alternative Approaches

5.1 Identified Approaches

We investigate different approaches of OTT-CSP and NSP coupling that would allow OTT-CSP to benefit from valuable network services while avoiding the issues of directly applying the managed VoIP principles to these actors. There are two alternative research approaches to offer a collaborative architecture in order to provide QoS or prioritisation of flows for OTT-CSPs: "in-network" and "over-the-network".

In the "in-network approach", NSPs would offer network or device APIs to CSPs (both Telco and OTT) in order to provide specialized treatment for their traffic. There are different available mechanisms and possible infrastructures that should be analysed to check the possibility of using them in future implementations.

- NSPs can provide media relays (i.e. TURN servers) for WebRTC communications. Deploying them close to the communicating end points may improve the QoS in comparison to using TURN servers deployed by OTT-CSPs, e.g. in the USA. TURN servers can be used like access SBCs, i.e. as systematic media relays in order to provide differentiated treatment to authorized media flows. This authorization can be done thanks to mechanisms such as the TURN extension for third party authorization [18]. However TURN servers are not currently meant to be used at the interconnection between NSP domains.
- In LTE an API can be opened on top of the PCRF so that media flows initiated by CSPs could benefit from specialized LTE bearer and be transported in dedicated VPNs.
- The Metadata-flow mechanism can provide a framework to enable exchanging communication information elements between applications and the network along the path. NSPs would have a better visibility of application flows and could assure their differentiated treatment. Proposed common information elements include bandwidth requirements and delay, jitter or packet loss tolerance. Also there is a possibility of application identification [14].
- Traditional IP routing uses static metrics, but a better distribution of the traffic could be achieved if a decision about the best route was taken based on statistics and metrics from edge routers or other network equipment. Such an approach is used in Cisco Performance Routing [15].
- Mechanisms for optimizing the co-existence of elastic elephant flows with real-time flows such as Cross-protect [19] or Fair Queuing (FQ) with Controlled Delay (CoDel) allows classifying packets into different flows in order to give low delays to flows that do not fill the buffers, e.g. real-time voice [16].
- Software Defined Networking (SDN) implementation may also be considered, e.g. UCI Forum's solution that exposes QoS network service app functionalities [17].

In the "over-the-network" approach, CSPs would work independently from NSPs. They could use big data processing of real-time network statistics collected from the end points (e.g. CSP software), various transport nodes (e.g. Multipoint Control Unit) and media relays (e.g. TURN). This data could be used to select the most advantageous path for the media (e.g. relayed media path vs peer-to-peer media path; use Wi-Fi vs cellular Internet access, etc.). The decision would be made by CSP with an optional NSP assistance, e.g. providing additional metrics.

5.2 Multi-criteria Analysis

It is not possible to use simple criteria (e.g. implementation cost, QoS/QoE improvement) to compare solutions listed above since they impact different actors (NSPs, CSPs and end users).

The solutions should be classified by taking into consideration two aspects: business models and network segments concerned by congestion points. When it comes to the business models and the impact on the business value chain, there are three possibilities:

- NSPs invest into improving their network performances for all services,
- OTT-CSPs pay for specialized network services provided by NSP,
- Partnership between different actors.

Network segments that above solutions are impacting can be divided into:

- Access: wireline or mobile,
- Peering: best-effort Internet or specialized tunnels.

However comparison based only on this classification is not enough. As a result a multi-criteria analysis is needed and more detailed, technical criteria should be selected to have a complete assessment of the solutions.

6 Conclusion

Telco-CSPs solutions inherit from traditional telephony. The advantage of managed solutions is that they ensure the end-to-end connectivity and provide high reliability and scalability. However they may be too specific and too dedicated in certain cases. The big success of unmanaged communication service solutions with emerging WebRTC technology may lead to marginalisation of SIP/IMS technology. WebRTC shows a completely new way of creating communication services, a way that is more "web" and more "developer friendly". OTT-CSPs thanks to their simplicity and a global reach may eventually gain an important part of the market. Even though the traditional telephony service is not the aim of this technology, it offers a conversation service that is rich, attractive and relevant to the users. As a result traditional telephony service seems poor and would be used only as a last resort, i.e. in case of bad network coverage or emergency calls.

The drawback is that WebRTC solutions may be considered by users as less reliable, especially for enterprises that strongly depend on the quality and reliability of communications. Also there exists no clear solution on how to implement QoS mechanisms. Especially managed VoIP design principles, which allow assuring end-to-end SLA, cannot directly apply to WebRTC.

We are witnessing a change in communication services. Instead of creating dedicated systems it is worth to collaborate and work on more global and interoperable solutions. Two possible research approaches were presented. They discuss possible collaborative architectures used to provide QoS or prioritisation of flows for OTT-CSPs solutions.

This article reveals several questions, especially implementation ones that should be answered in the future research. It presents research approached that would allow offering QoS and specialized network services to WebRTC communication. It proves that none of the identified implementations offers an end-to-end solution since they impact different network segments. As a result for the future work we will focus on multi-criteria analysis by taking into account different actors requirements.

References

1. Statovci-Halimi, B., Franzl, G.: QoS differentiation and internet neutrality. Telecommun. Syst. **52**(3), 1605–1614 (2011). Springer, Berlin
2. Barreiros, M., Lundqvist, P.: QOS-Enabled Networks—Tools and Foundations. Wiley, Chichester (2011)
3. Position Paper on CC for Interactive RT Communication. http://www.tschofenig.priv.at/cc-workshop/irtf_iab-ccirtcpaper23.pdf. Accessed 23 May 2014
4. WebRTC. http://www.webrtc.org/. Accessed 16 April 2014
5. Rtcweb Status Pages. https://tools.ietf.org/wg/rtcweb/. Accessed 16 April 2014
6. WebRTC 1.0: Real-time Communication Between Browsers. http://www.w3.org/TR/webrtc/. Accessed 16 April 2014
7. Study on Web Real Time Communication (WebRTC) Access to IP Multimedia Subsystem (IMS). http://www.3gpp.org/DynaReport/23701.htm. Accessed 16 April 2014
8. Bertin, E., Cazeaux S., Cubaud, S., Tuffin, S., Crespi, N., Beltran, V.: WebRTC, the day after: What's next for conversational services? In: 17th International Conference on Intelligence in Next Generation Networks (ICIN), pp. 46–52. IEEE (2013)
9. Interactive Connectivity Establishment (ICE). https://tools.ietf.org/html/rfc5245. Accessed 16 April 2014
10. Session Traversal Utilities for NAT (STUN). http://tools.ietf.org/html/rfc5389. Accessed 23 May 2014
11. Traversal Using Relays around NAT (TURN). http://tools.ietf.org/html/rfc5766. Accessed 23 May 2014
12. Packet-oriented QoS management model for a wireless access point. http://tools.ietf.org/html/draft-jobert-iccrg-ip-aware-ap-00. Accessed 23 May 2014
13. Singh, V., Lozano, A.A., Ott, J.: Performance analysis of receive-side real-time congestion control for WebRTC. In: 20th International on Packet Video Workshop (PV) 2013, pp. 1–8. IEEE (2013)

14. A Framework for Signaling Flow Characteristics between Applications and the Network. http://tools.ietf.org/id/draft-eckert-intarea-flow-metadata-framework-02.txt. Accessed 21 May 2014
15. PfR: Technology Overview. http://docwiki.cisco.com/wiki/PfR:Technology_Overview. Accessed 23 May 2014
16. FQ_CoDel. http://man7.org/linux/man-pages/man8/tc-fq_codel.8.html. Accessed 21 May 2014
17. Automating QoS UC SDN Use Case. http://ucif.org/Portals/0/documents/2014_02_27_Use_Case.pdf. Accessed 21 May 2014
18. TURN Extension for Third Party Authorization. http://tools.ietf.org/html/draft-reddy-tram-turn-third-party-authz-02. Accessed 24 May 2014
19. Cross-Protect. http://perso.rd.francetelecom.fr/oueslati/XP.html. Accessed 24 May 2014

Identifying Operating System Using Flow-Based Traffic Fingerprinting

Tomáš Jirsík[✉] and Pavel Čeleda

Institute of Computer Science, Masaryk University,
Botanická 68a, Brno, Czech Republic
{jirsik,celeda}@ics.muni.cz

Abstract. Many vulnerabilities are operating system specific. Information about the OS of all hosts in a network represents a valuable asset for network administrators. While OS detection in small networks is an easy task, expanding the same process on a large scale becomes a challenge. The weak performance, high speed traffic and large amount of hosts for OS detection are issues to overcome. In this paper we propose a flow based framework for large scale OS detection. Furthermore, we describe the framework implementation into a flow probe, provide performance comparison and share remarks on deployment in a real world network.

Keywords: OS fingerprinting · Passive · High-throughput · p0f · Flow

1 Introduction

Being aware of all operating system (OS) communicating in a network means an advantage for administrators protecting network security. Hosts with vulnerable OSs pose a serious threat to security as they could be misused as an entry-point to the network. This awareness also improves network management as any host with an outdated system can be easily identified (e.g., the recent termination of Windows XP support). Since 1994, when the main concept was introduced in [3], two main approaches to OS detection have emerged: active and passive.

The existing active OS detection tools such as *nmap* [5] launch a set of TCP, UDP and ICMP probes to a scanned host and detect OS system based on responses they receive. This approach provides high accuracy, but is also time demanding especially in large networks as we need to scan each host. Furthermore, it inserts other traffic into network, which increases bandwidth. This approach has the form of a network scan which, without permission, is legally questionable.

On the other hand, passive OS detection does not insert any packets into the network traffic. The OS type is determined based on the traffic captured from the network. One widely used passive OS detection tool is p0f [6], which employs data extracted from packet L3-L4 headers and even utilizes the content of application-level payload to detect OS. p0f is a cornerstone for other tools such as Ettercap, Disco, Yaf or Satori [6]. The advantages of passive fingerprinting are

© Springer International Publishing Switzerland 2014
Y. Kermarrec (Ed.): EUNICE 2014, LNCS 8846, pp. 70–73, 2014.
DOI: 10.1007/978-3-319-13488-8_7

that it does not leave any traces and does not modify the traffic. This approach is suitable for deployment in large networks as there is no necessity to actively probe each host.

We identify following the criteria for a OS detection tool working on large scale: easy deployment and use, passive detection, and high performance. High performance is desired in order to be able to scan large networks entirely and handle traffic incoming at high speeds. Passive detection is preferred to active because it does not affect the traffic in any way and is capable of monitoring large amount of hosts at the same time. Ease of deployment and use are required to save network administrators' time.

In this paper, we present a flow based OS detection framework for use on a large scale. We implement the framework into a flow probe, compare its performance with other OS detection tools and discuss some remarks on its deployment in a real network.

2 Flow Based OS Detection

In this section we describe a flow based framework for OS detection in large networks. Such an approach to OS detection has been chosen for following reasons. First, flow based monitoring [2] is widely used standard for monitoring large network infrastructures. This fact eases the deployment of our detection framework as there is no need to introduce a new monitoring infrastructure. Second, observation points for flow based monitoring are suitably situated. Usually, the points are placed on the main network traffic hubs and network borders. Therefore all hosts can be monitored at the same time. Moreover, we are able to detect the OS of all hosts in a network without accessing them. Lastly, the concept of flow based network traffic monitoring is designed to process network traffic even at high speeds of up to 100 Gbits/s, which makes it suitable for deployment in high speed networks.

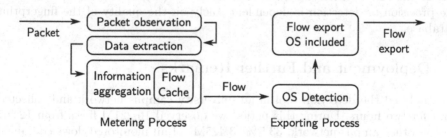

Fig. 1. Architecture of flow based OS detection framework

The proposed framework for large scale OS detection is described in Fig. 1. The most utilized part of the framework is the Metering Process as millions of packets per second are processed there. For this reason, we postpone all logic related to OS detection to less utilized processes. During the Metering Process packets are observed at the observation point (e.g., using TAPs). Each packet is processed and relevant data are extracted. Apart from the basic set of values needed for flow creation, we extract data necessary for OS detection, namely TTL, SYN packet size, initial size of TCP window and User Agent field from HTTP protocol. The number of values extracted from the packet can be easily increased by adding new rules into the Data extraction process. The gathered information is then aggregated in Flow Cache into flows. Anytime the inactive or active timeout is triggered, the flows are passed further onto the Exporting process. So far, there has been no logic to detect OS. This logic is part of the Exporting Process. The delay of logic for OS detection decreases the computational demands as the number of flows to process is significantly lower than the number of packets. The logic for OS detection can be represented by the comparison of gathered OS specific information with a database of OS fingerprints. The improvement of logic for OS detection is left for future work. When an OS is detected, OS information is added to flows and flows are exported to collector.

We have implemented the framework into FlowMon probe [4] as a set of processes and filter plugins.[1] Furthermore, we have benchmarked the tool at a set of 1068 packets (TCP SYN packets : HTTP GET packets : other TCP/UDP packets $= 1:1:1$), which were loaded in loop from memory to probe[2]. The FlowMon probe running without detection plugins processed 18.328 Mp/s. Using only OS detection based on User Agent field, the throughput dropped by 50.42 % to 9.087 Mp/s. Running the detection based on all fields (i.e. TTL, SYN size, TCP win. size) the performance decreased by another 6.49 % to 8.497 Mp/s.

The main contribution of our work is the framework design with high performance OS detection in large networks. Other passive OS detection tools such as p0f (or k-p0f) are able to process up to 0.05 Mp/s (or 0.6 Mp/s) [1]. Our approach benefits from flow monitoring framework specially designed for deployment in large networks. Therefore, we were able to increase the performance of OS detection remarkably. We do not evaluate the precision of the OS detection, since we collect the same entries from network traffic as (k-)p0f tool in [1]. Therefore the precision of detection is dependent solely on the quality of the fingerprint database.

3   Deployment and Further Remarks

We deployed the detection tool in an university campus network and collected data for two hours. During this period we observed 10.221M flows from 12 897 hosts in the campus network. 33.5 % (3.425M) of all monitored flows contained all the information needed for OS detection which represented 70.33 % (9 072) of all hosts. We observed that in some cases more than one OS was detected for one IP. The cause of this behavior could be dynamic addressing in networks. Therefore we removed all dynamically addressed subnets from evaluation.

---

[1] Description and sources available at http://is.muni.cz/th/359565/fi_b.
[2] Configuration: Intel Xeon CPU E31230 @ 3.20GHz, 15GB RAM, and Linux (64 bit).

Table 1. Number of unique OS detected at one IP: **A** - whole network, **B** - dynamically addressed subnets removed

# of unique OS	# of IP in A	% of all A	# of IP in B	% of all B
1	7898	87.059	3996	95.989
2	1071	11.806	159	3.819
3	80	0.882	7	0.168
>3	23	0.253	1	0.024
Total	9072	100 %	4163	100

The results (see Table 1) show, that the portion of the IP addresses with more than one detected OS has decreased after the removal of dynamically addressed networks. However, still 4 % of IP shows characteristics of two or more OS. This fact can be explained by the presence of more devices with different OS using the same IP address. This implies the presence Network Address Translation (NAT) devices. Therefore, the OS detection can be used also as NAT detection assuming that only a static addressed network is monitored.

The OS detection framework presented in this paper represents a useful tool for network administrators. It meets all previously defined requirements for deployment in large scale networks: easy deployment and use, passive monitoring, and high performance. The ease of deployment and use is ensured by taking advantage of existing flow based monitoring infrastructure commonly used in such networks. The design of the framework also ensures the flexibility and, as it has been shown, the increase in performance. In future work, we will focus on the OS detection logic. We would like to enlarge the database of fingerprints by adding OS specific elements and provide a new approach to fingerprints correlation, which should increase the precision of OS detection.

Acknowledgments. This material is based upon work supported by Cybernetic Proving Ground project (VG20132015103) funded by the Ministry of the Interior of the Czech Republic.

References

1. Barnes, J., Crowley, P.: k-p0f: a high-throughput kernel passive os fingerprinter. In: Architectures for Networking and Communications Systems (ANCS), 2013 ACM/IEEE Symposium on, pp. 113–114 (2013)
2. Claise, B., Trammell, B., Aitken, P.: RFC 7011: Specification of the IPFIX Protocol for the Exchange of Flow Information (2013)
3. Comer, D., Lin, J.C.: Probing tcp implementations. In: USENIX Summer, pp. 245–255 (1994). http://dblp.uni-trier.de/db/conf/usenix/usenix_su94.html#ComerL94
4. INVEA-TECH: FlowMon Exporter - Community Program. http://www.invea-tech.com, [cited 2014-04-15] (2013)
5. Lyon, G.F.: Nmap Network Scanning: The Official Nmap Project Guide to Network Discovery and Security Scanning. Insecure, USA (2009)
6. Zalewski, M.: p0f v3. http://lcamtuf.coredump.cx/p0f3/. Accessed 15 April 2014

Towards an Integrated SDN-NFV Architecture for EPON Networks

Hamzeh Khalili[⊠], David Rincón, and Sebastià Sallent

Deptartment of Telematics Engineering, Universitat Politècnica de Catalunya
(UPC) – BarcelonaTech, Castelldefels, Barcelona, Spain
{khalili.hamzeh, drincon, sallent}@entel.upc.edu

Abstract. SDN and NFV are two novel paradigms that open the way for a more efficient operation and management of networks, allowing the virtualization and centralization of some functions that are distributed in current network architectures. Optical access networks present several characteristics (tree-like topology, distributed shared access to the upstream channel, partial centralization of the complex operations in the OLT device) that make them appealing for the virtualization of some of their functionalities. We propose a novel EPON architecture where OLTs and ONUs are partially virtualized and migrated to the network core following SDN and NFV paradigms, thus decreasing CAPEX and OPEX, and improving the flexibility and efficiency of network operations.

Keywords: EPON · SDN · NFV · Scheduling

1 Introduction

Ethernet Passive Optical Network (EPON) is currently the cutting edge technology in access networks. It combines the high bandwidth of optical networks with the well-known Ethernet architecture and frame format. EPONs follow a point-to-multipoint topology which comprises: (1) a central unit called Optical Line Terminal (OLT) that connects the access network to the backbone, (2) a set of distributed Optical Network Units (ONUs) located at the customer's premises, and (3) optical fibres and passive optical splitters that connect the OLT and the ONUs in a tree-like topology [1]. The OLT centralizes the management of the EPON. The downstream channel is broadcasted from the OLT to the ONUs, while in the upstream channel arbitration procedures are performed in order to coordinate ONUs and to avoid collision between the data frames generated by the users (inter-ONU scheduling). The OLT is also capable of performing bandwidth allocation and flow prioritization inside each ONU (intra-ONU scheduling) via a set of class-based queues (for example, for real-time services such as IP Telephony or IP TV).

Software-Defined Networking (SDN) is a novel paradigm that decouples the control and data planes of network equipment, and concentrates the intelligence and complexity of devices in a centralized controller which has a global view of the state of the network [2]. The SDN/Openflow architecture defines a set of flow tables. When a packet arrives to an SDN switch, it is analyzed and forwarded to the flow table that

© Springer International Publishing Switzerland 2014
Y. Kermarrec (Ed.): EUNICE 2014, LNCS 8846, pp. 74–84, 2014.
DOI: 10.1007/978-3-319-13488-8_8

matches the packet headers. The table defines the actions to be executed on the packet, such as drop, forward to a certain port, or rewrite headers, for example. This opens the way to the programmability and global optimization of network operations, with the goal of maximizing reliability, balancing the load, minimizing delay, and optimizing energy consumption, to name a few possibilities. Openflow [3] is currently the de-facto standard interface between the SDN controller and the devices.

More recently, Network Functions Virtualization (NFV) [4] has been proposed in order to take further the programmability of the network by virtualizing network functions (such as NAT, firewalls, caching, or load balancers, for example) and running them in servers located inside the core network, thus decreasing the cost of the edge equipment and increasing the efficiency of network operations. Both SDN and NFV promise significant reductions in both Capital Expenditure (CAPEX) and Operational Expenses (OPEX) by reducing the complexity of devices, and they allow a more efficient way of managing networks by expanding the optimization offered by SDN.

Our proposal applies the aforementioned paradigms to the EPON scenario. Optical access networks present several characteristics (tree-like topology, distributed shared access to the upstream channel, partial centralization of the intelligence of the network in the OLT device) that make them appealing for the virtualization of some of their functionalities. The control plane of the OLTs of a large operator can be (partially) virtualized and centrally controlled via Openflow/SDN, thus opening the way to coordinated backbone/access network optimizations, dynamically adjusting the configuration to the traffic pattern, or end-to-end flow prioritization and QoS enforcement (to name a few examples) while reducing CAPEX and OPEX. The paper provides a preliminary analysis of such a scenario.

The rest of the paper is organized as follows. Section 2 introduces the main EPON-related concepts needed to understand the new architecture proposed. Section 3 provides a survey on the related work that has been done in the area of integrating SDN and PON. Section 4 details the proposed architecture and focuses on the new SDN-OLT architecture, its functionalities, and the new set of related actions. It also includes an example of how an EPON bandwidth allocation algorithm could be enhanced in the new architecture. Section 5 concludes the paper.

2   EPON Architecture

EPON follows the original architecture and keeps all the advantages of a Passive Optical Network physical layer (high data rates, cheap passive optical components) in the signal distribution network, while using easy-to-integrate, well-known Ethernet technology as the data link layer. The active components are (1) the OLT, located at the service provider's premises, at the top of the topology tree, and (2) the ONUs, located at the customer's premises [1], as illustrated in Fig. 1.

The main challenge for EPONs is how to organize the access control (MAC) to the shared optical transmission medium. The downstream channel is common and arrives at every ONU, while the upstream channel is arbitrated in order to avoid collisions between the transmission attempts of the ONUs.

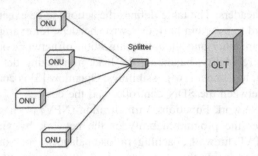

Fig. 1. Elements of the PON topology.

As shown in Fig. 2, the Multi-Point MAC control is composed of one or more MAC instances, where the number of MAC instances depends on the number of ONUs connected to the OLT. A functionality of the Multi-Point MAC control sublayer is the Multi-Point Control Protocol (MPCP), which is in charge of managing the exchange of messages between the OLT and ONUs during the initial registration phase, and also during normal operation. MPCP defines a state machine, messages and several timers to control access to the medium, one ONU at a time.

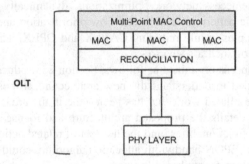

Fig. 2. Protocol architecture of an EPON OLT.

For the initial registration phase, the following messages are defined:

- REGISTER_REQ: unregistered ONUs use this message to respond to discovery GATE messages. In the downstream channel, the OLT sends GATE messages (explained later), which all the ONUs receive.
- REGISTER: the OLT uses this message to assign a unique identity to a newly registered ONU.
- REGISTER_ACK: sent by the ONU to the OLT as a final registration acknowledgment.

During normal operation after the ONU has been registered, there is a continuous exchange of GATE and REPORT messages (Fig. 3):

- REPORT messages: apart from carrying the amount of data (in the form of several Ethernet frames piggybacked to the REPORT message header), which were assigned previously by the OLT via a GATE message, this message is used by ONUs to request bandwidth from the OLT.
- The GATE message performs two roles: A discovery GATE message for the registration phase, and a normal GATE message that is used to assign the transmission time and bandwidth to each ONU. The timing is accurately calculated and coordinated by the OLT, depending on the distance and propagation delay from the OLT to each ONU, so that the transmissions from the ONUs do not collide in any of the passive splitters.

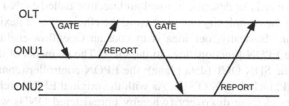

Fig. 3. OLT to ONU messages

3 Related Works

Few works have tackled the topic of applying the Software Defined Networking paradigm to Passive Optical Networks. The authors of [5] propose an SDN-based architecture for optical access networks by applying a centralized optical wavelength assignment mechanism that transfers to the OLT functionalities that are typically implemented in ONUs. It allows full virtualization of the optical spectrum space, thus allowing arbitrary wavelengths to be available on-demand through software reconfigurable control. With this technique, the physical upstream and downstream connections can be virtualized as logical flows between bidirectional Openflow port identifiers.

The discussion of how SDN principles might be applied to optical access and mobile backhaul networks is the focus of [6]. Regarding PONs, Software-Defined OLTs and ONUs are proposed, though few details are given. A "meta-MAC" algorithm (able to coordinate the medium access control algorithms of different PON technologies and/or physical layers) is presented as one of the applications of a centralized, SDN-based management of the network.

GPON (Gigabit Passive Optical Networks) are the focus of [7], where an extension of Openflow is proposed in order to provide traffic mapping and forwarding capabilities, while keeping its original functionality, architecture and capabilities. Accordingly, each OLT and ONU in the GPON contains flow tables and communicates over a secure channel with remote controller via the OpenFlowPLUS protocol. Three new actions are proposed, all of them related to the mapping of Ethernet frames to GPON logical ports, containers, and framing. Other functionalities of the OLT, such as ONU discovery, synchronization, or bandwidth assignment are not tackled.

An integrated management architecture for SDN-based access, metro and core networks is proposed in [8]. The access segment is enhanced with Openflow-enabled OLTs that pass bandwidth assignment information to the Metro segment (an optical ring of Openflow devices) and the Core segment (an IP/MPLS network with path computation network element (PCE)). A so-called Generalized SDN controller is responsible for the control planes of the global network and is potentially able to coordinate and optimize the end-to-end performance.

4   Proposed Architecture

4.1   High-Level Description and Discussion

The aim of this paper is to describe a novel architecture called SDN-EPON, with the goal of decreasing the complexity and increasing the efficiency and flexibility of EPON network operations. Basically, our idea is to take an Openflow-enabled switch as a base, then add the EPON functionalities to the OLT. The elements of the SDN-EPON architecture are: the SDN-OLT (data plane); the EPON-controller (control plane); and the EPON network, including N ONUs. As with the original EPON architecture, SDN-EPON coordinates element discovery (whereby unregistered ONUs will be added to the network); it synchronizes newly added ONUs; and it assigns transmission time slot and traffic volumes in order to transmit data within a specified time slot in the upstream direction in accordance with some policy defined by a bandwidth allocation algorithm. The novelty introduced by our architecture is the flexibility in defining operation policies, which is done by keeping the forwarding functions within the SDN-OLT switch and moving the management functions to the EPON-controller. Table 1 shows a summary of the comparison between EPON and SDN-EPON functionalities.

The NFV concept can also be applied by centralizing the controller of several EPON access networks in servers located in some Data Center (DC) in the cloud infrastructure of the operator. The aforementioned approach opens the way to coordinating the SDN-OLT(s) with the backbone network in order to improve the end-to-end quality of service and to manage resources efficiently. The centralization and consolidation of several EPON-controllers may raise concerns about reliability, but this can be solved by setting up a master-slave controller architecture. When the master controller fails, one of the slaves becomes a master for the network. Scalability concerns can also be solved by distributing the controllers hierarchically. Why, then, centralize the controllers if we later distribute the load between them? The reason is economy: EPON controllers will be virtual machines running in physical servers, and running them together (cloud paradigm) saves operation and investment costs.

As shown in Fig. 4, the SDN-EPON architecture is divided into three main parts. The first one is the EPON-controller, which concentrates the intelligence of the network and could be run on dedicated servers located within the network backbone or in the access provider's data centres. It dialogues with the data plane (SDN-OLT) and manages the bandwidth policies to be applied for each ONU/end user. It could also take advantage of its centralized view of the network to optimize several aspects, such as energy consumption, to name just one possibility. The second element is the SDN-OLT,

Table 1. Comparison of functionalities between EPON and SDN-EPON

EPON	SDN-EPON
• Element discovery	• Element discovery
o Register	o Register—flexible policy
• Synchronization	• Synchronization
• Topology management	• More flexible topology management
• Quality of service	• Quality of service
o Bandwidth allocation	o Bandwidth allocation
o Static policy	o Dynamic policy
	• Centralized/coordinated management of access network
	• Reduced operation and fixed cost

which concentrates the main functionalities of the EPON network. It is physically located between and both communicates with and allows communication between the EPON-controller, the EPON network and the core network. The SDN-OLT is an Openflow switch that emulates the forwarding function of the MPCP sublayer. The switch has N virtual ports (one per ONU), plus three ports which communicate with the core network, the EPON-controller, and the EPON network. The EPON port is synchronous, since the communications between the OLT and the ONUs have tight timing requirements. We propose splitting the functionality of the MPCP sub-layer of the OLT into two parts: the high-level policies, which can be migrated to the centralized controller; and the data plane functions, which can remain at the SDN-OLT. Finally, there is the third element of the EPON network (including optical links, splitters, ONUs and end users), which remains unchanged.

Focusing now on the SDN-OLT, our preliminary analysis identified the need for extending Openflow in order to facilitate the dialogue between the controller and the SDN-OLT. Basically, the new messages transport information about ONU registration, bandwidth assignment and scheduling. Timing can be a challenge, since processing the SDN dialogue between the controller and the SDN-OLT (which takes place at the scale of milliseconds) can delay certain key real-time interactions (such as those between ONUs and OLT, which take place at a much lower time scale, on the order of nanoseconds).

We now discuss how certain EPON operations can be executed and enhanced by the new SDN-based architecture.

4.2 Element Discovery

For the discovery and registration of ONUs, the SDN-OLT periodically broadcasts a discovery GATE message via the downstream channel. The new ONU responds with a REGISTER_REQUEST message via the upstream channel to indicate that it needs to register to the network. The SDN-OLT then asks the EPON-controller about the policy to apply to the user via an Openflow message. The controller defines the policy for the newly added ONU and sends an Openflow message with the policy parameters to the SDN-OLT; then the SDN-OLT responds to the ONU with a REGISTER message and, finally, the ONU sends a REGISTER_ACK message in the next time slot allocated by

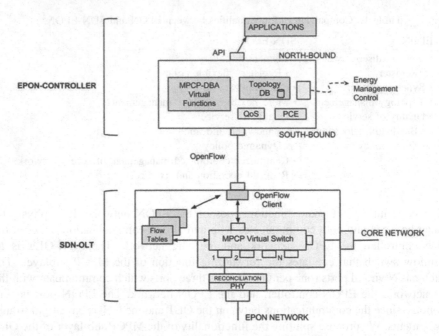

Fig. 4. SDN-EPON architecture.

the SDN-OLT. This allows the SDN-OLT to modulate its policy in terms of the requirements of the SDN controller. In this case, the time scale is not an issue, since the registration and acceptance of a new ONU is not a time-critical operation.

4.3 Bandwidth Management Mechanism

The synchronous EPON port in the SDN-OLT is responsible for the exchange of GATE and REPORT messages with the ONUs. Since Openflow tables do not include synchronous capabilities, we have to extend them with timestamp information, as we will see later. Besides, this is one of the operations that cannot be executed at the EPON-controller, due to the much faster time scales at which the process must be run. Therefore, it must be executed entirely in the SDN-OLT, although the bandwidth allocation policies can be modified at longer time scales, as described in Sect. 4.4.

The SDN-OLT can identify the ONU that sent any message by means of the ONU-ID (identifier), which is carried in the header of the REPORT message. Therefore, the packets coming from a certain ONU can be matched against one of the flow entries of the main flow table, which then defines the actions to be taken. Each flow table contains flow entries and each flow entry is composed of a set of fields, such as the one shown in Table 2:

- Match fields: to match against packets and include packet headers fields and ingress port.
- Priority: match preference of flow entries.

- Counters: use for each matched packet and flow
- Action set: action set consists of a set of actions to apply to the packet.
- Timers: store the arrival and send time of REPORT and GATE messages, respectively.

Table 2. Flow entry in the SDN-OLT main flow table

Match fields	Priority	Counters	Action set	Timers

We assume the existence of one flow entry per ONU, which therefore allows the execution of differentiated policies per user. This does not exclude the possibility of nesting flow tables to further differentiate between traffic flows generated by the same ONU. Since the OLT operations are synchronous, the first thing the SDN-OLT must do upon arrival of a REPORT message is to store the arrival time t_1 in a received-timestamp field, and then strip the EPON-specific header. Then, two different actions are performed: (1) the Ethernet frames carried by the REPORT message are forwarded to the appropriate port, and (2) the information present in the REPORT header, related to the bandwidth requested by the ONU for the new cycle, is processed following some bandwidth allocation policy (to be described in detail later). Following this, both the volume of data and the time t_3 at which the data will be sent by the ONU are calculated. The GATE message with the two aforementioned parameters (volume and time) and the EPON-specific header must be sent ahead in time (at least two propagation times before the calculated time), and it is therefore scheduled to be sent at time t_2. The strip-header/add-header actions require the standard Openflow action set to be extended.

4.4 Bandwidth Allocation

4.4.1 Introduction

Regarding the upstream Dynamic Bandwidth Allocation (DBA) algorithm, we define some policies for both inter-ONU and intra-ONU scheduling at the controller. We maintain the main DBA algorithm in the SDN-OLT and migrate some high-level policies to the controller. The DBA algorithm is implemented by extending the Action Set, Experimenter message, and creating a Bundle message to apply synchronous change to our virtual switch. Furthermore, Openflow messages are extended to include the particularities of the EPON primitives. We focus on the deployment of the Distributed Dynamic Scheduling for EPON (DDSPON) DBA algorithm [9, 10] in the SDN architecture.

Regarding intra-ONU scheduling, the proposed architecture allows for easier management of quality of service. For example, the operator can allocate different policies for each class of queues (i.e., Expedited Forwarding, Assured Forwarding, and Best Effort). Similarly, in inter-ONU scheduling we can allocate different weights to each queue based on their priority. As an example, Fig. 5 from [9] illustrates the typical upstream traffic variation pattern during the day for each type of ONU (business and home customers). By deploying a time-dependent policy, the SDN controller can optimize the resource allocation. For instance, daytime bandwidth and QoS for business customers can be prioritized, while residential users can be assigned a better service at night and on weekends.

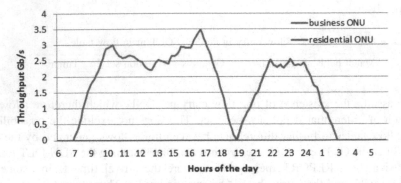

Fig. 5. Daily traffic patterns at the ONU.

As in the case of the Element discovery, the time scale at which the DBA policies change is not critical, since we are speaking of time scales on the order of hours. Therefore, the role and time scale of the EPON-controller is perfectly compatible with the procedures, while the synchronous, time-tight operations (such as the GATE-REPORT exchange) are performed by the data plane of the SDN-OLT at a much higher frequency, as shown in Fig. 6.

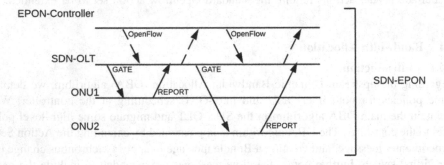

Fig. 6. SDN-OLT to ONU messages in the proposed architecture.

Example. In the DDSPON algorithm [9, 10], bandwidth allocation is based on assigning weights to the ONUs, so every final user is assigned a specific bandwidth during each upstream transmission cycle. Weight assignment to each ONU is shown in Eq. (1) and Table 3. In the new architecture, the weight value is initialized as a DBA parameter for each ONU and maintained dynamically in a Virtual MPCP (VMPCP) in the controller, and it is managed in real time by the extended flow tables in the SDN-OLT. The EPON-controller can change the weights dynamically, and therefore apply different global policies depending on time (i.e., days, week, and weekend), and different type of users (i.e., business/home). This capability of adaptation is difficult to achieve in the current EPON architecture.

$$\varphi_i \rightarrow w_i = \frac{\varphi_i}{\sum_{i=0}^{n=N} \varphi_i} w_{max} \qquad (1)$$

Table 3. Notation in the bandwidth allocation Eq. (1)

Notations	Value
• N	• Number of ONUs
• φ_i	• Set-up weight value of the ONU_i
• w_i	• Transmission window size of the ONU_i computed in cycle n
• w_{max}	• Maximum transmission window size (bits)

4.4.2 Implementation Details

The main challenge to solve here is how to carry out changes in the SDN-OLT configuration in a way that is fast enough so that the EPON operations are not compromised. Openflow 1.4 offers some solutions, such as Action Set and Bundle Messages.

Action Set allows the controller to define the set of required actions to be performed on each flow entry of the flow table inside the SDN-OLT. In this way, the controller can change the behavior of each flow by applying a different set of actions for each user.

Bundle Messages are a group of sequenced action set modification requests that are performed as a single operation in the virtual switch. Upon receiving a bundle message from the EPON-controller in the SDN-OLT, both the message and the modified parameters are stored in the temporary memory of the virtual switch. Then, a new bundle-id is created and attached to the current connection. The controller can send a completely new OLT behavior encoded in the actions. Eventually, the controller can commit the bundle at a specified time in order to apply all messages and state modifications in the vSwitch (flow tables, for example). Bundle messages are therefore useful for radical reconfigurations of the bandwidth allocations, such as those illustrated in the example in Fig. 5.

5 Conclusions

We propose a novel architecture for reducing the complexity of the EPON operation, together with the OPEX and CAPEX, while also introducing the possibility of dynamically optimizing the use of resources. This can be applied for many goals: joint optimization of traffic scheduling by several OLTs working in a federated way; global optimization of end-to-end quality of service for premium flows; minimization of energy power consumption; or the dynamic adaptation of traffic plans depending on the time of the day, as described in our example.

The proposed scheme is based on the SDN and NFV concepts, by splitting some functionality of the MPCP sub-layer between a centralized controller and a modified SDN-OLT. Defining a new instruction extension, Bundle message and QoS in the virtual switch of the SDN-OLT gives the ability to schedule and allocate the required bandwidth to each ONU and end user.

Our future research will focus on a detailed analysis of functionalities, as well as the messaging and timing issues involved in real-time operation, in order to provide a complete description of the elements, messages, and algorithms involved. This will require the development of a simulation scenario based in OPNET [11], so that we can evaluate the real-time constraints. Once the feasibility of the approach is verified, we will develop a prototype of the proposed architecture using the OpenDayLight controller [12] and Mininet [13]. Further research is needed regarding which and how functionalities can be run following the NFV paradigm. We also want to extend our proposal to scenarios including access and core networks (such as that described in [8]), and propose algorithms and SDN-based signalling (federation of controllers, for example) that are able to globally optimize the network resources and improve end-to-end QoS performance for the end users. Finally, we would like to extend our architecture to other synchronous, next-generation optical networks.

Acknowledgement. This work is partially supported by the Spanish government under project TEC2013-47960-C4-1-P.

References

1. Kramer, G.: Ethernet Passive Optical Networks. McGraw-Hill, New York (2005)
2. Feamster, N., Rexford, J., Zegura, E.: The road to SDN: an intellectual history of programmable networks. ACM Queue **11**(12), 20–32 (2013)
3. Open Networking Foundation: Openflow specifications. https://www.opennetworking.org/sdn-resources/onf-specifications/openflow
4. Network Function Virtualisation: ETSI introductory white paper. http://portal.etsi.org/NFV/NFV_White_Paper.pdf. October 2012
5. Cvijetic, N., Tanaka, A., Ji, P.N., Sethuraman, K., Murakami, S., Wang, T.: SDN and Openflow for dynamic flex-grid optical access and aggregation networks. IEEE J. Lightwave Technol. **32**(4), 864–870 (2014)
6. Cvijetic, N.: Software-defined optical access networks for multiple broadband access solutions. In: OptoElectronics and Communications Conference (OECC), paper TuP2_1, pp. 1–2, June 2013
7. Parol, P., Pawlowski, M.: Toward networks of the future: SDN paradigm introduction to PON networking for business applications. In: Proceedings of the Federated Conference on Computer Science and Information Systems (FEDCSIS), pp. 829–836 (2013)
8. Sgambelluri, A., Paolucci, F., Cugini, F., Valcarenghi, L., Castoldi, P.: Generalized SDN control for access/metro/core integration in the framework of the interface to the Routing System (I2RS). In: IEEE Globecom Workshops, pp. 1216–1220 (2013)
9. Garfias, P.: Resource management research in ethernet passive optical networks. Ph.D. thesis, Universitat Politècnica de Catalunya UPC-BarcelonaTech (2013)
10. De Andrade, M., Gutierrez, L., Sallent, S.: DDSPON: a distributed dynamic scheduling for EPON. In: Proceedings of ICSPC 2007, pp. 840–843, Nov 2007
11. OPNET Application and Network Performance. https://www.opnet.com/index.html
12. OpenDayLight, Linux Foundation Collaborative Project. http://www.opendaylight.org/
13. Mininet. http://mininet.org/

Towards Validation of the Internet Census 2012

Dirk Maan$^{(\boxtimes)}$, José Jair Santanna, Anna Sperotto, and Pieter-Tjerk de Boer

Design and Analysis of Communication Systems (DACS), University of Twente,
Enschede, The Netherlands
h.c.maan@student.utwente.nl,
{j.j.santanna,a.sperotto,p.t.deboer}@utwente.nl

Abstract. The reliability of the "Internet Census 2012" (IC), an anonymously published scan of he entire IPv4 address space, is not a priori clear. As a step towards validation of this dataset, we compare it to logged reference data on a /16 network, and present an approach to systematically handle uncertainties in timestamps in the IC and reference data. We find evidence the scan indeed took place, and a 93 % match with the /16 reference data.

Keywords: Internet census · Scan · Validation

1 Introduction

In March 2013, an anonymous researcher published the result of a project called *Internet Census 2012* (IC) [2]. The project was based on a scan of the entire IPv4 addresses space (i.e., an Internet-wide scan). A scan is created by sending probe packets to hosts, using one probing host or a distributed network of hosts controlled by a central server. Technical issues that could prevent accurate results are packet loss, or bot misconfiguration. The anonymous author claims his 9 Tbytes of raw log files are the most recent and accurate census of the Internet.

Active scans on the Internet are certainly an important source of information, as several studies have demonstrated that they can help reveal new kinds of vulnerabilities, monitor deployment of mitigation, and highlight hidden distributed ecosystems [5–7,10]. However, the IC results were published anonymously, and the methodology only partially described, which, as pointed out by the Cooperative Association for Internet Data Analysis (CAIDA) [1], leads to some important questions, such as: how does one know that the IC scan actually happened, and if it did, how does one know that the resulting data is correct?

In this paper we extend the work of CAIDA [1] by proposing a methodology to validate the Internet Census in third-party networks and datasets. We then applied our methodology to the /16 network address block of the University of Twente (UT), and found a match of about 93 % between the considered Internet Census data and our reference data.

The scientific community has ethical (and legal) concerns about the IC. There are concerns about network-wide scanning in general; discussions so far have not

© Springer International Publishing Switzerland 2014
Y. Kermarrec (Ed.): EUNICE 2014, LNCS 8846, pp. 85–96, 2014.
DOI: 10.1007/978-3-319-13488-8_9

led to clear concensus. In the case of the IC, this is exacerbated by the fact that the IC was performed using a botnet consisting of around 420 thousand compromised systems. In this paper, we sidestep these concerns by limiting ourselves to comparing this dataset to reference data of our own, with the sole purpose of finding out to what extent the IC dataset actually reflects reality.

The remainder of this paper is organized as follows. Section 2 discusses related work, and is followed by a characterization of the IC dataset in Sect. 3. Section 4 describes our proposed methodology, which is analyzed in Sect. 5. Finally, in Sect. 6 we summarize our findings and highlight future work.

2   Related Work and Background

Since the beginning of the Internet, scans have been performed to obtain information about the end hosts. RFC-832 [11] describes the first documented scan of the Internet. At that time, in 1982, 315 hosts were probed to see if they use the TCP protocol. The scan took roughly one day.

In [6], Heidemann et al. presented a study of the active Internet over the period 2003–2008. The presented census highlighted anomalies in the un-allocated address space and indicates the percentage of usage for allocated network blocks. The observations from this scan were validated by comparing them to scans of smaller address blocks. This study only considers ICMP probes, as TCP is considered too resource-consuming for the scanned hosts.

Furthermore, Holz et al. conducted HTTPs scans of the top million popular hosts over a timespan of 1.5 years [8]. These scans were horizontal, as only port 443 was probed, scanning for certificates. The IC differs by probing the top 100 and several other random ports.

Another Internet-wide scan which is similar to the IC was performed by Durumeric et al. [4]. To the best of our knowledge, it is the most recent documented scan of the complete Internet. The authors developed a scanning tool, ZMap, specifically designed to perform fast scans at a large scale. Differently from the IC, the scans performed by Durumeric et al. are targeted at the study of specific protocols, showing that the authors are cautious to avoid more scanning activities than needed.

Internet-wide scans are unfortunately not only used for Internet measurements. In [3], Dainotti et al. describe a scan of the entire IPv4 address space performed by the Sality botnet. It is estimated that the botnet has scanned approximately 3 million distinct IP addresses over a period of 12 days, scanning both port 5060 (SIP) and port 80.

3   Characterization of Internet Census 2012

The dataset provided by the IC is composed of seven sets of traces, as summarized in Table 1. Each entry of each trace contains three elements: (1) the IP address of the probed device, (2) a timestamp indicating the moment of probing, and (3) the result of the scan, which depends on the scan method used in each trace.

Table 1. Traces in IC

#	Trace	Content	Size
1	ICMP ping	Responsiveness and latencies	1.8 TB
2	Reverse DNS	DNS records	366 GB
3	Serviceprobes	Services behind open ports	5.5 TB
4	Hostprobes	Responsiveness	771 GB
5	Syncscan	State of ports	435 GB
6	TCP/IP Fingerprint	Type of device and operating system	50 GB
7	Traceroute	Path of data packet	18 GB

For example, the ICMP scan indicates if a host is reachable, while the Synscan trace lists the status of the scanned ports.

In our research, the traces *'icmp_ping'*, *'hostprobes'* and *'syncscan'* are of special interest, because these traces indicate if a device was active or not at a certain timestamp. These three traces will be the only traces considered in the following sections.

3.1 Trace Overview

Figure 1 shows the time distribution of the probes that reached the UT /16 netblock accordingly to the IC. They are clustered in three main periods, namely April–July 2012, August–October 2012 and mid-December 2012. IP address are generally probed more than once per trace, as shown in Fig. 2. The x-axis of this figure is the number of probes sent to an IP address, while the y-axis displays the respective frequencies. For example, in the hostprobes trace more than 35000 IP addresses were probed five times. In the syncscan, most IP addresses are probed only once or twice, while icmp_ping has around 13 probes per IP address.

3.2 Timestamp Rounding

The IC paper does not much provide information about the probe timestamps reported in the datasets. Based on the format, the timestamps used in the IC

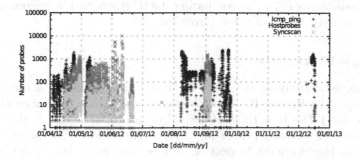

Fig. 1. Number of probes per day for 130.89.0.0/16

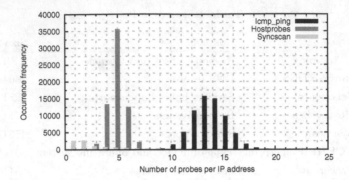

Fig. 2. Occurence frequency of the number of probes per IP address

are assumed to be in standard Unix time format (i.e., seconds since Jan. 1, 1970). The source of the timestamping is unclear: they might be the probing bots themselves, or some central server collecting the data. Especially in the former case, timestamps may be off and inconsistent due to the respective bot's clock not being set correctly.

Furthermore, it is notable that each timestamp value in the IC is an odd multiple of 900 s; in other words, each timestamp is either exactly 15 min before or after a full hour. Apparently, the actual timestamps of the probes have been rounded in some way, presumably for anonimization. The rounding strategy is not described; obvious possibilities are always up, always down, or to nearest. This leads to a total uncertainty of 3600 s, ranging from 1800 s before the IC timestamp to 1800 s after it. We will take this observation into account in the validation of the IC traces performed in Sects. 4 and 5.

4   Methodology

Our validation methodology consists of two parts. First, we verify that probes from the IC have indeed reached hosts at the UT. We do this by analysing packet traces that were collected at the time of the scan for a particular IP address. Secondly, we validate the information of the IC for the /16 netblock of the UT, which we indicate as IC_{UT}, by comparing the IC traces with a reference dataset based on the ARP tables of the UT routers.

4.1   Single-IP Analysis

For the single-IP analysis, the trace of all incoming traffic to a server at the UT is compared with the IC data. (We only had such a trace available for a single machine.) The best trace of the IC to use for this goal is the syncscan trace, because of its many probes in a short time interval. The hostprobes and icmp_ping IC traces are not inspected, because, due to the timestamp rounding and the frequency of ICMP packets in the host trace, it was not possible to

Table 2. Overall comparison of the ARP and IC_{UT} datasets

Subset	Definition	Description
Subset A	$ARP - IC_{UT}$	UT IP addresses are active but not included in the IC
Subset B	$ARP \cap IC_{UT}$	UT IP addresses are active and included in the IC
Subset C	$IC_{UT} - ARP$	UT IP addresses are not active but included in the IC

match ICMP packets in the trace to the IC with certainty. From the syncscan trace the probed ports and the time of probing are known. This is enough data to filter the IC probes from other incoming traffic at the server. To validate each entry that corresponds to the analysed IP, we consider the following: first, it is checked if the machine was actually approached by the IC at the stated timestamp; second, the state that was reported in the IC is checked to be equal to the actual state of the machine.

4.2   UT Address Block Analysis

Reference Dataset. To validate the IC data, we need a reference dataset indicating, for a certain moment in time, which IP addresses are active in the /16 UT networks. The dataset used in this paper is a consolidated snapshot of the ARP table of the UT routers, referred as ARP, during the period April 2012–December 2012. From the analysis of the ARP tables we determine that the UT /16 block has a utilization of about 53 %. We are aware that the ARP tables can introduce some measurement imprecisions. For example, an IP would typically remain in the ARP tables for some time after it has disconnected. Furthermore, several gaps in the dataset are present, due to SNMP timeouts that occurred or because the database table space was temporarily full. However, considering that we are analyzing IC data over a period of 8 months, we believe that these imprecisions only have a limited impact on the validation.

We first investigate the intersection and, respectively left and right difference between the IP sets in IC_{UT} and ARP, as indicated in Table 2. Subsets A and C report errors in the IC, namely active IP addressed that have not been reported or, conversely, inactive IP addresses that have been wrongly included in the IC. In the case of Subset B, we proceed as described in the following subsection.

Subset B Timestamp Analysis. Although in principle Subset B is the intersection of IC_{UT} and ARP, this is not sufficient to state that these IP addresses are correctly reported. For example, an IP could have been listed in the IC at a moment in time in which it was not active, or viceversa. To investigate this issue, we perform the following analysis on the ARP and IC timestamps.

First, we consider the complete interval in which the IC probe can be sent. Due to the timestamp rounding in the IC, every timestamp t is expanded to create an interval with start time $t - 1800\,s$ and end time $t + 1800\,s$. For the ARP tables this is not necessary, since they already report the start and end time of activity for a certain IP. Comparing the interval of the ARP table with the interval of the IC will result in four possible outcomes, referred as overlaptypes (see Fig. 3) with four different conclusions.

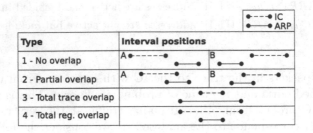

Fig. 3. Different overlap possibilities.

No overlap: This situation occurs when an IP address was registered according to the ARP table, but the IC probed the IP address outside the ARP interval. Therefore, the IC should not state this IP address as being alive.

Partial overlap: If the intervals overlap only partially, it is not clear whether the probe was sent within or outside the ARP registration interval, so no conclusion can be drawn.

Total IC overlap: In this case, the IC interval is completely contained in the ARP registration interval. The information in the IC must therefore contain an indication of the IP address being alive. If the IC states that the host is unreachable, this is an error.

Total IC overlap: The last case is characterized by the ARP registration interval being completely overlapped by the IC trace interval. The IC trace interval itself is partially overlapped, so it is not clear whether the probe was sent within or outside the ARP registration interval and no conclusion can be drawn.

Validation. In this study, we focus in particular on the erroneous entries in the IC, because they are an indication of the reliability of the IC. An erroneous entry is defined as an entry that contradicts the data in the ARP tables of the UT.

Basically, the comparison consists of the following steps, which will be elaborated further on:

– Split the IC trace into unreachable and alive subtraces; this step is necessary to correctly analyze the IPs in Subset B.
– Determine the appropriate subset for each entry.
– Count probes per subset.

In order to clarify the comparison in a more visual way, we refer the reader to the flowchart in Fig. 4. This figure shows how an IC probe is categorized in a certain subset. Furthermore, it shows what type of IC probes are erroneous, as can be deduced from Sect. 4.2.

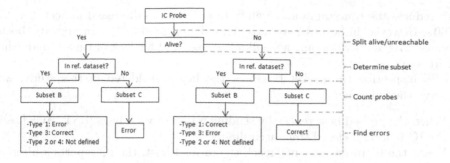

Fig. 4. Flowchart of the comparison process

5 Results

Similar to Sect. 4, the results are described in two parts and ordered in the same way, first the single-IP analysis is discussed, followed by the results of the /16 address block analysis.

5.1 Single-IP Analysis Results

Performing the method described in Sect. 4.1 on the given traces, results in the conclusion that the IC records concerning the server correspond to the traffic traces of our server. Indeed, the IP of the server turns out to be present in the IC records of the syncscan trace. Furthermore, in the incoming traffic of the server packets have been identified that match the timestamp and portnumbers listed for scans of this machine in the IC. As an aside, it turns out that when the IC scanned several ports within a short timeframe (same rounded timestamp), these scans came from the same IP address, while scans farther apart came from different IP addresses. Most probes were replied to with a packet having the RST and ACK flags set, revealing that the probed host exists but has these ports closed. These ports of the server IP were marked as 'closed' in the IC, which is as expected. One port was correctly marked as open in the IC. In the remaining cases, the IC marks ports for our IP as 'filtered', and indeed no corresponding incoming sync packet could be found.

By comparing the timestamps of the packet traces of the single host to the probe timestamps in the IC, the rounding of IC timestamps can be studied. It turns out that the timestamps in the IC are between 200 and 900 s lower than the timestamps in the packet trace. From this we can conclude that out of the three options mentioned in Sect. 3.2, only the round "always down" and "to nearest" are compatible with the data. (Note that we could distinguish between these remaining two options if we had timestamps in the first or third quarter of the hour, but apparently our server was only probed in the second and fourth quarter of the hour.) Although we only have this data of one IP and one trace, it is assumed that all timestamps in the IC are rounded the same way. In principle, this reduces the timestamp uncertainty from 3600 s as discussed in Sect. 3.2, to 2700 s. However, in Sect. 4.2 we have used the original 3600 s uncertainty, both because 2700 s provides only a small advantage and for lack of time to redo the entire analysis.

By inspecting the packet traces of the host considered in this study, we observe the following:

- When the probed host replies by sending a packet with flags [RST, ACK] set, the IC reports a closed state accordingly.
- When the IC probe does not reach the probed host, the IC reports a filtered state accordingly.
- When the IC probe reaches the probed host and the host does not reply but drops the probe, the IC reports a filtered state accordingly.
- Some ports are probed multiple times.

Since each probe of our server in the IC, reporting a different state than filtered, indeed can be matched to a packet in our trace, we can conclude that the scan did indeed happen (confirming findings of [1]), and did indeed reach our network. Furthermore, we have obtained partial knowledge of the timestamp rounding.

5.2   /16 Address Block Analysis Results

In conformity with the division in subsets of Sect. 4.2, the results of the /16 address block analysis are split in three parts, because each of these parts requires a different analysis. The result of the interval comparison in subset B is an overview of the occurrence of different overlaptypes described in Fig. 3.

Subset A. All hosts registered in the ARP tables were present in icmp_ping and hostprobes traces, resulting in an empty subset A for these traces. By analysing the comparison of the syncscan trace, 71.4 % of the IPs in ARP do not appear in the IC_{UT}. Since the author of the IC paper states that a syncscan was limited to about 660 million IP addresses [2], we consider our observation in line with the IC description.

Subset C. The percentage of the entries in subset C with respect to the total probes in each subtrace (e.g. hostprobes_alive or icmp_unreachable) is shown in the first column of Table 3.

According to the characteristics described in Sect. 4.2, no IC entries marked as alive should be in this subset. As shown in Table 3, the alive subtraces of hostprobes, icmp_ping and syncscan contain 5.31 %, 2.82 %, and 3.94 % respectively nonmatching IP addresses. These are considered erroneous. However, further analysis shows that several alive IP addresses of trace icmp_ping that are categorized in this subset are actually broadcast addresses or network addresses. The UT has about 200 of these addresses in the /16 address block. These addresses are categorized in subset C, because they are not included in the ARP table of the UT. The IC reported these addresses as alive, due to the reply of some UT routers that received the probe. In addition, several hosts reported as alive in this subset were probed close in time to moments where ARP table errors occurred. This can be another reason why some IP addresses in the /16 address block that were alive according to the IC are not present in the ARP table. From this observation is concluded that alive entries in this subset are not necessarily errors in the IC.

Figure 5 shows that more than 50 % of the probes in the unreachable subtraces of hostprobes and icmp_ping do not match the IP addresses of the ARP table. These probes are consistent with the ARP data, due to the fact that IP addresses can not be alive without them being registered in the ARP table. Hence these probes are considered correct.

Subset B. By categorizing the records of subset B into separate overlaptypes, the validity of each subtrace can be determined. The result is a table with the number of probes that is counted for each overlaptype, as shown in Table 3.

Table 3. Result of comparison per subtrace of IC with ARP table

Subtrace	Subset C	Subset B				Total
	noipmatch	no_overlap	partial_overlap	totaltraceoverlap	totalregoverlap	
hostprobes alive	1192 [5.31%]	1573 [7.01%]	411 [1.83%]	18945 [84.46%]	311 [1.39%]	22432
hostprobes unreachable	170565 [55.80%]	118078 [38.63%]	2775 [0.91%]	13481 [4.41%]	769 [0.25%]	305668
icmp alive	1497 [2.82%]	1010 [1.90%]	1176 [2.22%]	48406 [91.30%]	930 [1.75%]	53019
icmp unreachable	458833 [55.27%]	310824 [37.44%]	8688 [1.05%]	49048 [5.91%]	2721 [0.33%]	830114
syncscan alive	670 [3.94%]	839 [4.94%]	264 [1.55%]	14930 [87.90%]	282 [1.66%]	16985

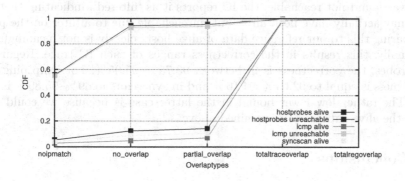

Fig. 5. Cumulative Distribution Function of overlaptypes in subtraces

Figure 5 shows the same data as Table 3, but now as a cumulative distribution function. On the x-axis are the possible overlaptypes, ordered roughly by increasing quality of the match; the y-axis displays the percentage of probes having up to that kind of match. The following two paragraphs summarize the observed distribution of the subtraces based on the probe states. Errors and correctness are discussed afterwards.

Unreachable. As seen in Fig. 5, the largest increase of the unreachable subtraces occurs in between overlaptypes noipmatch and no_overlap. Because these traces add up to more than 90 % of all probes in these traces, we can conclude that most of these probes did indeed not reach active hosts. About these probed IP addresses it can be said that their unreachable state is noted correctly in the IC.

Alive. Another observation from Fig. 5 is the large percentage of the total-traceoverlap in traces hostprobes_alive, icmp_alive, shown by a clear increase from overlaptype partial_overlap to totaltraceoverlap. The share of total probes in these subtraces in overlaptype totaltraceoverlap of subset B is 84.46 % and 91.30 % respectively. The probes of these traces in this category are correct. A similar percentage of 87.90 % totaltraceoverlap is observed in the syncscan_alive subtrace.

Trace Correctness. In order to give an overall correctness indication for each IC trace for this /16 block, we take together the statistics for the unreachable and the alive subtraces of each trace. The cases which are counted as correct are marked green in Table 3: unreachable and either noipmatch or no_overlap, or alive and totaltraceoverlap. The cases which are counted as incorrect are marked red in the table: alive and either noipmatch or no_overlap, or unreachable and totaltraceoverlap. In the remaining cases, no correctness conclusion can be drawn due to the timestamp uncertainties. Thus, we cannot calculate the overall correctness percentage as a single value, but as a range to represent the uncertain cases.

A further difficulty occurs in the case of the syncscan trace: here we only have an alive subtrace and not an unreachable subtrace. This is because when a port was found not reachable, the IC reports it as 'filtered', indicating that the host may actually have been alive, but unreachable due to a filter on the path. Comparing this to our reference data of alive hosts clearly is not meaningful.

Finally, this results in the correctness ranges of each IC trace. Regarding hostprobes, the correctness is in between 93.75 %–95.05 %. For icmp_ping this correctness is equal to 92.63 %–94.16 % and in syncscan, 40.69 %–95.89 % is correct. The rather low lower bound in the latter case is because we could only check the alive subtrace, as explained above.

6   Conclusions

In this paper, we have validated a /16 block from the "Internet Census 2012" by comparing it to locally logged data from that /16 block, and introduced a method to deal with the uncertainties in both the timestamps of the IC and the reference data.

Using the incoming traffic traces of a single host, it was validated that the IC scan included devices in the /16 address block of the UT. We were able to identify the syncscan probes of the IC in the normal server traffic, which is a strong indication that the IC indeed was performed on the UT network. We showed that the syncscan probe timestamps were either rounded down or to nearest with respect to the probe timestamp as observed on our server.

After verifying that the scan has taken place at the UT network, our analysis of the complete UT /16 address block has shown that about 93 % of the IP addresses utilization in this block are correctly reported by the IC, by comparing them to logged ARP tables. Although this results indicates that the census has the possibility of depicting an accurate picture of the Internet utilization, it is also important to notice that, on a large scale this potentially amounts to several millions of incorrectly classified hosts. Also, we reckon that the accuracy could be influenced by specific network settings, therefore we do not extrapolate from these results to wider conclusions.

Many error sources could have affected the IC scan when it was performed. Some of the possible error causes might be packet loss or bot misconfiguration. Missing information could for example lead to an incorrect unreachable state of an IP address in the IC. In contrast to the hostprobes and icmp_ping traces, the syncscan trace has only been validated for about 40 %. Many probes of this trace were ignored in the process, e.g. UDP probes and probes that have the state 'filtered' in the IC. Therefore, we consider this result as not really accurate and think it should not be used as a measure for correctness of the entire syncscan trace.

There are several opportunities for future work. By using traces of incoming traffic of more hosts, if available, the rounding method of the IC timestamps can be identified, and the accuracy of the timestamps studied further. If the rounding method is known, the accuracy of the proposed validation method can be increased. Furthermore, other address blocks of the IPv4 address space can be validated using the proposed method. When more address blocks in the IC are validated, a better conclusion about the validity of the entire IC can be drawn. Another possibility for future research is the validation of IC traces that were skipped in our research. The serviceprobes and tcp_ip_fingerprint traces for example contain Nmap data about the devices that were scanned.

Acknowledgements. Special thanks goes to Jeroen van Ingen at ICTS (University of Twente) for providing the ARP data. This work was funded by the FP7 Network of Excellence project FLAMINGO (ICT-318488).

References

1. Alistair, A.: Carna botnet scans confirmed (2013). http://blog.caida.org/best_available_data/2013/05/13/carna-botnet-scans/
2. Anonymous.: Internet census 2012 (2013). http://internetcensus2012.bitbucket.org/paper.html
3. Dainotti, A., King, A., Claffy, K., Papale, F., Pescapè, A.: Analysis of a "/0" stealth scan from a botnet. In: Proceedings of the 2012 ACM Internet Measurement Conference, pp. 1–14. IMC '12. ACM, New York (2012). http://doi.acm.org/10.1145/2398776.2398778
4. Durumeric, Z., Wustrow, E., Halderman, J.A.: Zmap: fast internet-wide scanning and its security applications. In: 22nd USENIX Security Symposium, pp. 605–619 (2013)

5. Eckersley, P., Burns, J.: An observatory for the SSLiverse. Talk at Defcon 18 (2010). https://www.eff.org/files/DefconSSLiverse.pdf
6. Heidemann, J., Pradkin, Y., Govindan, R., Papadopoulos, C., Bartlett, G., Bannister, J.: Census and survey of the visible internet. In: Proceedings of the 2008 ACM Internet Measurement Conference, pp. 169–182. ACM, Vouliagmeni, Greece (2008). http://www.isi.edu/~johnh/PAPERS/Heidemann08c.html
7. Heninger, N., Durumeric, Z., Wustrow, E., Halderman, J.: Mining your ps and qs: detection of widespread weak keys in network devices. In: 21st USENIX Security Symposium (2012)
8. Holz, R., Braun, L., Kammenhuber, N., Carle, G.: The SSL landscape: a thorough analysis of the x.509 PKI using active and passive measurements. In: Proceedings of the 2011 ACM Internet Measurement Conference, pp. 427–444. IMC '11. ACM, New York (2011). http://doi.acm.org/10.1145/2068816.2068856
9. Maan, H.C.: Validation of internet census 2012. BSc thesis, University of Twente, The Netherlands (2014)
10. Moore, H.: Security flaws in universal plug and play: unplug, don't play (2013). http://community.rapid7.com/servlet/JiveServlet/download/2150-1-16596/SecurityFlawsUPnP.pdf
11. Smallberg, D.: Request For Comment 832: Who talks TCP. RFC 832, December 1982. https://tools.ietf.org/html/rfc832

Development and Performance Evaluation of Fast Combinatorial Unranking Implementations

András Majdán$^{(\boxtimes)}$, Gábor Rétvári, and János Tapolcai

Department of Telecommunications and Media Informatics,
Budapest University of Technology and Economics, Budapest, Hungary
{majdan,retvari,tapolcai}@tmit.bme.hu

Abstract. Compressed bitmaps have been long used in computer science and today it seems they conquer more and more fields of networking. The goal of this paper is to provide fast combinatorial unranking implementations for use in bitmap data compression. Within this context, unranking refers to the operation of obtaining a bit vector given its rank in a particular enumeration of all bit vectors of the same size with respect to a given order. Easily, the simplest way to accomplish this task is to use a lookup table. However, for large block sizes such a table may not fit into the memory. Efficient combinatorial unranking algorithms, which eliminate large lookup tables, are therefore essential in practice. Taking the textbook combinatorial unranking schemes, in this paper we develop very fast combinatorial unranking implementations and we introduce a comprehensive performance evaluation and profiling toolkit to measure their efficiency. Our benchmarks show that our optimized implementations improve the performance of the naive combinatorial unranking implementations by 39%, almost attaining the performance of simple lookup tables.

1 Introduction

Bit vectors, or *bitmaps*, are amongst the most frequently used data structures in the theory and practice of computer science and, more closely, in the networking area. Applications range from storing allocation tables invirtual memory and virtual file systems, raster images in computer graphicsor, more generally, storing arbitrary sets over a fixed (large) universe. Today's massive applications, big data analytics softwares, and large-scalenetwork services, however, require fast and efficient operations onenormously large bitmap instances, significantly increasing the computational burden implied by this simplistic data structure.

Storing a bitmap is trivial if memory cost is not to be considered. However,in practice we are often obliged to save space by using bitmap compression algorithms, because the uncompressed bitmap image would simply not fit into the main memory. Recently, bitmap compression algorithms have been demonstrated to effectively reduce the memory footprint of bitmaps without significant performance penalty on standard operations, like random access [1]. This holds much

© Springer International Publishing Switzerland 2014
Y. Kermarrec (Ed.): EUNICE 2014, LNCS 8846, pp. 97–108, 2014.
DOI: 10.1007/978-3-319-13488-8_10

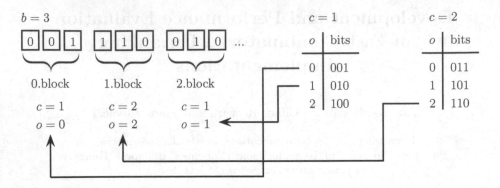

Fig. 1. Bitmap Block Compression Scheme.

promise to application developers, as a way out of the compelling scalability issues caused by today's massive input datasets. For instance, lately compressed bitmaps have been used to squeeze Internet forwarding tables, comprising hundreds of thousands IP address prefix to next-hop associations, to just a couple of hundred kilobytes of memory without any decrease in lookup performance [2].

Consider the following simple bitmap compression algorithm, called the Bitmap Block Compression Scheme (BBCS) (see Fig. 1):

1. Divide a bitmap with size 'n' into blocks of size 'b'.
2. Count the number of 1s in each block and assign this to the block as its class (c).
3. Index the block in a fixed enumeration of all bit vectors of the same class and call it the offset (o).
4. Store the class and the offset of each block sequentially.

Curiously, already this simple block compression scheme can reduce the space requirement of bitmaps to the theoretical minimum (up to lower order error terms). Consider the following result from [3].

Proposition 1. *Given a bitmap of size n and zero-order entropy H_0, the size of the representation compressed by he BBCS algorithm is at most $nH_0 + o(n)$ bits.*

Proof. Block i of the bitmap is represented by the pair (c_i, o_i), where c_i is the number of 1s in the i-th block and o_i is the id of the block within class c_i. Observe that the offset of the i-th block o_i can take $\binom{b}{c_i}$ different values, and hence each o_i can be stored on $\log \binom{b}{c_i}$ bits. Adding this up, for storing the offsets we need

$$\sum_{i=1}^{\lceil \frac{n}{b} \rceil} \binom{b}{c_i} \leq \log \binom{b(n/b)}{c_1 + \dots + c_{n/b}} \leq nH_0 \tag{1}$$

bits, using the fact that $\log \binom{b}{c_1} + \log \binom{b}{c_2} \leq \log \binom{2b}{c_1+c_2}$. The class ids c_i are stored on $\log(b+1)$ bits each, which add up to

$$\sum_{i=1}^{\frac{[n]}{b}} \log(b+1) \le (n+1)\frac{\log(b+1)}{b} = o(n). \tag{2}$$

Thus, we need at most $nH_0 + o(n)$ bits to store the bitmap, which finishes the proof. $\qquad\square$

Easily, the key to the BBCS scheme and many more sophisticated bitmap compression schemes based on the same block compression principle, like RRR [1], is step 3. Here, the task is to compute the offset of a given block of 1s and zeros in some fixed enumeration of all bit vectors of the same class. This task is called *combinatorial ranking* [4–6]. The reverse operation, that is, the reconstruction of a bitmap block given its class and rank within the enumeration, is called *combinatorial unranking*.

As compression algorithms are usually asymmetric, with more emphasis on decompression speed than on compression, combinatorial unranking is the operation with more stringent performance requirements. Hence, in this paper we will focus on fast and efficient combinatorial unranking schemes.

In some cases it is not required to decompress a full block but only a position within. For example, consider a bitmap for a memory allocation table, where each bit represents whether or not a particular memory page is allocated. If we would like to know if a page is free we just have to get the corresponding bit in the bitmap. We shall see later that if we need to only partially reconstruct bitmaps we can get better performance with combinatorial unranking algorithms.

The simplest way for combinatorial unranking is using a lookup table (like in Fig. 1). This, as we shall see, is currently the fastest option available. Lookup tables, however, need storing vast bitmap-to-rank mappings in main memory, ruining cache-friendliness of bitmap compression. Depending on the block size b, the whole lookup table might not even fit into the memory (observe that the size of the table needed is $O(2^b)$ bits). Combinatorial ranking/unranking eliminate tables alltogether, by providing the bitmap-to-offset mapping *algorithmically*. This, however, may cause substantial computational overhead.

The main questions we ask in this paper are *(i)* whether the improved cache-friendliness of combinatorial unranking compensates for the computational overhead as compared to lookup tables and *(ii)* to what extent the overhead can be reduced by optimized implementations. To answer these questions, we have developed very fast combinatorial unranking implementations for use in bitmap decompression, we created a comprehensive performance evaluation and profiling toolkit to compare these implementations to each other, and we used this tool to benchmark our implementations in extensive performance evaluations.

The rest of this paper is structured as follows. In Sect. 2, we introduce the theoretical background, in Sect. 3 we present our implementations and optimization strategies, in Sect. 4 we briefly discuss the performance evaluation toolkit, which is followed by the measurements in Sect. 4. Finally, in Sect. 5 we sum up the main findings and describe directions of future work.

2   Combinatorial Ranking and Unranking

In this section, we discuss several combinatorial ranking/unranking implementation directions. In particular, we shall look into the following techniques:

- Precomputed lookup tables.
- Combinatorial unranking over lexicographically ordered bitmaps (lex).
- The above over co-lexicographic order (colex).

Other combinatorial unranking algorithms, like Cool-lex [7], are for further study.

2.1   Lookup Tables

The trivial method of combinatorial unranking is to use two lookup tables (see Fig. 2): an OFFSET_TABLE that stores class offsets, and a BITVECT_TABLE that stores the bit vectors themselves. The OFFSET_TABLE holds exactly b (block size) plus one elements, as there are $b + 1$ classes[1]. The BITVECT_TABLE has $\binom{b}{0} + \binom{b}{1} + \dots + \binom{b}{b-1} + \binom{b}{b} = 2^b$ number of elements because it stores all combinations of bit vectors. The pseudo-code for trivial implementation is given in Fig. 3a.

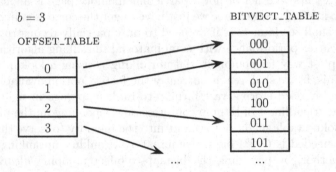

Fig. 2. Lookup tables

As we increase the block size b, the exponential growth of memory consumed by BITVECT_TABLE limits its usage. On smaller scales, when the full table fits into the processor cache[2], lookup tables can be very fast, while on larger scales the lookup table itself might not entirely fit into the main memory, causing cycle hungry memory swapping. Easily, there is a middle ground where only a portion of the table fits into the processor cache but it otherwise fits into the RAM entirely. We shall take a closer look on the performance of lookup tables in this particularly important and interesting operational regime in Sect. 4.

---

[1] Plus one, because of the zero class which means none of the bits is set.
[2] In this paper, we mean last level cache if it is not otherwise stated.

```
uint_fast8_t
table_unrank_onebit(
  uint_fast64_t rank,
  uint_fast8_t weight,
  uint_fast8_t bit) {
  return !!(
    bitvect_table[offset_table[weight]+rank]
    & (uint_fast64_t)1<<bit);
}
```

(a) Bit vector lookup table bit unrank (table-bit-onebit)

```
uint_fast8_t
lexico_unrank_onebit(
  uint_fast64_t rank,
  uint_fast8_t weight,
  uint_fast8_t width,
  uint_fast8_t bit) {
  uint_fast64_t v;
  while(weight) {
    // shifted binom table
    v = binom[width][weight];
    if(v>rank) {
      if(!bit) return 1;
      --weight;
    } else rank -= v;
    if(!bit--) return 0;
    --width;
  }
  return 0;
}
```

(b) Optimized lexicographic bit unrank (lex-bit-opt3-onebit)

Fig. 3. Bit unrank implementations for table lookup and lex-oder.

2.2 Lex

Interestingly, the mapping from class-offset pairs to bit vectors (and vice versa) can be done algorithmically. The idea is as follows. Suppose we need to enumerate all b-bit bitmaps of class c (recall, this means that there are c bits set to 1 in the block) and determine the position of any given bitmap t in this enumeration (i.e., we do combinatorial ranking). Instead of the bitmap t, we are going to rank its position vector $[t_1, t_2, \ldots, t_c]$, which encodes the position of 1s within t. Easily, there are $\binom{b}{c}$ bitmaps on class c and the same number of position-vectors, so the mapping from bitmaps to position vectors and reverseis one-to-one.

Our enumeration (for now) will be based on the ordering of position vectors of class c in lexicographic order. Now, given a position vector $[t_1, t_2, \ldots, t_c]$, we need to determine how many position vectors there are in the lexicographic order *before* this vector. This is the sum of all the position vectors $[u_1, u_2, \ldots, u_c]$, with $u_1 < t_1$, or $u_1 = t_1$ but $u_2 < t_2$, or $u_1 u_2 = t_1 t_2$ but $u_3 < t_3$, etc. One easily sees that the number of such position vectors (and so the rank r of t) is

$$r = \sum_{i=1}^{c} \left(\sum_{j=t_{i-1}+1}^{t_i-1} \binom{b-j}{c-i} \right). \tag{3}$$

Unranking, that is, determining the position-vector given its rank r in the lexicographic order, is a bit more involving. The main idea is that we go through all $i = 1, \ldots, c$ and all particular positions $j = 1, \ldots, b$ and we decide whether or not the i-th bit set to 1 can appear in position j. This can only happen if $r > \binom{b-j}{c-i}$. For a more in-depth discussion, refer to [4–6].

```
uint_fast64_t
colex_unrank_bitvect(uint_fast64_t rank, uint_fast8_t weight) {
  int_fast8_t i=weight-1, p;
  uint_fast64_t res=0, mask=1;
  while(i>=0) {
    p=i;
    while(binom[p][i+1]<=rank)
      ++p;
    res |= mask<<(p-1);
    rank-=binom[p-1][i+1];
    i-=1;
  }
  return res;
}
```

Fig. 4. Colexicographic bit vector unrank (colex-bit)

2.3 Colex

Colexicographic unranking is similar, but it is based on a colexicographic order instead of a lexicographic order. Here, colex order is essentially a reversal of the lex order. Interestingly, just this simple modification creates a whole lot of optimization chances, as we shall see in the next section when we discuss our implementations (Fig. 4).

3 Implementations and Optimization

We present optimized lookup table based, lex and colex unranking algorithms. Optimization is performed in an iterative way, trying out multiple tactics and verifying the results by a profiler. We aim to use as few variables, and operations on them, as possible, and eliminate temporary values by using increment and fetch operator. We also take care of counting towards zero in loops so we cut down cycles. Our working platform has an x86-64 instruction set, so we do not have to address penalty caused by function parameter passing. The compiler always passes parameters in registers, which would conventionally require stack operations (because of the small register file).

3.1 Table

For the lookup table we only present the bit access code (see Fig. 3a), because getting the bit vector is trivial. Double logical negation is used on the masked bit vector for getting proper boolean output (zero or one) instead of zero or many. One negation can be saved by storing a table of inverted bit vectors, however in this case compiler's optimization fails and generates a longer assembly code. This code can be also written without logical negations:

```
bitvect_table[offset_table[weight]+rank]>>bit & (uint_fast64_t)1 .
```

This is what the compiler does anyway after optimization.

```
uint_fast64_t
lexico_unrank_bitvect(
  uint_fast64_t rank,
  uint_fast8_t weight,
  uint_fast8_t width) {
  uint_fast8_t i=0, t=0;
  uint_fast64_t v, res=0, mask=1;
  while(i<weight) {
    v = binom[width-1-t][weight-i-1];
    if(v>rank) {
      res |= mask<<t;
      ++i;
    }
    else rank -= v;
    ++t;
  }
  return res;
}
```

(a) Lexicographic bit vector unrank (lex-bit-normal)

```
uint_fast64_t
lexico_unrank_bitvect(
  uint_fast64_t rank,
  uint_fast8_t weight,
  uint_fast8_t width) {
  uint_fast64_t v, res=0, mask=1;
  while(weight) {
    // shifted binom table
    v = binom[width][weight];
    if(v>rank) {
      res |= mask;
      --weight;
    }
    else rank -= v;
    --width;
    mask<<=1;
  }
  return res;
}
```

(b) Optimized Lexicographic bit vector unrank (lex-bit-opt3)

Fig. 5. Lexicographic bit vector unrank implementations

3.2 Lex

For the lexicographic unranking code, we do the optimization for both kinds of lookups (i.e., the lookup for the complete block and the simple one-bit access form). See Fig. 5. Note that we implement the reverse variant of lex which means it should be read from the less significant bit to the most significant bit (to be in lexicographic order). In the optimized algorithm, the binomial coefficients table has to be shifted bottom-right by one element to be able to save some subtractions.

The function parameters are the following:

- *rank*: the rank value need to be unranked (same as relative offset o for each class c in OFFSET_TABLE lookup table);
- *weight*: the number of ones in the bit vector (previously referred to as the class c);
- *width*: length of the bit vector (i.e., the block size b).

To find whether a bit is zero we iterate until we have found *weight* number of ones. The maximum number of iterations is *width* and each iteration decides one bit of the bit vector. In each iteration we compare a chosen binomial coefficient to the current rank value. If rank is less it means a bit set to 1 in the bit vector, otherwise it is set to zero and rank has to be decreased by this coefficient.

The row of chosen binomial coefficient is started at $width-1$ and decreases in each iteration (may reach row zero if the most significant bit is one). The column of the chosen binomial coefficient is initiated to $weight-1$ and decreases only on bits that are set to 1 (reaching always column zero). This essentially means that the algorithm can walk through $width * weight$ sized rectangle in the binomial coefficients table (see more on this "geometrical" view in [6]).

If we are interested in only one bit, as in Fig. 3b, we can save time by stopping the algorithm in the right column.

In addition to our optimized implementation of *lex-bit-opt3*, we also created an even faster implementation we shall call *lex-bit-opt4*. To save space, we do not present this algorithm separately. The idea is similar, but the code contains optimization for the case when *weight* is larger than the half of *width*, using the fact that $\binom{a}{a-b} = \binom{a}{b}$. This part of the code creates normal lexicographic ordering, so this unrank technique is a mixed variant of reverse and normal lexicographic ordering.

3.3   Colex

The algorithm, presented in Fig. 4, is similar to the lexicographic unrank algorithm, except that it finds the 1s corresponding row by increasing from row zero (instead of the decreasing property of lex) and by this design the *width* parameter is not required. We look for the highest value in the current column of the binomial coefficients table which can be subtracted from the current rank and results in a natural number. Then we step to the previous column and do the same until reaching the last column. Each row iteration during finding that value results in a zero bit, while each column change corresponds to a one bit in the resulting bit vector.

4   Performance Evaluation and Profiling

In order to measure the performance of our implementations, we created a comprehensive benchmarking framework (called `Cyclecount`) and profiling scripts using the `Callgrind` tool. The `Cyclecount` framework can provide cycle accurate measurements and also creates diagrams for them. `Callgrind` is an extension to `Cachegrind` and part of the sophisticated `Valgrind` [8] profiling tool suite.

`Cyclecount` is based on the excellent measurement library [9] of Agner Fog and it includes a kernel driver and a user space program. The library contains instruction latency and throughput tables [10] for different processor architectures. The elapsed cycles measured using the processor's Performance Monitor Counter (PMC) and the emptiness of the pipeline is guaranteed by using the CPUID[3] instruction. PMC is an internal hardware counter for measuring events like elapsed cycles, cache misses, failed branch predictions, etc. The framework runs the test cases multiple times and calculates mean values to eliminate spikes that may be caused by interrupts. Because we measure clock cycles instead of elapsed time, the frequency scaling property of the CPU cannot alter the results.

For compiling and measuring the code with different parameters we have introduced a special `interval` precompiler macro. This macro is processed by our framework and, besides replacing it with the corresponding precompiler

---

[3] Normal usage of this instruction is to determine features of the CPU, however it also has a property of flushing the pipeline.

macro for optimization, it also automatically orders the tests into groups in the diagram. Multiple output formats are supported, like simple text file for human reading, XML file for machine processing, and plot files for diagrams using GNUPlot in PNG and EPS formats. Cyclecount is written in C++ and Python, and runs on Linux exclusively.

The profiling script uses Callgrind to measure the consumed cycles. Unfortunately, Callgrind simply returns event numbers but it does not calculate total cycles for us. We used the metric of KCachegrind to calculate the estimated cycles caused by cache misses: 10 cycles for a level-1 miss and 100 cycles for a last-level miss. The profiling script has an option to compare the output of the profiled programs to ensure that the optimized program generates the same output as the normal program. In this case, the seed of the randomization is not the time but a predefined value (12345). The script comes in the form of GNU Makefiles and use only standard Unix utilities, hence it should run on any Unix-llike platform where Valgrind is available.

The measurements are done on an Intel Core 2 Quad Q6600 processor with Fedora Linux 19 (x64) and GCC 4.8.2 compiler (with -O2 and -march=core2 optimizations). The tests are done using random (but valid) ranks and using 1 million unrank operations.

Our benchmarking suite together with all the source codes is available for download at https://github.com/andmaj/eunice2014article, so one can independently verify the results.

4.1 Results

In Fig. 6, we present the performance of unranking techniques with random classes but fixed block size using the two performance evaluation tools. The block

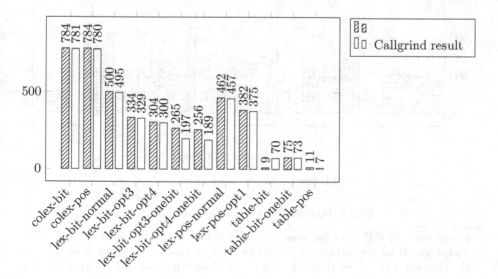

Fig. 6. Performance of unranking techniques (block size = 25, random classes)

size b is 25 bytes because in this case the 268MB lookup table would certainly not fit the processor's cache but can be easily fit into the RAM. The values are quite close in most cases so Callgrind does a good job on simulating the processor. However in case of *lex-bit-opt3-onebit* and *lex-bit-opt4-onebit* Callgrind shows a value 26 % lower than the result of the real world Cyclecount test and there is a big difference between the *table-bit* results too. We have also implemented the unranking techniques in terms of position vectors[4]. Unfortunately, the results could not be included in the paper due to space limits, so we only sketch some results in Fig. 6b.

Figure 7a shows the dependence on the block size of the unranking performance with random classes, while in Fig. 7b the focus is on class dependence with fixed block size.

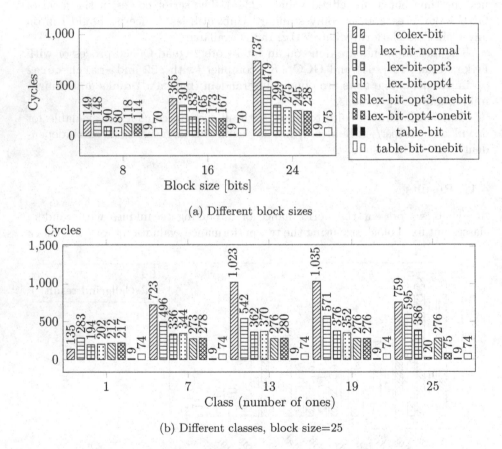

(a) Different block sizes

(b) Different classes, block size=25

Fig. 7. Performance of unranking techniques

---

[4] Recall that the difference between a bit vector and a position vector is that a bit vector stands for the bitmap itself and can be represented by a 64 bit integer, while the position vector is an array of 8 bit integers, each representing the position of a bit set to 1.

4.2   Table

Interestingly, we found the *table-pos* technique to be the fastest amongst the unranking techniques. As it just returns a reference of a position vector, the simplicity of the *table-pos* buys performance. Note that in common applications, where one used to make a copy, it would be slower than other lookup table methods. In other cases, however, table-based unranking is still a very reasonable choice, despite the promise of the other purely algorithmic techniques.

Curiously, we found that a *table-bit* unrank query terminates in only 9 cycles in the `Cyclecount` test, but when bit manipulation takes place on this data (like in the case of *table-bit-onebit*) this jumps to 75 cycles. We believe that there may be an optimization in this processor family on simple memory copy operations, or it can arrange the micro-operations in a way that the query runs quasi-parallel with the random number generation functions. The operations are certainly completed because we have also tested summarizing the returned values. It also seems that the performance of lookup tables is independent of the class and block sizes.

4.3   Lex

Our optimized lex unranking algorithm *lex-bit-opt4* can attain 304 cycles which is 39 % faster than the plain version *lex-bit-normal* as seen in Fig. 6. Further, if we are interested in only one bit of the bit vector performs even better, reaching 256 cycles as *lex-bit-opt4-onebit*. The performance of lex shows the same trends as that of colex for growth of block size, however it increases logarithmically with the class size. However, the optimizations in *lex-bit-opt4* and *lex-bit-opt4-onebit* result in a linear decrease of cycle count with the class parameter, after the class becomes larger than half of the block size.

4.4   Colex

As can be seen in Fig. 6, colex can be considered a very bad choice for combinatorial unranking in terms of speed, with only 784 cycles per unrank operation. The number of CPU cycles consumed by colex grow linearly with block size (see Fig. 7a). It is interesting that for different classes it shows a wave like behavior but never forms a half period (see Fig. 7b).

5   Conclusion

At the moment, it seems that combinatorial unranking algorithms cannot replace simple lookup tables in compression/de-compression codes, at least as long as the block size is small enough for the lookup table to fit entirely into the RAM. However, they may still find their use for larger block sizes, that is, when the exponential growth of lookup tables would cause the table to overflow the main memory and swapping would ruin the process. For such cases, our optimized combinatorial unranking codes seem to present a decent choice for implementors.

Even so, we have not given up yet the possibility that a hardware-assisted implementation would be able to reach the performance of lookup tables someday. This presents a great opportunity for future research.

Acknowledgements. András Majdán was supported by the Google Faculty Research Awards programme "Searchable Compressed Data Structures for the Mainstream". Gábor Rétvári was supported by the OTKA/PD-104939 grant.

References

1. Raman, R., Raman, V., Srinivasa Rao, S.: Succinct indexable dictionaries with applications to encoding K-ary trees, prefix sums and multisets. ACM Trans. Algorithms **3**(4), 43 (2007)
2. Rétvári, G., Tapolcai, J., Kőrösi, A., Majdán, A., Heszberger, Z.: Compressing IP forwarding tables: towards entropy bounds and beyond. In: Proceedings of the ACM SIGCOMM 2013 Conference on SIGCOMM, pp. 111–122 (2013)
3. Mäkinen, V., Navarro, G.: Dynamic entropy-compressed sequences and full-text indexes. ACM Trans. Algorithms **4**(3), 32 (2008)
4. Knuth, D.E.: The Art of Computer Programming: Combinatorial Algorithms, Part 1. Addison-Wesley, Boston (2011)
5. Kokosiski, Z.: Algorithms for unranking combinations and other related choice functions. http://riad.pk.edu.pl/~zk/pubs/95-1-006.pdf (1995)
6. Tomic, R.V.: Quantized indexing: background information. http://www.1stworks.com/ref/TR/tr05-0625a.pdf (2005)
7. Ruskey, F., Williams, A.: The coolest way to generate combinations. Discrete Math. **309**(17), 5305–5320 (2009)
8. Valgrind Instrumentation Framework. http://valgrind.org/. Accessed 18 July 2014
9. Fog, A.: Test programs for measuring clock cycles and performance monitoring. http://www.agner.org/optimize/testp.zip. Accessed 18 July 2014
10. Fog, A.: Lists of instruction latencies, throughputs and micro-operation breakdowns for Intel, AMD and VIA CPUs. http://www.agner.org/optimize/instruction_tables.pdf (2014)

YouQoS – A New Concept for Quality of Service in DSL Based Access Networks

Sebastian Meier$^{(\boxtimes)}$, Alexander Vensmer, and Kristian Ulshöfer

Institute of Communication Networks and Computer Engineering (IKR),
University of Stuttgart, 70569 Stuttgart, Germany
{sebastian.meier,alexander.vensmer}@ikr.uni-stuttgart.de,
kristian.ulshoefer@gmail.com

Abstract. Today's Internet users typically own multiple devices and consume several services simultaneously. Due to this usage pattern, bandwidth in *Access Network* (ANs) is often insufficient. Increasing bandwidth is not always feasible or economic. A well-known approach to cope with limited bandwidth is *Quality of Service* (QoS) enforcement. However, today's QoS solutions are neither accepted by providers nor by users. Users are concerned because of network neutrality. Operators hesitate adopting QoS frameworks because they typically require end to end deployment. In this paper we present YouQoS – a solution, which addresses operators' as well as users' concerns by providing a QoS solution, which works locally in the AN based on user defined QoS policies. We introduce our evolutionary approach to QoS management in today's *Digital Subscriber Line* (DSL) based ANs by utilizing and enhancing existing QoS mechanisms. Furthermore, we provide an initial proof of concept with a Linux demonstrator.

Keywords: Quality of service · Access networks

1 Introduction

Bottlenecks in packet switched networks negatively influence QoS. In particular they have impact on packet loss, delay, and bandwidth. In the past, many approaches (such as IntServ [5] and DiffServ [4]) have been proposed to migrate from best effort to QoS enabled networks. QoS architectures have been deployed to some extent in ANs to manage services offered by the *Internet Service Provider* (ISP) (e.g. IP telephony). However, to the best of our knowledge these approaches have not been deployed widely for managing QoS of *Internet* traffic in the AN. One of the reasons for not adopting these approaches (in particular IntServ) is that they typically assume end to end deployment.

However, in today's networks, bottlenecks are commonly located in the ANs. Particularly in rural areas, many households are connected to the Internet with

---

Kristian Ulshöfer–At the time of writing, Kristian Ulshöfer was a student at the IKR.

© Springer International Publishing Switzerland 2014
Y. Kermarrec (Ed.): EUNICE 2014, LNCS 8846, pp. 109–120, 2014.
DOI: 10.1007/978-3-319-13488-8_11

low bandwidth. A Study for DSL ANs in Germany has shown that 38 % of subscribers are connected to the Internet with as little as 6 MBit/s. The "ICT Facts and figures" report from 2014 [9] shows that these observations can be transferred to other countries, as well.

These conditions are insufficient for today's user behavior, which is characterized by consuming several services (e.g. VoIP and Download) and using several end-devices simultaneously. We assume that this problem persists even with improving (e.g. very high speed digital subscriber lines [11]) and new AN technologies (e.g. gigabit passive optical networks [10]) as service demands will increase as well (e.g. 4K video streaming).

In contrast to previous end to end QoS approaches we propose a QoS solution, which operates locally in the AN based on user defined policies. This approach is promising, since it has several advantages for network operators as well as users (subscribers) as outlined in the following.

On the one hand, our approach supports gradual deployment as YouQoS extensions can be limited to a single AN. In the simplest case, upgrading a single AN device is sufficient. On the other hand, user satisfaction can be increased by efficient QoS management without having to increase the subscriber's bandwidth.

Furthermore, the user is able to specify the prioritization of the services she consumes. This is beneficial in two ways. On the one hand, the user knows best, which services are important compared to others. On the other hand, enabling the user instead of the service provider to influence service prioritization mitigates the problem of network neutrality.

Our solution enforces QoS on the last mile, which is usually the *Local Loop* (LL) in DSL ANs The last mile is typically assigned to an individual subscriber. In contrast to DiffServ we therefore can trust a user's prioritization as his decisions only impact his services but never influence the services of other users.

The remainder of this paper is structured as follows. Section 2 gives an overview of the state of the art of QoS management in DSL ANs. Section 3 presents an overview of the YouQoS architecture, its functional blocks and their placement.We detail the architecture of the functional block for YouQoS Policy Selection in Sect. 4, and its implementation in Sect. 5. In Sect. 6 we conclude the paper and discuss our next steps.

2   State of the Art of QoS Management in DSL ANs

Figure 1 depicts the basic structure of a DSL AN. Although we simplified the topology, it contains all relevant network elements, including the Local Area Network (LAN) of a residential customer.

A *Home Gateway* (HG) connects one or several *User Devices* (UDs) (e.g. PC, smart TV, mobile) to the network. Today's HGs usually deploy basic QoS mechanisms (e.g. stochastic fairness queuing [12]). Although statically configured, they guarantee some fairness between several UDs or services competing for upstream bandwidth.

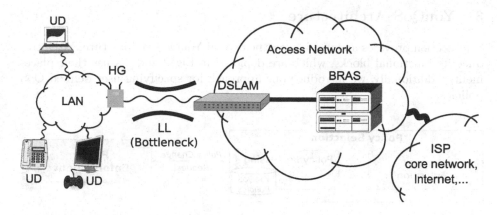

Fig. 1. DSL Access Network

A *Digital Subscriber Line Access Multiplexer* (DSLAM) terminates DSL LLs of several subscribers. Depending on the deployment model, a DSLAM connects from several dozens subscribers (decentralized outdoor deployment) up to several thousand subscribers (central office deployment) [14]. First generation DSL ANs utilized *Asynchronous Transfer Mode* (ATM) on the data link layer. Although ATM offers sound QoS mechanisms, network operators typically made little use of ATM's QoS features in DSLAMs. Today's Ethernet based DSLAM become increasingly sophisticated. Recently, IP functionality is being added to DSLAMs. This trend is motivated by operators' demand for "Broadband Remote Access Server (BRAS) offloading", i.e. moving functionality from BRAS to DSLAMs. Offloading may include QoS differentiation, e.g. based on priority levels of virtual LAN tags [8].

A BRAS connects DSLAMs to the ISP's core network. It may handle up to 128.000 subscribers [13]. Since the introduction of "Triple-Play", the BRAS plays a central role in managing QoS for downstream traffic [2,13]. Early architecture proposals [2] envisioned the BRAS to perform scheduling on packet level based on policies associated with subscriber sessions. However, these policies were rather static and only able to apply QoS differentiation to a small set of services offered by the ISP (e.g. IPTV). They didn't cover Internet traffic, which was always classified as best effort traffic. New proposals [6] identify requirements regarding extensions to the existing multi-service architecture, e.g. "QoS on Demand" and "near real time QoS changes". These proposals introduce sophisticated queuing and scheduling hierarchies within a BRAS for QoS enforcement on subscriber and even application level. These architecture extensions would allow applying QoS differentiation to Internet services and applications.

However, to the best of our knowledge, there are still plenty of open issues regarding the specification and realization of this architecture. In this paper we tend to go beyond the state of the art by providing a solution for swift determining and signaling of application QoS requirements.

3   YouQoS Architecture

This section provides an overview on the overall YouQoS architecture. We introduce its functional blocks, which are depicted in Fig. 2 and discuss their placement. Additionally, we introduce our approach for specifying user defined QoS policies.

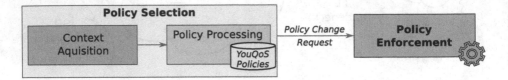

Fig. 2. Functional blocks of the YouQoS architecture

3.1   YouQoS Policies

YouQoS Policies are user defined rules for specifying the prioritization of the services that the user consumes. The underlying assumption is that there doesn't exist a "one size fits all" QoS parameterization. For instance, a gamer might be interested in prioritizing gaming traffic while a home office user might want to prioritize video conference calls.

Furthermore, we assume that QoS prioritization depends on context information. For instance, a video stream played back on a smart phone might decrease in priority, if the user places the phone screen side down on a table. Detecting this kind of dependencies automatically can be challenging if not impossible.

Therefore, our YouQoS policy approach combines context information as well as user preferences for determining QoS prioritization. To achieve this task, we propose a policy based approach. A YouQoS Policy consists of attributes and a prioritization result. Attributes may match on flow state and properties as well as device state and properties, see Table 1 for examples. Currently, a policy's prioritization result encodes a relative priority.

The following subsection details, how our architecture selects YouQoS Policies and utilizes their prioritization result for policy enforcement.

Table 1. Attributes of YouQoS policies (excerpt)

Policy attribute	Examples
User name	Sebastian, Alexander, Kristian
User activity	Foreground tab in browser, screen saver state
Application name	Chrome, Skype
Flow information	Transport layer port, source IP address

3.2   Policy Selection

This functional block selects YouQoS Policies based on context information. It consists of the two sub functions: *Context Acquisition* and *Policy Processing*.

Context Acquisition keeps track of all information, which is relevant to policy attributes, in particular state changes in the system. This includes system wide state information (e.g. active/visible application) on the one hand, as well as flow related state information (e.g. application name) on the other hand.

Policy Processing is triggered by Context Acquisition. Based on the trigger it searches for policies, which are sensitive to the state changes discovered by Context Acquisition. Based on matching policies the selection block generates *Policy Change Requests*, which are signaled towards the functional block *Policy Enforcement*.

A *Policy Change Request* specifies a QoS priority and defines, which packets should be treated with the designated priority. For the latter, a Policy Change Request provides a flow definition consisting of source/destination IP address, source/destination port, and transport layer protocol.

3.3   Policy Enforcement

The main task of *Policy Enforcement* is to differentiate the priority of flows. Policy Enforcement achieves this by creating an artificial, yet fully controllable bottleneck. With this approach, QoS differentiation can be achieved by dropping, delaying or preferring individual packets. These tasks are typically carried out by packet schedulers whose internal algorithms decide the order in which packets from each flow are transmitted on the link.

As shown in Sect. 2, QoS adaptations become increasingly dynamic. We therefore assume that network devices (e.g. BRAS) provide interfaces for configuration and parameterization of their queues and schedulers. These interfaces may be proprietary or device specific and their realization is out of our scope.

With QoS Policy Change Requests, we provide a device independent description for signaling per flow prioritization information. Concerning packet processing on the data plane, little extensions to a network device are required. A small extension for translating between our device independent QoS Policy Change Requests and proprietary packet scheduler interfaces is sufficient.

Enforcement of QoS Policy Change Requests should only affect traffic of the user that created the request and must not interfere with the QoS perceived by other subscribers. Typically, this requirement is implicitly fulfilled by the AN topology, in which the LL is the bottleneck and other shared resources are over-dimensioned. In case of oversubscribed ANs, the provider typically enforces fair sharing of available resources by traffic shaping. Regarding QoS Policy Change Requests, the network operator has to ensure, that operator defined traffic shaping has precedence over user defined policies. This ensures, that user defined QoS policies cannot impact the QoS of other subscribers.

Since network operators are likely critical of user initiated QoS Policy Change Request signaling, special care has to be taken regarding the control plane.

Although control plane details are out of scope of this paper, we have identified several challenges which we intend to address, e.g.:

– *Authentication and authorization of QoS Policy Change Requests.* In case of DSL ANs, reuse of existing infrastructure for subscriber management seems feasible at first glance. However, a more thorough evaluation of our assumption is necessary.
– *Robustness in terms of signaling and processing load.* Network devices are typically dimensioned to handle a predefined number of policies per subscriber on the one hand, and a maximum signaling rate on the other hand. Suitable mechanisms are required to enforce these limitations, preventing a (misbehaving) user to compromise the stability of the system. For our scenario, a very simple approach for achieving this goal is discarding QoS Policy Change Requests, in case a user violates any of the aforementioned constraints.

3.4 Placement of YouQoS Functional Blocks

As Fig. 3 depicts, we consider the following devices for functional placement: UD, HG, DSLAM, and BRAS. Regarding the functions we differentiate between *Context Acquisition* (CA), *Policy Processing* (PP), and *Policy Enforcement* (PE). In this section we discuss, which devices are suitable for hosting which functional blocks.

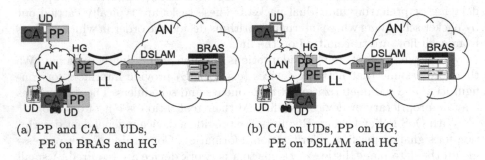

(a) PP and CA on UDs,   (b) CA on UDs, PP on HG,
    PE on BRAS and HG   PE on DSLAM and HG

Fig. 3. Functional placement examples

Context Acquisition is typically carried out on UDs, as necessary information is only available there. We acknowledge the existence of legacy devices, which might not be able to perform context acquisition themselves (e.g. IP telephones). We cover that case in our Policy Processing function, which we explain in the following.

Policy Processing can be performed on all considered devices, in principle. However, there are advantages and disadvantages regarding each choice.

Processing on the UD has the advantage that the policies are always available, independently of UD location, which facilitates using YouQoS on mobile devices. On the other hand, keeping policies on separate UDs is cumbersome, in case a user owns several UDs (e.g. smart TV, smart phone, laptop). Furthermore, following this approach strictly, would exclude consideration of legacy devices.

Processing on the HG has the advantage that devices are managed centrally from the user's point of view. Keeping a central repository facilitates management of YouQoS Policies for devices present in a user's LAN. A HG could furthermore support management of legacy devices such as IP telephones, for instance by defining static device policies.

Processing on the DSLAM or BRAS (i.e. on devices owned by the network operator) is possible in principle. However, changes in context information may occur frequently. As these changes trigger Policy Processing, signaling these frequent changes introduces overhead. This overhead might be acceptable while being local to a device or LAN. However, we assume that the overhead becomes unacceptably high, if signaling has to traverse the LL bottleneck. Therefore, we don't consider DSLAM or BRAS as suitable candidates for Policy Processing.

Policy Enforcement has to be placed before the bottleneck. As "before" depends on the traffic direction, we discuss upstream and downstream traffic separately.

For prioritizing upstream traffic HG and UD are suitable candidates. In a LAN environment, typically multiple devices compete for bandwidth on the LL bottleneck. Therefore, policy enforcement is best placed at an element, which has full control over this bottleneck. In our scenarios, this element is usually the HG.

For prioritizing downstream traffic, BRAS and DSLAM are suitable candidates. In contrast to the upstream direction, selecting the best location is less obvious. The decision depends on factors such as network topology, network size, number of subscribers, network element capabilities, and network operator preferences.

In the next section we detail the design of our architecture's functional blocks. Since Policy Enforcement is usually a simple translation between QoS Policy Change Requests and internal scheduler interfaces (see Sect. 3.3), we focus on the Policy Selection functional block in the following.

4 Policy Selection Block Architecture

4.1 Basic Principles

Regarding the Policy Selection block, our main goal is to provide an easy to use, application independent solution.

Easy to use means that complexity is hidden from the user. We do not expect that a user knows, whether his services are sensitive to packet delay, loss, or bandwidth. Particularly, we do not want users to define QoS targets (e.g. delay, loss) on a flow basis. Instead, we intend to provide a simple interface to the user, which allows intuitive prioritization, i.e. a "priority dial" for applications. Special care has to be taken that a user can always undo any priority changes, in case they have unforeseen or unintended impact.

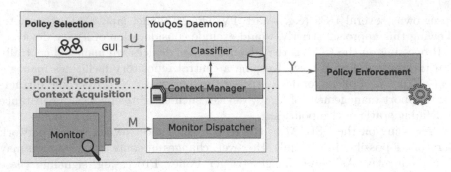

Fig. 4. Functional block for Policy Selection

Application independent means that we don't intend to patch applications for providing YouQoS functionality. Instead our approach is to utilize existing operating system interfaces for acquiring system and application state information. A *YouQoS Daemon* collects and processes this information.

The advantage of this approach is that all applications that run on a YouQoS enabled platform may benefit from our QoS policies. Although our initial design was intended for Linux, our approach is generic enough for being ported to other platforms, such as iOS or Android, for instance.

The following subsection details the internals of the YouQoS Daemon and its interaction with external entities.

4.2   Components and Interfaces

Figure 4 shows the three core components (*Monitors*, *YouQoS Daemon*, and *GUI*) as well as external interfaces (*U, M, Y*) of the YouQoS *Policy Selection* block.

Monitors are the main component of Context Acquisition. They are responsible for collecting state information related to the entire system, particular applications, or individual flows. Each individual Monitor is responsible to collect exactly one type of state information (e.g. active network flows).Monitor implementations may differ in many aspects, such as exported data (kind, frequency, amount), privileges (user privileges, root privileges), or environment (kernel space, user space). Despite those differences, the YouQoS Daemon provides a unified interface M for interacting with Monitors. Our approach was to define a simple yet flexible and extensible message based protocol for the M interface. In the current implementation of our architecture, we utilize this interface for *Inter-process communication* (IPC) between Monitors and the YouQoS Daemon. However, the design approach supports information exchange across system boundaries, in principle. This allows to carry out Context Acquisition and Policy Processing on different systems, which gives us more degrees of freedom for functional placement, see Sect. 3.4.

The ***YouQoS Daemon*** consists of three sub-components: a *Monitor Dispatcher* for managing Monitor instances, a *Context Manager* for keeping track of state information, and a *Classifier* for selecting policies. It relies on these components to generate Policy Change Requests, which are signaled over the Y interface to the Policy Enforcement. We provide a more detailed description of these sub-components in the following.

The **Monitor Dispatcher** selects Monitors, which are suitable for the system environment. For instance, on a Linux system with an X Window System, the Monitor Dispatcher selects a Monitor instance for capturing X Window events (e.g. foreground window). Furthermore, the Monitor Dispatcher parameterizes properties of Monitors. Properties are typically related to the kind and amount of data a Monitor exports. For instance, a Monitor that provides flow information may be configured to not export information about short-lived flows (e.g. DNS requests).

The **Context Manager** creates for each application, which is managed by the YouQoS Daemon, context information necessary for policy management. This includes keeping track of and acting upon state changes. However, the Context Manager doesn't perform actions on its own. It rather creates and dispatches events based on context changes and selects suitable sub-components for event handling. For instance, a new connection typically requires classification for QoS policy selection. Therefore, in this example the Context Manager would trigger the Classifier component for further processing. Other events, e.g. when the user closes an application require policy deletion, which is handled by another sub-component (not depicted).

The **Classifier** has an internal database for storing user-defined YouQoS Policies. Based on trigger events from the Context Manager, the Classifier creates database requests for retrieving matching policies. A YouQoS Policy matches if and only if all of its attributes coincide with the current system state and application specific context information. In case multiple policies match, the Classifier may select a subset based on further criteria such as policy priorities, or number of exactly matching attributes. The classification result is signaled to the Policy Enforcement by an additional sub-component (not depicted).

The **GUI** provides user friendly access to the U interface, which allows to list, add, edit, and delete user defined YouQoS Policies. Similar to the M interface, the U interfaces relies on a simple protocol for managing YouQoS Policies. The architecture doesn't have any constraints regarding the realization of the GUI - in particular neither where nor how the GUI should be implemented.

5   Policy Selection Block Implementation

We implemented a fully functional prototype of the YouQoS Daemon for a Linux system. In addition to the daemon we also implemented two monitors and a web based graphical user interface.

For functional evaluation of interaction between Policy Selection (i.e. YouQoS Daemon) and Policy Enforcement we relied on the Linux traffic shaping framework [1]. This framework is powerful enough to emulate the scheduling capabilities of a DSLAM or BRAS.

In the following we present selected components and aspects of our implementation.

5.1 Functional View

The *X Server Monitor* is realized as a user space process. By using the Xlib helper library it queries information about the graphical user interface environment from the X Server [7]. It monitors which application is running in foreground and whether the screen saver is active.

The *Connection Monitor* is implemented as a Linux kernel module. It utilizes information gathered by the Linux kernel Conntrack subsystem [15], which keeps track of a computer's connections by inspecting network packets.

We implemented the M interface, which we utilize for communication between YouQoS Daemon and Monitors by relying on Netlink [3]. Netlink provides socket oriented communication, which supports IPC between user space processes, as well as exchanging information between user space and kernel space.

The YouQoS Daemon is implemented as a user space process. For our prototype, the Classifier uses a SQL based database as a backend for storing and retrieving YouQoS Policies. We decided to provide a web based graphical user interface and therefore utilize HTTP for the U interface. This enables a user to list, add, delete, and edit YouQoS policies conveniently by using a browser. Therefore, our implementation includes a simple web server for translating between SQL database entries and Ajax enriched HTML.

5.2 Information Flow

In the following we outline interactions and information flow in our prototypic implementation of the YouQoS architecture by using a small example. We consider a UD, which hosts the YouQoS Policy Selection consisting of YouQoS Daemon, Monitors and GUI. Our starting point is that the YouQoS Daemon is running and its initialization (e.g. Monitor setup) is complete. We assume that the user previously defined two simple YouQoS Policies: a gaming policy which gives high priority to an online game application and a second policy giving low priority to FTP downloads. Now, the user starts an online game, while an FTP download is running in the background.

Figure 5 depicts the procedure from initial connection detection until Policy Change Request signaling in the YouQoS architecture.

The Connection Monitor detects a connection establishment of the online game and extracts a 6-Tuple consisting of source and destination IP address, source and destination port number, transport protocol, and process ID. It encapsulates this information in a Netlink messages and forwards this message from kernel space to the user space YouQoS Daemon.

The Monitor Dispatcher receives the message, extracts its payload and forwards the extracted state information to the Context Manager.

The Context Manager checks, whether there already exists a context for association of the received state information. In our example that's not the

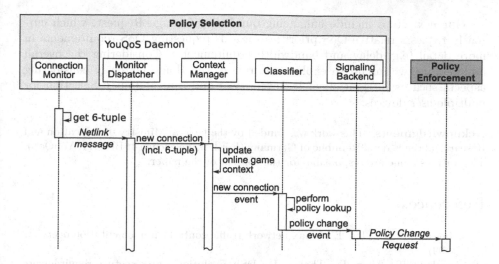

Fig. 5. Message sequence chart for triggering a Policy Change Request

case. Therefore, the Context Manager creates a new application context and assigns related state to the newly created context (e.g. connection information). Furthermore, the Context Manager performs a lookup based on the process ID for identification of the application name. Afterwards, the Context Manager creates an event which triggers the Classifier to perform a policy lookup.

For determining matching YouQoS Policies, the Classifier performs a database lookup. The database query is based on the application's context which includes information about it's connections, but also about the overall system state. In our example we assume that the Classifier finds a matching policy. It triggers the Signaling Backend to create a Policy Change Request for the online game, which is sent to the Policy Enforcement.

The Policy Enforcement point receives the Policy Change Request and extracts all required information for identifying packets belonging to the online game's connection. It parameterizes its internal packet scheduler to treat online game traffic with a higher QoS priority than packets belonging to the FTP download. Therefore, the user is able to enjoy the online game, without being impaired by the FTP transfer running simultaneously.

6   Summary and Future Work

In this paper we introduced our YouQoS architecture, its functional blocks and their placement for user defined Quality of Service enforcement in DSL access networks. Based on the current state of the art, we presented how our architecture utilizes and enhances existing QoS mechanisms. We detailed the design of the YouQoS Policy Selection block and demonstrated its feasibility by a prototypic Linux implementation. It is worth considering, whether our approach can be transferred to other access network technologies beyond DSL, as well.

Our next steps include enhancing our Policy Change Request, which currently requests relative QoS priorities towards requesting QoS requirements in more detail (e.g. delay and bandwidth requirements). Considering the overall architecture, we intend to explore the role of the Home Gateway considering aspects such as integration of legacy devices and central Policy Selection for multiple user devices.

Acknowledgments. This work was funded by the Federal Ministry of Education and Research of the Federal Republic of Germany (Förderkennzeichen 16BP1211, YouQoS). The authors alone are responsible for the content of the paper.

References

1. Almesberger, W., Ica, E.: Linux network traffic control - implementation overview (1999)
2. Anschutz, T., Allan, D., Thorne, D.: DSL Evolution - architecture requirements for the support of QoS-enabled IP services. Technical Report, DSL Forum
3. Ayuso, P.N., Gasca, R.M., Lefèvre, L.: Communicating between the kernel and user-space in Linux using Netlink sockets. Soft. Pract. Exp. **40**(9), 797–810 (2010)
4. Blake, S., Black, D., Carlson, M., Davies, E., Wang, Z., Weiss, W.: An architecture for differentiated services (1998). http://www.ietf.org/rfc/rfc2475.txt
5. Braden, R., Clark, D., Shenker, S.: Integrated services in the internet architecture: an overview. RFC 1633 (1994)
6. Cui, A., Allan, D., Thorne, D.: Broadband multi-service architecture and framework requirements. Technical Report, DSL Forum
7. X. Org Foundation: Homepage of X.Org Project (2014). http://www.x.org/
8. IEEE: 802.1Q-2011: Media access control (MAC) bridges and virtual bridged local area networks. IEEE Standard 802.1Q-2011 (2011)
9. ITU: The world in 2014: ICT facts and figures. Technical Report, ITU
10. ITU-T: G.984.1: Gigabit-capable passive optical networks (GPON): general characteristics. ITU-T Recommendation G.984.1 (2008)
11. ITU-T: G.993.2: Very high speed digital subscriber line transceivers 2 (VDSL2). ITU-T Recommendation G.993.2 (2011)
12. McKenney, P.E.: Stochastic fairness queueing. In: INFOCOM'90, Ninth Annual Joint Conference of the IEEE Computer and Communication Societies. The Multiple Facets of Integration. Proceedings, IEEE. pp. 733–740. IEEE (1990)
13. Shrum, E., Allan, D., Thorne, D.: Broadband remote access server (BRAS) requirements document. Technical Report, DSL Forum
14. Agilent Technologies: Understanding DSLAM and BRAS access devices. White Paper (2006)
15. Welte, H., Ayuso, P.N.: Homepage of Netfilter project (2014). http://conntrack-tools.netfilter.org/

Compressing Virtual Forwarding Information Bases Using the Trie-folding Algorithm

Bence Mihálka[✉], Attila Kőrösi, and Gábor Rétvári

Department of Telecommunications and Media Informatics,
Budapest University of Technology and Economics, Budapest, Hungary
{mihalka, korosi, retvari}@tmit.bme.hu

Abstract. In the latest years network virtualization and virtual routers have gained considerable attention, because with their aid it is possible to realize multiple virtual topologies on the same physical network. This plays a key role in cloud-based systems and VPN (Virtual Private Network), amongst others. In order to be able to forward IP packets according to multiple topologies, the router needs to store numerous Forwarding Information Bases (FIBs), which can lead to memory scalability issues. We address this issue by applying the well-known "trie-folding" FIB compression method to the case of multiple virtual FIBs (VFIBs). We propose two novel approaches to perform the compression, based on different virtual router architectures. We introduce a further opportunity for optimization, based on the distribution of next-hop labels. We formulate a minimization problem using entropy measure, and we provide a heuristic approach of solving the problem. We present numerical evaluations including lookup speed, memory size of compressed VFIBs, and their corresponding entropies. Based on these results and the underlying theoretical reasoning, we can safely say that the presented techniques are not only able to resolve the memory scalability issues of modern virtual routers, but they also improve lookup speed considerably, one of the most important performance measures in a core router, be it virtual or not.

Keywords: Virtual router · Forwarding information base · IP lookup · Trie-folding

1 Introduction

Network virtualization techniques, and specifically the use of virtual routers, are promising technology, because a lot of network-related problems are easily solvable with its help, including user-specific or rule-based routing. Moreover, they play a crucial part in the workings of VPNs, and cloud-based systems.

The key to realizing these virtual routers is to run multiple instances of them on a single physical device. When an incoming packet arrives, the router inspects its header information (for example its MPLS label, or Ethernet VLAN tag, etc.) and decides which virtual instance it is intended for. Next, the router uses the appropriate VFIB (Virtual Forwarding Information Base) to determine which neighbor should the packet be forwarded.

© Springer International Publishing Switzerland 2014
Y. Kermarrec (Ed.): EUNICE 2014, LNCS 8846, pp. 121–133, 2014.
DOI: 10.1007/978-3-319-13488-8_12

When implementing these functions in a real device, one of the most pressing bottlenecks in the system is the memory size of the router. In order to minimize packet forwarding delay it needs to be very fast, and it also needs to maintain all VFIBs simultaneously. These two factors lead to scalability issues, severely limiting the possible number of virtual router instances a physical device can host.

A viable answer to this problem is to compress the VFIBs. In other words, the task is to rearrange their data structures in such a way, that after the compression they still provide exactly the same forwarding logic as before, but consuming significantly less memory. The basic idea, independently of the router being virtual, is of course in widespread use in today's routers [1–3, 13–17]. In this paper we shall apply a well-known algorithm, called "trie-folding" to the case of the virtual FIB instances. We chose this particular algorithm because it is proven to be able to compress FIB data to within a constant factor of its entropy bound [4]. As the original algorithm was designed to compress the FIBs of physical routers, we shall propose below a number of improvements to adapt it to the special needs of compressing VFIBs.

It is a crucial architectural decision in router design whether or not the virtual router instances can exchange data with each other. If the virtual router instances run separately in their own namespaces then, naturally, their VFIBs need to be compressed separately and hence all the resultant data structures need to encode the forwarding logic of that virtual router entirely. On the other hand, if information can be shared between the virtual routers then the VFIBs can be compressed jointly, this way greatly reducing the memory footprint [5]. In this paper, we observe, however, that without careful intervention the entropy of the combined VFIBs may increase drastically, limiting the compression efficiency and hence the size of the compressed VFIBs. As main contributions, we define an entropy-minimization problem to overcome this issue, we give a through mathematical analysis, and we propose a novel next-hop relabeling heuristics that, according to our numerical evaluations, efficiently improves the compressibility of real-life VFIBs.

The rest of the paper is organized as follows: Sect. 2 describes the background, Sect. 3 introduces the different virtual router architectures, and methods of applying the trie-folding algorithm. In Sect. 4 we present the entropy-minimization problem, and describe our heuristic approach for solving it. In Sect. 5 we present our numerical evaluations, along with the description of the measurement environment and the origins of the utilized FIB data. Finally, in Sect. 6 we conclude the paper.

2 Background

In this section we will introduce the concept of IP FIBs, and describe the most frequently used data structure for its storage, the prefix tree. We will also mention a regularized form of this tree called the leaf-pushed prefix tree. This is crucial because based on it we can provide an entropy measure, which yields an important lower bound for the memory requirement of the data structure, and thus, a lower bound for the size of the FIB.

2.1   FIB, Prefix Trees

Be it a virtual or a real forwarding information base (FIB), it is the data structure responsible for forwarding an inbound IP packet to the appropriate neighbor. Its input data consists of entries which assign a next-hop label to an IP address and corresponding prefix length. The next-hop label is the IP address of one of the routers' neighbor. As an example we show the entries of two FIBs in Table 1. In these examples we denote next-hop labels with integer values instead of IP addresses. As we will see later on this provides an opportunity for further optimization of the compression.

The next-hop labels in the entries of a FIB are in effect IP addresses, so we need to pair the integer identifiers to the actual IP addresses in a small auxiliary data structure (or in the case of multiple VFIB instances, one for each). The memory and time consumption of this additional lookup table are negligible, since a typical router has no more than a few hundred neighbors.

Table 1. The entries of two VFIBs

VFIB #1		VFIB #2	
IP address/ prefix length	Next-hop	IP address/ prefix length	Next-hop
0.0.0.0/1	3	0.0.0.0/3	1
64.0.0.0/2	1	0.0.0.0/2	2
128.0.0.0/2	2	0.0.0.0/1	3
160.0.0.0/3	3	64.0.0.0/3	2
192.0.0.0/3	3	128.0.0.0/1	1
192.0.0.0/2	1	128.0.0.0/2	2

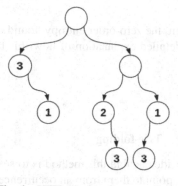

Fig. 1. VFIB #1 stored as a prefix tree

The two main required operations on the data structure are the lookup and update functions. The lookup function returns the appropriate next-hop value based on the destination IP address of the packet. If more than one entry matches the destination IP address, then the most specific entry is the correct output. This problem is solved by LPM (Longest Prefix Match). The other important function is the update, which can add, modify or delete entries as needed.

The most widely used data structure for storing FIBs is the binary prefix tree, also known as a trie. Figure 1 shows the trie constructed from the entries of VFIB #1 from Table 1. Taking the IP address as a binary number we step in the tree left (0) or right (1), and at the depth described by the prefix length we store the next-hop label.

2.2   Leaf-Pushing

It's important to note that the trie-folding algorithm includes another algorithm, called leaf-pushing. It transforms the trie so that every interior (non-leaf) node of the trie has exactly two children (so it becomes a well-formed prefix tree), and only the leaves contain next-hop labels. Every trie can be transformed into such a structure as follows.

First, traversing the tree in preorder we create another child for nodes with only one child and we keep pushing the next-hop labels downstream. Next, we use a postorder traverse to identify leaves of the same parent that hold identical next-hop label and we delete them, storing the label in the parent.

2.3   Entropy of Leaf-Pushed Tries

Given an IP FIB V, let the leaf-pushed prefix tree representation of V be T_V. Let n be the number of leaves in T_V and let Σ denote the set of next-hop labels. Additionally, let p_s denote the probability that some next-hop $s \in \Sigma$ appears as a leaf label and let H_0 denote the Shannon-entropy of the probability distribution p_s, $s \in \Sigma$:

$$H_0 = p_s * log_2 \left(\frac{1}{p_s}\right) \tag{1}$$

Then, the zero-order entropy bound of T_V (denoted by Z_V) can be calculated using (2): A detailed explanation of how this bound is formulated can be found in [4].

$$Z_V = 2n + nH_0 [bit] \tag{2}$$

2.4   Trie-folding

The idea behind this method is to search for equivalent subtrees, store them only once, and point to them from all occurrences of this subtree. Two leaves are equivalent if they hold the same next-hop label, and two interior nodes are equivalent if and only if their left and right subtrees are equivalent. The resulting data structure will not be a tree any more, instead it becomes a DAG (Directed Acyclic Graph). If we apply trie-folding to the trie depicted in Fig. 1, we get the result shown in Fig. 2.

There are many algorithms in the literature for reducing the memory consumption of FIBs [13–17]. Trie-folding, however, is unique, in that it was shown to admit the FIB entropy bound (2) up to a small constant factor. (In particular, for a leaf-pushed FIB with n leaves and entropy H_0, the expected size of the compressed FIB is roughly $5nH_0$ plus some lower order terms. For this reason, we shall use the trie-folding algorithm for compressing VFIBs henceforth.

The required lookup and update operations need to be defined on the compressed data structure as well. The implementation of the lookup function is quite straight-forward. Even though our data structure is now a DAG, stepping left and right according to the destination IP address, starting from the root, and finding the most specific entry works exactly the same way as in a trie. Moreover, because we can represent the VFIBs with fewer bits, a larger portion of the data structure can be loaded into the cache, yielding faster lookup operation. For a lack of sufficient space, we do not treat the update operation to any detail here. For a precise description, see [4].

3 Applying the Trie-folding Algorithm to Different Virtual Router Architectures

In this section we turn to our main contributions. We will introduce two different virtual router architectures, which differ in the handling of the IP packets' virtual router identifiers. We examine the possibility of applying the trie-folding algorithm in both of these cases, and also provide entropy measures for the different VFIB structures.

3.1 Virtual Router Architectures

The naive approach for implementing virtual routers would be to store the virtual instances separately from one another, and handle their input and output by a pre-processing system based on a demultiplexer and a multiplexer, which passes the IP packet to the appropriate VFIB by examining the packet header. This scheme is illustrated on Fig. 3. In this paper we denoted the ID of the virtual router as VNID (Virtual Network Identifier), but in real life it is often determined by Ethernet VLAN tags or MPLS labels. In this arrangement the VFIBs are composed of entries identical to the above examples, and need to support the same operations as well.

However, there is another possible architecture for virtual routers. We connect all VFIBs together under a common Virtual Root (VR), allowing them to share data amongst themselves. It is illustrated in Fig. 4. This way the handling of the VNID becomes part of the LPM algorithm, which is easily implementable. It has been shown that this architectural setup promotes a more efficient compression [5].

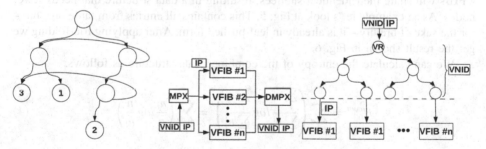

Fig. 2. Trie-folded prefix tree   **Fig. 3.** Separated VFIBs   **Fig. 4.** Combined VFIBs

3.2 The Case of Separately Compressed VFIBs

If the structure of the physical device does not allow VFIBs to share their data, then we can only apply trie-folding to them one-by-one. We have already seen the trie-folded version of VFIB #1 in Fig. 2, and the second example can be constructed in the same way. As we will see later on, this method is not as effective as the others, but it has the definite advantage that it can be applied in almost any virtual router device without any architectural change.

In order to be able to compare the effectiveness of the different compression schemes, we need to define an entropy measure for this separated case also, which we based on the entropies of separately leaf-pushed tries. Each VFIB is weighted in the sum by the ratio of the number of its own leaves to the number of leaves in the whole virtual router. Let n denote the number of next-hop labels in all VFIBs, let n^i denote the number of leaves in the ith VFIB, n_j^i denote the number of times next-hop label j appears in the ith VFIB, and let H_0^i denote the entropy of the ith VFIB. Using this notation, the entropy of the separately compressed VFIBs is:

$$H_0^{sep} = \frac{\left(\sum_i n^i H_0^i\right)}{n} = \frac{\left(\sum_i \sum_j n_j^i log\left(\frac{n^i}{n_j^i}\right)\right)}{n} \tag{3}$$

Along the same lines, the entropy bound Z_V is simply $2n + n * H_0^{sep}$. If we apply (3) to our example, we get the result of 1.459147 bits for the entropy.

3.3   Compressing VFIBs Combined via VR

There are a lot of studies regarding the compression of virtual routers [7–12], but they typically don't make use of the fact that these virtual routers have a lot of similarities, which can be utilized in order to attain a more efficiently compressed data structure.

If the architecture of the router does allow VFIBs to be connected under a common virtual root, then we can apply trie-folding to the whole data structure. This way all VFIBs will share their identical subtrees, resulting in a data structure that needs fewer nodes. As an example let's look at Fig. 5. This contains all entries from table one, but – for the sake of brevity – it is already in leaf-pushed form. After applying trie-folding we get the result shown in Fig. 6.

We can calculate the entropy of the combined data structure as follows:

$$H_0^{com} = \sum_j \left(\frac{\sum_i n_j^i}{\sum_i n^i} log \frac{\sum_i n^i}{\sum_i n_j^i}\right) = \sum_j \left(\frac{n_j}{n} log \frac{n}{n_j}\right) \tag{4}$$

This is technically the same as (1) applied for the VR. Applying (4) to the given examples we can calculate that the entropy of the whole data structure is 1.584962.

We observe that, curiously, the combined VFIBs exhibit larger entropy. This implies that even though the size of the jointly compressed VFIBs will be smaller than that of the separately compressed ones the trie-folding algorithm will not be able to realize its full potential, due to the large entropy of the underlying data. The reason behind this is that the next-hop labels of the VFIBs are mixed in the combined VFIB in a completely random fashion, this way compensating the bias in the individual next-hop label distributions and increasing entropy. This idea is formalized in the below important result.

Theorem 1:

$$H_0^{sep} \leq H_0^{com}$$

Refer to the appendix for the proof.

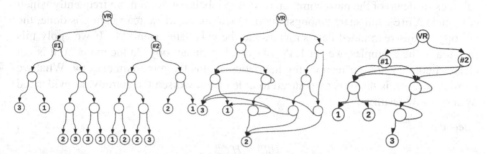

Fig. 5. VFIBs after trie-folding together with rearranged next-hop labels

Fig. 6. Combined VFIB compression

Fig. 7. Combined VFIBs with rearranged next-hop labels, after the trie-folding algorithm

4 Minimizing the Entropy of Joint VFIB Compression

Our main goal is to minimize the size of the VFIBs by using trie-folding algorithm, which is proven to be able to compress FIB data to within a constant factor of its zero-order entropy bound, which in turn is highly affected by the distribution of next-hop labels. This line of thought leads us to the idea of trying to minimize the entropy of combined VFIBs by rearranging their next-hop labels, yielding smaller size. This minimization problem can be formulated as follows.

First, let us set up some notation. Let N be the number of VFIBs. As before, let Σ denote the set of next-hop labels, and l denote the number of labeled nodes. Let P_i denote the set of all possible permutations of next-hop labels in the ith VFIB ($i = 1,.., N$), and $P_i, P_{i-1} \in P_i$ denote the inverse permutation of each other. Also, let $c(s)$ denote the count of next-hop label's. With these notations we can describe the entropy of all combined VFIBs, as being a function of the applied permutations:

$$H_0^{rea}(P_1, P_2, \ldots, P_N) = \sum_{s \in \sum} \sum_{i=1}^{N} c(P_i^{-1}(s)) log_2 \frac{1}{(c(P_i^{-1}(s)))} \tag{5}$$

Now we are ready to formulate the minimization problem:

$$minH_0^{rea}(P_1, P_2, \ldots, P_N) : P_i \in \prod_i, i-1..N \tag{6}$$

This means we are looking for a permutation of next-hop labels in each VFIB, so that the resulting entropy of the whole data structure is minimal.

Instead of trying to solve this problem directly, we present a heuristic approach. Its central idea is to rearrange the next-hop labels so that the most frequently occurring label will become '1', the second one will be '2', and so on. We expect that by using this scheme we can obtain a more memory-efficient FIB compression, because the subtrees made up of the most common next-hop labels can form more frequently which combined VFIBs can share amongst them. Once this heuristic rearranging is done, the entropy of this rearranged data structure can be calculated using (4). If we apply this formula to the examples, we get 1.459147 bits for the entropy. At the moment, it is not clear whether or not our rearranging heuristics attains the minimum entropy. What we know, however, is that it is guaranteed to at least not worsen the entropy, as evidenced by the below result:

Theorem 2:

$$H_0^{rea} \leq H_0^{com}$$

It turns out, however, that the efficiency of our rearranging algorithm is fundamentally limited by the entropy of the original VFIBs. Consider the below result:

Theorem 3:

$$H_0^{sep} \leq H_0^{rea}$$

If we rearrange the next-hop labels in Fig. 5 according to incidence, we get the result shown in Fig. 7.[1] So in this example we managed to reduce the number of nodes necessary for describing these two VFIBs.

5 Numerical Evaluations

In this section we first describe our measurement setup, then we present the results of the simulations and evaluate them. These include the effectiveness of the various compression methods, and the lookup speed of the resulting VFIBs.

5.1 Measurement Bases

In order to be able to measure the effectiveness of these algorithms and techniques we implemented them in simulation software. After running the various compression methods we gathered statistics about the resulting data structures. The most important numerical results for us in this paper are the memory needed for storing them, and also the entropy and zero-order entropy bound of VFIBs. We have already seen how to calculate entropy using formulas (3) and (4) and the bound derived from it, using (2).

---

[1] VFIB #1: $3 \to 1$, $1 \to 2$, $2 \to 3$; VFIB #2: $2 \to 1$, $1 \to 2$, $3 \to 3$.

We calculated the memory size for a VFIB using the following formula, where M is the size of the memory in bits, P is the number of pointers used, N is the number of nodes in the VFIB, and NH is the number of next-hop labels.

$$M = P \log_2 N + NH \log_2 NH \tag{7}$$

Our input data came from two sources: firstly,[2] we used numerous real-life FIBs that were originally used by international telecommunication service providers in the access network. We created three different VFIB batches from these input FIBs. They are called access, hbone, and internet2, and they contain 6, 10, and 10 FIBs respectively. In addition, we also used synthetic VFIBs to confirm our hypothesis mentioned above. In particular, we reassigned the next-hop labels in our FIBs according to a uniform and power-law distribution.

Table 2. Numerical results of simulations. H_0: Entropy [bit], Z: Zero-order entropy bound [kB], M: Memory [kB]

	Original	Separated			Combined			Rearranged		
	M	H_0	Z	M	H_0	Z	M	H_0	Z	M
access	2574	1.44	285	765	1.76	242	626	1.72	240	632
hbone	4606	1.86	428	1284	2.49	497	743	2.03	447	711
internet2	1585	1.47	142	559	1.61	148	310	1.52	144	296
Power	3427	1.68	309	1221	2.28	360	1154	1.68	309	1055
Uniform	4335	2.58	480	1898	2.58	480	1681	2.58	480	1681

5.2   Memory, Entropy and Zero-Order Entropy Bound of VFIBs

The results of these measurements are summarized in Table 2. It shows that the presented theorems about the entropies hold true for all cases. The uncompressed and separated entropies are always equal because they are both calculated based on the separately leaf-pushed VFIBs. Looking at the memory consumption after the different methods of compression we can see that - with the exception of "access" - the most efficient method is to combine all VFIBs with rearranged next-hop labels. The slight increase of memory consumption in the case of access shows that the method is truly a heuristic approach, not an optimal one, but a useful one nonetheless. If we examine the ratio of memory and zero-order entropy bound, we find that the uncompressed VFIBs use 10.3 times more memory than the bound; the separately compressed VFIBs require 3.2 times memory, while the compressed combined VFIBs require about 2.07 times memory, regardless of rearranging. However, in most cases the compression did manage to achieve smaller memory sizes when we applied the rearranging heuristics.

The last two rows of the table were generated with a script, and they contain entries that yield uniform and power-law distributions of next-hop labels. Using these inputs, we were able to test our hypotheses mentioned in Sect. 4. We can observe that with

---

[2] The FIBs with some statistics are available at http://lendulet.tmit.bme.hu/fib_comp.

power-law distribution the rearranging of next-hop labels yields almost the same entropy as in the separately measured case, while a uniform distribution prevents any significant difference. Luckily, next-hop label distributions in real-life FIBs tend to be based on power-law.

We also wanted to determine how the compression schemes hold up as we load more and more VFIBs. For this we used the above mentioned hbone FIBs, each containing about 470–490 K entries. The results are shown in Table 3.

Table 3. Memory consumption of hbone FIBs in [MB]

#VFIBs	Uncompressed	Separated	Combined	Rearranged
5	10.6494	1.1757	0.8906	0.8496
10	34.333	2.3535	1.4179	1.2011
15	51.5341	3.5214	1.7636	1.4101
20	68.5996	4.6865	2.0527	1.6953
25	85.9281	6.1347	2.3291	1.9570
30	104.748	7.5742	2.5810	2.1992

We can clearly see that the uncompressed VFIBs use a huge amount of memory: loading only 30 VFIBs demanded more than a 100 MB, while the compressed VFIBs remained much more manageable. Also, the advantage of the fact that the VFIBs can share common subtrees with each other shows quite strikingly, as well as the use of our novel approach of next-hop rearrangement.

5.3   IP Lookup Performance

We conducted measurements in order to determine how the compression affects the lookup speed. We ran one million random lookups multiple times on each data structure from using various real FIBs. Normally the VFIBs would be stored on the line cards of the router, which can perform much faster, so we present our results in percentage, the uncompressed data structure being 100 %.[3] On average, running the lookups on the separately compressed VFIBs required 80.5 % of time, the combined VFIBs required 68.6 %, while after the rearranging heuristic it only required 66.8 % of time.

So it appears that by compressing the VFIBs we not only can store them using much less memory, it also helps along the lookup performance. Because our data structure uses less memory, a bigger part of it can be loaded into the cache hierarchy, which provides faster memory operations, improving lookup speed.

Based on these simulations we can declare that the implemented compression methods are highly effective. Not only do they squeeze the size of VFIBs to a fraction of the original uncompressed data structure, they also improve lookup time, and thus they can be used in real-life routers to overcome the scalability problems posed by the use of VFIBs.

---

[3] For the record, using conventional PC memory running at 1600 MHz the simulator could perform one million lookup in less than a second.

6 Conclusions

In this paper we described how we can apply the well-known FIB compression method - trie-folding – to the case of virtual FIBs, and we saw that it is applicable remarkably well. We also introduced another aspect of optimizing the compression algorithm, the rearranging of next-hop labels. We described a minimization problem regarding the possible permutations of next-hop labels, and proposed a heuristic approach for solving it. We corroborated these ideas from a theoretical standpoint by establishing entropy and zero-order entropy bound measures of VFIBs for both kind of virtual router architectures. We also put forth three theorems that compare the amount of entropy in each case. In our numerical evaluations we showed that compressing the VFIBs with either method also helps along lookup performance.

In our future work we will implement the update algorithm described in [4], with the addition of VNID handling, so we can carry out time measurements of the update as well. We also plan to generalize the trie-folding algorithm to be able to handle level-compressed prefix trees [6]. Later on we would like to implement it in the form of a Linux kernel module, so these methods can be tested in real-life conditions.

Acknowledgments. Gábor Rétvári was supported by the OTKA/PD-104939 grant. This work was partially supported by the European Union and the European Social Fund through project FuturICT.hu (grant no.: TAMOP-4.2.2.C-11/1/KONV-2012-0013) and the High Speed Networks Laboratory.

Appendix

Proof of Theorem 1:

$$H_0^{sep} = \frac{\left(\sum_i \sum_j n_j^i log\left(\frac{n_j^i}{n_j}\right) \right)}{n} = \sum_j \left(\frac{n_j}{n}\right) \sum_i \left(\frac{n_j^i}{n_j} log\left(\frac{n^i}{n_j^i}\right)\right) \leq \sum_j \left(\frac{n_j}{n} log \sum_i \left(\frac{n^i}{n_j}\right)\right)$$
$$= H_0^{com}$$

This is true, because the log function is concave: $\sum a_i = 1 \Rightarrow \sum a_i log x_i \leq log \sum a_i x_i$, which proves that $H_0^{sep} \leq H_0^{com}$.

Proof of Theorem 2:

If we allow the permutation of next-hop labels in each VFIB then we can reduce the entropy of H_0^{com}:

$$H_0^{rea} = \sum_j {}^{`} \left(\frac{\sum_i m_j^i}{\sum_i n^i} log\left(\frac{\sum_i n^i}{\sum_i m_j^i} \right) \right) = \sum_j \left(\frac{m_j}{n} log \frac{n}{m_j} \right)$$

We achieve this by rearranging the characters in each string according to their incidence, where m_j^i denotes the incidence of the jth next-hop label in the ith VFIB. Since this transformation has no effect on H_0^{sep}, it follows that $H_0^{sep} \leq H_0^{rea}$.

Proof of Theorem 3:

For this we only need to show that if not all next-hop labels of all VFIBs are ordered according to incidence, then we can decrease the entropy by changing the order of them. In other words, i_1, i_2, j_1, j_2 exist such that $n_{j1}i_1 <= n_{j2}i_2$ and $n_{j1}i_2 > n_{j2}i_2$ while $n_{j1} <= n_{j2}$. Swapping j_1 and j_2 in i_2 the entropy is decreasing. For the sake of simplicity let p denote $n_{j1}i_2 - n_{j2}i_2$:

$$\frac{n_{j1}}{n}\log\frac{n}{n_{j1}} + \frac{n_{j2}}{n}\log\frac{n}{n_{j2}} > \frac{(n_{j1}-p)}{n}\log\frac{n}{(n_{j1}-p)}\log\frac{n}{(n_{j1}-p)} + \frac{(n_{j2}+p)}{n}\log\frac{n}{(n_{j2}+p)}$$

$$(n_{j1}-p)\log(n_{j1}-p) + (n_{j2}+p)\log(n_{j2}+p) > n_{j1}\log n_{j1} + n_{j2}\log n_{j2}$$

This is satisfied because $x\ log(x)$ is convex. This proves that $H_0^{rea} \leq H_0^{com}$.

References

1. Song, H., Kodialam, M., Hao, F., Lakshman, T.V.: Building scalable virtual routers with trie braiding. In: INFOCOM, 2010 Proceedings IEEE. IEEE (2010)
2. Ferragina, P., Luccio, F., Manzini, G., Muthukrishnan, S.: Compressing and indexing labeled trees, with applications. J. ACM (JACM) 57(1), 4 (2009)
3. Draves, R.P., et al.: Constructing optimal IP routing tables. In: INFOCOM'99, Proceedings of Eighteenth Annual Joint Conference of the IEEE Computer and Communications Societies, vol. 1. IEEE (1999)
4. Rétvári, G., Tapolcai, J., Kőrösi, A., Majdán, A., Heszberger, Z.: Compressing IP forwarding tables: towards entropy bounds and beyond. In: Proceedings of the ACM SIGCOMM 2013 Conference on SIGCOMM. ACM (2013)
5. Fu, J., Jennifer, R.: Efficient IP-address lookup with a shared forwarding table for multiple virtual routers. In: Proceedings of the 2008 ACM CoNEXT Conference. ACM (2008)
6. Rétvári, G., Csernátony, Z., Körösi, A., Tapolcai, J., Császár, A., Enyedi, G., Pongrácz, G.: Compressing IP forwarding tables for fun and profit. In: Proceedings of the 11th ACM Workshop on Hot Topics in Networks. ACM (2012)
7. Chowdhury, N.M., Raouf, B.: A survey of network virtualization. Comput. Netw. 54(5), 862–876 (2010)
8. Le, H., Prasanna, V.K.: Scalable tree-based architectures for IPv4/v6 lookup using prefix partitioning. IEEE Trans. Comput. 61(7), 1026–1039 (2012)
9. Huang, K., Xie, G., Li, Y., Liu, A.X.: Offset addressing approach to memory-efficient IP address lookup. In: INFOCOM, 2011 Proceedings IEEE. IEEE (2011)
10. Luo, L., Xie, G., Uhlig, S., Mathy, L., Salamatian, K., Xie, Y.: Towards TCAM-based scalable virtual routers. In: Proceedings of the 8th International Conference on Emerging Networking Experiments and Technologies. ACM (2012)

11. Luo, L., Xie, G., Salamatian, K., Uhlig, S., Mathy, L., Xie, Y.: A trie merging approach with incremental updates for virtual routers. In: INFOCOM, 2013 Proceedings IEEE. IEEE (2013)
12. Song, H., Kodialam, M., Hao, F., Lakshman, T.V.: Efficient trie braiding in scalable virtual routers. IEEE/ACM Trans. Networking (TON) **20**(5), 1489–1500 (2012)
13. Nilsson, S., Karlsson, G.: IP-address lookup using LC-tries. IEEE JSAC **17**(6), 1083–1092 (1999)
14. Gupta, P., Prabhakar, B., Boyd, S.P.: Near optimal routing lookups with bounded worst case performance. In: IEEE INFOCOM, pp. 1184–1192 (2000)
15. Ioannidis, I., Grama, A.: Level compressed DAGs for lookup tables. Comput. Netw. **49**(2), 147–160 (2005)
16. Zhao, X., Pacella, D.J., Schiller, J.: Routing scalability: an operator's view. IEEE JSAC **28** (8), 1262–1270 (2010)
17. Song, H., Kodialam, M.S., Hao, F., Lakshman, T.V.: Scalable IP lookups using shape graphs. In: IEEE ICNP, pp. 73–82 (2009)

Survey on Network Interface Selection in Multihomed Mobile Networks

Pratibha Mitharwal$^{(\boxtimes)}$, Christophe Lohr, and Annie Gravey

Télécom Bretagne, Brest, France
pratibha.mitharwal@telecom-bretagne.eu

Abstract. This survey is focused on providing a cruising ship with Internet access facilities. On a ship, the entire network infrastructure (networks, subnets, devices, terminals, etc.) is subject to mobility. Multiple connections (e.g., satellite, LTE, 3G, WiFi, etc.) can provide Internet access, thus making the ship multihomed, but the different connections may be sporadic, and provide different services in terms of bandwidth, throughput, cost. The user may thus need to dynamically select one connection among those that are available, according to its preferences. This paper presents a survey of network interface selection in existing mobility and mutlihoming protocols to provide multihomed network mobility to a cruising ship, or to any vehicle (e.g., train, car, airplane, etc.).

1 Introduction

In early days computers were very heavy to move around and had only one interface. Therefore, it was easy to identify any computer with a single Internet address. With the evolution of technology, computers can be easily moved around (i.e., they are mobile) and are connected through several network interfaces simultaneously (i.e., they are multihomed). Mobility and multihoming are closely related to each other with respect to IP addressing. Concerning mobility, IP address changes due to changing network attachment point (location) of the host (interface), whereas in multihoming, IP addresses change while changing communication paths (the selected network interface). Changes in IP address cause connection disruption as upper layers sockets are bound to IP addresses.

Multihomed mobile hosts such as smartphones, tablets etc. commonly use a single link at a given time. The network selection for every data connection on such technologies is based on "the best availability" or "on user choice". These two choices do not provide the user with cost effective benefits of multihoming scenario, e.g., one link may be free of charge but with a poor connection while another may provide dedicated services, a managed quality of service, etc., and be costly with a specific cost scheme (by volume of data, time of the day, distance, etc.).

Similarly, in multihomed mobile networks (e.g., train, ship, airplanes etc.), there are many users and every user will have different requirements. These user requirements (influenced by user & application preferences) and network characteristics (e.g., price, bandwidth, quality etc.), can be used to select the best

© Springer International Publishing Switzerland 2014
Y. Kermarrec (Ed.): EUNICE 2014, LNCS 8846, pp. 134–146, 2014.
DOI: 10.1007/978-3-319-13488-8_13

available interface. If the interface selection is done appropriately it can improve the performance of network applications [2]. Interface selection mechanism combines two steps: taking the decision on interface selection, and enforcing the decision. In mobile networks, the decision enforcement is located at the edge router (i.e., mobile router) of the network. Therefore, a interface selection mechanism which can communicate with the users and the mobile router, is required.

During mobility, the availability of network interfaces and also the characteristics of access networks are constantly changing as the system moves. Whenever this happens, one may want to transfer the ongoing communication from one network interface to another interface. Multihoming uses same scenario to provide best available connection. This paper discusses about network interface selection mechanism in the existing protocols for mobility in multihomed context.

The remainder of the paper is organized as follows. In Sect. 2, we explain about the project and requirements. Section 3, explains functionality of multihomed mobility protocols with provided interface selection mechanism (if any) and Sect. 4 concludes this paper.

2 Context of Study and Requirements

This study is part of TMS (Terminal Marine Stablise) project[1], which aims to design a ship terminal facilitating broadband access for cruising ships. The major requirements of this project are explained in following subsections. An overview of all these requirements is given in Table 1.

Table 1. Requirements of TMS project

$\mathcal{R}1$: Network mobility	Reachability, session continuity, security, handover, roaming
$\mathcal{R}2$: Network multihoming	Session continuity, handover, security
$\mathcal{R}3\mathcal{S}$: static interface selection	Decision enforcement, binding of packet flows
$\mathcal{R}3\mathcal{D}$: Dynamic interface selection	User preferences, service provider's constraints, network administrator preferences

2.1 Mobility

Mobility refers to a situation where an end-host changes its topological point of attachment to the Internet. Whenever a host moves, its network layer address changes. Thus, in order to continue to communicate, the host must be able to signal the changes in its addresses to its active peers. This signaling must be secure since non-secured signaling can lead to an unauthorized traffic diversion and denial-of-service attacks. If end user hosts are mobile it is considered as "*host mobility*", and if border routers and interconnected edge network hosts are mobile it is considered as "*network mobility*".

---
[1] The project is supported by the French Government (Direction Generale des Enterprises).

Requirement 𝑅1: Network Mobility. First requirement for TMS project is, network mobility management. The network mobility management [7,20] needs to provide support for handover management to forward the packets towards new location for an ongoing communication imposing minimal disconnection time for reducing unacceptable data loss, reachability to mobile network's new location, support for existing applications and services without any change, transparency to user applications about mobility, minimal infrastructure changes, roaming agreement and authentication process while switching network interfaces between different operators to avoid security concerns, e.g., address stealing, address flooding which cause Denial-of-Service, man-in-middle etc. In TMS project, mobile networks are ship based where network changes does not happen too often, so handover speed is of minor interest.

2.2   Multihoming

Multihoming refers to a situation where an end-point has several parallel path for communication with rest of the Internet [12]. This situation can be characterized as the host being reach-able through several topological paths (with multiple network layer addresses) which are completely independent of each other. When a host is connected with several different edge networks it is known as *"host multihoming"*, and when an edge network is interconnected to the core redundantly with multiple connections via multiple borders or via multiple interfaces of a border router it is known as *"site multihoming"*.

Multihoming helps to achieve redundancy and fault tolerance, increase bandwidth, balance the load inside the access network and provide traffic engineering by stripping the flows over all existing paths, using user defined rules [22].

Requirement 𝑅2: Multihoming. Second requirement for TMS is multihoming management. The multihoming solutions [46] needs to provide support for interface selection mechanism required when a communication is established (e.g., when a TCP connection is opened for an outgoing & incoming traffic), a secure recovery mechanism for handover management and session continuity to divert ongoing communication from one interface to another in case of failure with minimal delay, a mechanism to handle growth of routing tables in case of aggregated routes, a mechanism to handle change of traffic characteristics, and a mechanism for controlling the load balance (symmetric flow of packets across all existing paths) based on address assignment.

2.3   Interface Selection

Interface selection refers to the selection of source IP address among all existing interfaces for a connection association or indirectly selection of first hop router influenced dynamically by user application preferences. In mobile networks, user's participation can play an important role in interface selection as shown in [4]. However, this experiment is done considering static scenarios. In interface selection mechanism first step would be to specify interfaces that can be used on account of a user/application's, operator's or peer node's requirements. Then, a policy set is created prioritizing the interfaces based on policies. A policy set contains filtering rules which can be stored as table distribution mechanism [21] or database [48]. After the policy set is created, these filtering rules can be used as input at OS level filtering frame work such as APIs, which will then enforce the decision in packet routing.

Requirement $\mathcal{R}3$: Interface Selection. Third requirement for TMS project is Interface selection which can be divided into static interface selection ($\mathcal{R}3\mathcal{S}$) and dynamic interface selection ($\mathcal{R}3\mathcal{D}$). Static interface selection can be managed by putting some filtering rules in OS whereas the management of dynamic interface selection is a challenge in multihomed mobile networks due to frequent changes of topological location of interface, changes in application requirement or change in availability of access, so it requires a way to manage these operations. Dynamic network interface selection decisions lie on the various information such as user preferences, application requirements, hardware capacity, available network's characteristics, service provider's constraints, network administrator preferences etc. [48]. So there is a need for decision modules which will have all the available information from link layer (network signal quality and related metrics), several attributes like source address destination address from IP layer, information about cost, bandwidth and availability of Internet access from network service provider (and constraints if any), information originated from user & applications etc.

3   Multihomed Mobile Networks

There exists several proposals on how to take decisions with respect to interface selection and most of them follow the policy filtering rules. Some approaches use Multiple Attribute Decision Making (MADM) algorithms for decision making about best available network, such as Analytical Hierarchical Process (AHP) [31], Grey Relation Analysis (GRA) [36] and Technique for Order Preference by Similarity to Ideal Solution (TOPSIS) [42]. A MADM algorithm first creates a decision matrix by measuring values of each criterion and then the effect of parameters scales and units is eliminated by normalization. Next the final decision scores are calculated to take the decision. An architecture is proposed in [40] for automatic network interface selection and allow user to stay connected with best available access network. The selection decision algorithm uses classical weighting objective method for decision making, considering multiple network and application preferences in account. The interface selection module for multihomed mobile hosts based on policy management and flow distribution were proposed in [2,23,34,40], but none is standardized. The following subsection details about the dynamic enforcement of interface in various network and transport layer multihomed mobility protocols.

3.1   Mobile IP with Extensions

Mobile IP is a network layer protocol, which enables mobile host to leave its home network and continue to receive packets at its home address irrespective of its current location. Each mobile host is identified by its home address. A new entity called *home agent* (HA) is introduced, which is a router at a static location in the host's home network for supporting mobility services. HA intercepts the packets destined to mobile host's home address when it is away. The idea was standardized for IPv4 (Mobile IPv4, MIPv4) in RFC 3344 [28] and IPv6 (Mobile IPv6, MIPv6) in RFC 3775 [15]. The protocol offers transparent movement of a mobile host to transport layer protocols and applications.

When the host moves to another network, it acquires a new address called a care-of address (CoA) through either stateless or stateful auto-configuration. The mobile host then informs the home agent of its current address. A binding is created between mobile hosts home address and care-of address. Any host communicating with mobile host is known as a corresponding node (CN). The CN uses the mobile host's permanent home address (belongs to the network associated with HA) as the destination address. Normal IP routing mechanisms forward these packets to the home agent. HA then redirects these packets to care-of-address through the IP tunnel by encapsulating the datagram with a new IP header using the care-of address of mobile host.

Hierarchical Mobile IPv6 (HMIPv6) was defined in RFC 5380 [35], is an extension to MIPv6. It aims to improve performance of MIPv6 by reducing signaling traffic and by optimizing delays that are introduced by binding updates. There is another extension for fast handover in MIPv6 [17] to reduce handover-latency.

Proxy Mobile IPv6 (PMIPv6), specified in RFC 5213 [10], extends MIPv6 signaling and reuses many concepts such as the home agent functionality. It is a network based mobility management solution which frees mobile host from participating in any mobility related signaling. The proxy mobile agent in the serving network performs mobility related signaling on behalf of mobile host. However, this protocol does not support multihoming.

Network Mobility (NEMO) Protocol was specified in RFC 3963 [3,6]. NEMO basic support also extends the idea of MIPv6 to support connectivity of network which moves. It contains a mobile router which is in charge of the mobility operation on behalf of all the hosts located in the moving network. In order to fulfill requirement $\mathcal{R}1$, NEMO ensures session continuity and reliability into a mobile network while moving transparently to the mobile network nodes(MNNs) with help of mobile router (MR). The mobile router works as a normal IPv6 router in its home network, i.e., routes all the traffic using traditional routing methods. When mobile router is connected to another IPv6 network it acquires a care-of-address (CoA), which represents its current location in the Internet. Then mobile router like mobile host in MIPv6, registers care-of-address to its home agent (a router located in mobile router's home network). Whenever mobile router is away from home network, home agent maintains the binding between home address, care-of-address and the prefix advertised in the mobile network (known as mobile network prefix (MNP)). A bi-directional IPv6-in-IPv6 tunnel is used to maintain connectivity between mobile router and home agent.

Multiple care-of addresses registration (MCoA) is an extension for MIPv6 and NEMO that was standardized in RFC 5648 [45]. In MIPv6 and NEMO care-of-address is a single point of failure for the whole network, so MCoA mechanism allows multiple care-of-addresses registration with mobile host's or network's home agent. In MCoA, a new binding identification (BID) generated by mobile host/router for each care-of-address, is used as unique key to distinguish multiple bindings that are registered by the same mobile host. The home agent caches the received binding identifications in a binding table and is therefore able to distinguish the multiple care-of-addresses of the mobile host/network. MCoA enables Mobile IPv6 and NEMO to support multihoming, which fulfills requirement $\mathcal{R}2$.

Flow binding is also an extension for MIPv6 and NEMO that was standardized in RFC 6089 [43] which allows hosts to bind one or more flows to a care-of address. These extensions allow multihomed hosts to instruct home agents and other Mobile IPv6 entities to direct inbound flows to specific addresses. In flow binding extension user can define any policies at OS level (fulfills $\mathcal{R}3\mathcal{S}$), but not in real time. It is assumed that the policies are configured on the mobile host's packet filtering tool [30] and the rules specified by the user are according to interface and binding, so the rules are protocol specific [23].

3.2 Location Independent Network (LIN6)

LIN6 [41], follows the idea of identifier and locator separation [18]. It introduces an identifier for each host known as LIN6 ID which is independent of its location and interfaces. It also defines two types of network addresses: the LIN6 generalized ID and LIN6 address. The LIN6 generalized ID is formed by concatenating a constant value called the LIN6 prefix before the LIN6 ID which is used at the transport layer to identity the connection. Whereas, the LIN6 address is formed by concatenating the network prefix (changes according to the mobile host's current network) and LIN6 ID which is used to route packets over network layer. The generalized IDs are then stored into DNS, together with the address of a mapping Agent. Since the generalized IDs are globally unique and permanent, the communicating hosts use them as endpoint identifiers. Apart from this, a mapping agent is used in LIN6 for queries related to mobile host's current address. LIN6 also supports multihoming through a single GI to be associated with several real addresses (fulfills $\mathcal{R}2$). There is no explicit way for interface selection mechanism in LIN6 for multihomed mobile hosts.

3.3 Locator Identifier Separation Protocol (LISP)

LISP achieves site-multihoming through core-edge separation and provides end-to-end packet delivery [8, 14, 32]. It follows three simple principles: address role separation, encapsulation, & mapping. To achieve first principle, LISP splits the semantics of IP addresses into endpoint identifiers (EID) and routing locators (RLOC). RLOCs are assigned to border routers by ISPs and EIDs are assigned inside edge networks. In LISP, the packets are created with EIDs in source and destination addresses, then these are encapsulated in a UDP segment with LISP header and finally forwarded through tunnels between edge networks. Border routers of the packet source are known as ingress tunnel routers (ITR), which perform encapsulation and the border routers of the destination site are known as egress tunnel routers (ETR), which perform the decapsulation. A mapping system (like DNS) is created for the mappings between EIDs & RLOCs. LISP's tunnel routers can query the mappings for specific EIDs and the system returns all the related mappings. LISP provides improved traffic engineering capabilities and multihoming (fulfills $\mathcal{R}2$). LISP mobile host [47] receives an EID from its home network and an address inside foreign network which can be used as RLOCs. Whenever mobile host moves and its RLOC changes, it registers the new mapping into the map server of its home network. LISP extension for network mobility (fulfills $\mathcal{R}1$) has been proposed in [5]. This locator identifier split can improve Internet scalability but it has deployment constraints. LISP does not provide any interface selection mechanism considering user preferences.

3.4   Host Identity Protocol

Host identity protocol (HIP) [24–26] has been developed to solve security, mobility and host multihoming issues in an integrated concept. It separates host identification & location, and introduces a new namespace, namely the host identity (HI). The purpose of HI is to support trust between systems, enhance mobility, and greatly reduce the DoS attacks to provide better security than other multihomed mobility solutions. HIP introduces a new host identity layer (layer 3.5) between the IP layer (layer 3) and the upper layers to avoid a dual role of IP address as endpoint and forwarding identifier. In HIP, upper layer sockets are bound to HI instead of IP addresses. In addition, the binding of these host identities to IP addresses is done dynamically. A great advantage in this mobility solution is that the hosts can easily have both the IPv4 and the IPv6 addresses. Furthermore, there is no need to change the current routing methods. Multihoming (fulfills $\mathcal{R}2$) and avoiding man in the middle(MitM) attacks are the other features offered by HIP. The HIP authenticates the connection and establishes security associations for a secure connection with IPsec ESP. For this purpose it uses a four-way handshake with Diffie-Hellman key exchange.

During mobility, HIP protocol is needed to take care of the dynamic binding between the hosts IP address and HI as HIs are used to identify the mobile host instead of IP addresses, the location of the host is not bound to the identifier. When one of the communicating peers changes location, it simply sends a HIP readdress (REA) packet through the secured ESP channel. However, if both of the peers change location at the same time (the double jump problem), a rendezvous server (RSV) is needed [19]. RSV is a packet forwarding agent which simply temporarily forwards the initial HIP packet to the responder.

For HIP an interface selection mechanism was defined in shim API [16], which enables participation from applications in interface selection per packet flow basis for both peers (fulfills $\mathcal{R}3\mathcal{D}$).

3.5 Site Multihoming by IPv6 Intermediation (SHIM6)

The SHIM6 protocol is another multihoming (fulfills $\mathcal{R}2$) host-centric solution [13,27,29]. It also introduces a new shim sublayer within the IP layer. It supposes that each host in the network owns multiple global IPv6 address. Each IPv6 address can be used as *locator* for IP routing and identifier or ULID (upper layer ID), for upper layer identification. It also maintains a mapping between locators and ULIDs in all active connections between two hosts. In SHIM6 operation, firstly a normal TCP connection is established between two hosts, then hosts exchange SHIM6 context. At this point, ULIDs and locators have same IPv6 addresses. For failure detection and recovery, SHIM6 uses REAP (REAchability Protocol). In case of any failure, ULIDs will remain same to the upper layers but the underlying locators will change and SHIM6 manages this mapping between locators and ULIDS. Thus the change of locators are transparent to the upper layers. SHIM6 provides denial-of-service (DoS) attack protection to the responder. Although this security measure does not fully preclude the possibility of DoS attacks, at least it imposes an additional effort for the attacker and provides some tracing capabilities.

Interface selection mechanism (fulfills $\mathcal{R}3\mathcal{D}$) is defined in shim API [16], which provides applications the liberty to choose preferred locators for both source & destination host and allows to perform per packet flow distribution.

3.6 Stream Control Transmission Protocol

Stream Transmission Control Protocol (SCTP) is a connection-oriented protocol for the transport layer [9,37,38], similar to TCP, but provides message-oriented data transfer, similar to UDP. It provides reliable transmission control, flow and congestion control same as TCP but offers new features such as unordered delivery, multi-streaming and multihoming (fulfills $\mathcal{R}2$). A key difference to TCP is the concept of several streams (sequence of messages) within a connection which are known as associations. During association startup, a list of IP address-port pairs is provided between the communicating hosts. These addresses are used as the endpoints of different streams. One of the addresses is selected as initial primary path, which is used as destination address for all packets and may be changed later if needed. A host has one primary path and zero or more alternative paths. Alternate addresses are used to retransmit packets when any failure occurs on the primary path. The Dynamic address reconfiguration (ADDIP) [44] extension for SCTP enables this protocol to add, delete, and change the IP addresses during an active connection. The SCTP with the ADDIP extension is called mobile SCTP (mSCTP), and provides a seamless handover for mobile hosts that are roaming between IP networks. The protocol is mainly targeted for client-server services, in which the client initiates the session with a fixed server.

For supporting peer-to-peer services, the mSCTP must be used along with an additional location management scheme. SCTP is also incompatible with all old applications.

Being a transport layer protocol, SCTP has the advantage to use security services, offered by the network layer but some vulnerabilities still exist to Men-in-the-Middle attacks. Socket API extension for SCTP [39] describes about implementing interface selection mechanism (fulfills $\mathcal{R}3\mathcal{D}$) but at application level which may not be very efficient.

3.7 MultiPath TCP

Multipath TCP [1,11] also extends the idea of TCP to add the capability to establish and use multipath between communicating hosts. If the legacy applications want to use all the new features of MPTCP, they would require some changes. The use of an MPTCP socket API being one of them. MPTCP is backward compatible with conventional TCP [33]. The connection establishment in MPTCP begins the same way as in conventional TCP. Signaling messages are used to inform the end user host about MPTCP compatibility. If both endpoints are MPTCP capable and multiple path exists, additional TCP sessions are created on each of the existing path, combining them with existing connection. These additional TCP sessions are also called as sub-flows. In end users network stack applications treat aggregated sub-flows as single MPTCP connection. To exchange available addresses, additional signaling messages are used. Each sub-flow is identified by a five-tuple compound of source and destination address and port as well as used protocol. Sub-flows can be added or removed also after connection establishment.

MPTCP supports concurrent multipath transfer (fulfills $\mathcal{R}2$) using a packet scheduler which divides the byte stream. The byte stream flows through application into segments and allocates these segments to the sub-flows. At the receiver reordering of these segments can be done using sequence numbers. Congestion control across the sub-flows have been proposed in RFC [33]. Multihoming capability of host can support mobility, i.e., if one path fails (or address changes due to host mobility), other paths will still be available but this is a special case in multihoming scenario. For full mobility support the sub-flow disruption due to address changes must be handled which is not provided by MPTCP.

The MPTCP API [33] contains a minimum set of functions which does not allow a user to express preferences about the management of paths or the scheduling of data.

4   Conclusion

This paper has surveyed protocols providing (partial) solutions to interface selection and session continuity in the context of a multihomed mobile network. Multihomed mobile networks & host will be connected through different access technologies and access networks, which offer different services in terms of bandwidth, cost, QoS etc. In order to provide the best available network services, the network interface selection should be influenced dynamically by user preferences, policies, service provider's and network administrator's constraints to adapt the real time environment.

Table 2 summarizes all the multihomed mobility approaches detailed in the previous section. The main results are summarized as:

- Locator/identifier separation approaches such as LISP, HIP, LIN6, SHIM6 are promising to solve mobility and multihoming, but come at the cost of modifying end user hosts or of deploying new network entities such as mapping systems or specialized borders as in LISP.
- Transport layer approaches as SCTP and MPTCP support concurrent multipath transfer, but do not address mobility and multihoming.
- NEMO, together with the MCoA extension, does support network mobility and multihoming but dynamic interface selection is missing.

Table 2. Summary of multihomed mobility approaches

	Approach		MIPv6 +Ext	NEMO	LIN6	LISP	HIP	SHIM6	SCTP	MPTCP
Features	No modification at host network stack		Yes	Yes	No	Yes	No	No	No	No
	Transparency to Application Layer		Yes	Yes	Yes	Yes	Yes	No	No	No
	Additional or modified network entities		HA	HA & MR	mapping agent	border routers, mapping system	PKI, RSV	NA ^{2}	NA ^{2}	NA ^{2}
	Tunneling		Yes	Yes	No	Yes	No	NA ^{2}	NA ^{2}	NA ^{2}
Requirements	Network Mobility $\mathcal{R}1$		No	Yes	No	Yes	No	No	No	No
	Multihoming $\mathcal{R}2$		Yes with McoA	Yes with McoA	Yes	Yes	Yes	Yes	Yes	Yes
	Interface Selection	$\mathcal{R}3S$	Yes with Flow binding	Yes with Flow binding	No	No	No	No	No	No
		$\mathcal{R}3D$	No	No	No	No	Yes with (API)	Yes with (API)	Yes with (API)	No

^{2}NA: Not Applicable

The filtering mechanism (common feature of all protocols) can help in interface selection by applying specific rules for the flow of packets. The configuration of such rules can be done in two ways, either by using socket API extensions or by relying on inbuilt packet filtering (e.g., NetFilter). A connection socket is identified by associating source & destination IP addresses and ports. The flow binding extensions for Mobile IPv6 and NEMO provide better interface selection mechanism using inbuilt packet filtering at network layer among all surveyed protocols. In HIP and SHIM6, Socket APIs are defined for interface selection. The SCTP API for interface selection supports path maintenance but does not describe the exchange of filtering rules between peers. NEMO together with its flow binding extension for nearly fulfills all the requirements of our project except dynamic interface selection. Therefore, our next step is to experiment with interface selection using the flow binding extension of NEMO which is dynamically influenced by user-application preferences, network characteristics, service provider's constraints etc.

In mobile networks, the interface selection requires a communication between user and mobile router. We plan to implement an API, which can communicate between user/application preferences and network level characteristics. Policy management will also be the part of this API, which will store all the required information from user, application, network, service operator, etc. Having all the attributes we would then design an algorithm to select the best available interface for any packet flow. The last step would be to enforce the decision in real time.

We intend to perform feasibility studies of the implemented solutions in terms of scalability, QoS, throughput under various mobility scenarios.

References

1. Barré, S., Paasch, C., Bonaventure, O.: MultiPath TCP: from theory to practice. In: Domingo-Pascual, J., Manzoni, P., Palazzo, S., Pont, A., Scoglio, C. (eds.) NETWORKING 2011, Part I. LNCS, vol. 6640, pp. 444–457. Springer, Heidelberg (2011)
2. Ben Nacef, A., Montavont, N.: A generic end-host mechanism for path selection and flow distribution. In: IEEE. PIMRC (2008)
3. Bernardos-Cano, C.J., Soto-Campos, I., Calderón-Pastor, M., von Hugo, D., Riou, E.: Nemo: Network mobility in ipv6. IPv6 More than A Protocol (2005)
4. Boutet, A., Le Texier, B., Montavont, J., Montavont, N., Schreiner, G.: Advantages of flow bindings: an embedded mobile network use case (2008)
5. Coras, F., Jakab, L., Lewis, D., Domingo-Pascual, J., Cabellos-Aparicio, A.: Lisp network element deployment considerations (2014)
6. Devarapalli, V., Wakikawa, R., Petrescu, A., Thubert, P.: Network mobility (nemo) basic support protocol. RFC 3963 (2005)
7. Eddy, W.M.: At what layer does mobility belong?. Communications Magazine. IEEE (2004)
8. Farinacci, D., Lewis, D., Meyer, D., Fuller, V.: The locator/id separation protocol (lisp) (2013)
9. Fu, S., Atiquzzaman, M.: Sctp: state of the art in research, products, and technical challenges. Communications Magazine. IEEE (2004)
10. Gundavelli, S., Leung, K., Devarapalli, V., Chowdhury, K., Patil, B.: Proxy mobile ipv6. RFC 5213 (2008)
11. Handley, M., Raiciu, C., Ford, A., Iyengar, J., Barre, S.: Architectural guidelines for multipath TCP development. RFC 6182 (2011)
12. Hurson, A.: Connected Computing Environment. Academic Press, San Diego (2012)
13. Huston, G.: Architectural commentary on site multi-homing a level 3 shim (2005)
14. Iannone, L., Saucez, D., Bonaventure, O.: Implementing the locator/id separation protocol: design and experience. Comput. Netw. **54**, 948–958 (2011)
15. Johnson, D., Perkins, C., Arkko, J.: Mobility support in ipv6. RFC 3775 (2004)
16. Komu, M., Bagnulo, M., Slavov, K., Sugimoto, S.: Socket application program interface (api) for multihoming shim. draft-ietf-shim6-multihome-shim-api-03 (2007)

17. Koodli, R.: Mobile ipv6 fast handovers. RFC 5568 (2009)
18. Kunishi, M., Ishiyama, M., Uehara, K., Esaki, H., Teraoka, F.: Lin6: A new approach to mobility support in ipv6. In: WPMC (2000)
19. Laganier, J., Eggert, L.: Host identity protocol (hip) rendezvous extension (2008)
20. Le, D., Fu, X., Hogrefe, D.: A review of mobility support paradigms for the internet. IEEE Commun. Surv. Tutor. **8**, 38–51 (2006)
21. Matsushima, S., Telecom, S., Okimoto, T., West, N., Wing, D.: Ipv6 multihoming without network address translation. RFC 7157 (2014)
22. Mihailovic, A., Leijonhufvud, G., Suihko, T.: Providing multi-homing support in ip access networks. In: IEEE. PIMRC (2002)
23. Mitsuya, K., Kuntz, R., Sugimoto, S., Wakikawa, R., Murai, J.: A policy management framework for flow distribution on multihomed end nodes. In: ACM/IEEE International Workshop on Mobility (2007)
24. Moskowitz, R., Nikander, P.: Host identity protocol architecture. RFC 4423 (2006)
25. Moskowitz, R., Nikander, P., Jokela, P., Henderson, T.: Host identity protocol. RFC 5201 (2008)
26. Nikander, P., Gurtov, A., Henderson, T.R.: Host identity protocol (hip): connectivity, mobility, multi-homing, security, and privacy over ipv4 and ipv6 networks. In: IEEE Communications Surveys & Tutorials. IEEE (2010)
27. Nordmark, E., Bagnulo, M.: Shim6: Level 3 multihoming shim protocol for ipv6. RFC 5533 (2009)
28. Perkins, C.: Ip mobility support for ipv4. RFC 3344 (2002)
29. Rahman, M.S., Atiquzzaman, M.: Semo6-a multihoming-based seamless mobility management framework, milcom. In: IEEE (2008)
30. Ropitault, T., Montavont, N.: Implementation of flow binding mechanism. In: IEEE PerCom (2008)
31. Saaty, T.L.: How to make a decision: the analytic hierarchy process. Eur. J. Oper. Res. **168**, 557–570 (1990)
32. Saucez, D., Iannone, L., Bonaventure, O., Farinacci, D.: Designing a deployable internet: the locator/identifier separation protocol. IEEE Internet Comput. **16**, 14–21 (2012)
33. Scharf, M., Ford, A.: Multipath tcp (mptcp) application interface considerations. RFC 6897 (2013)
34. Shen, C., Du, W., Atkinson, R., Kwong, K.H.: Policy based mobility and flow management for ipv6 heterogeneous wireless networks. Wireless Pers. Commun. **62**, 329–361 (2012)
35. Soliman, H., Bellier, L., Elmalki, K., Castelluccia, C.: Hierarchical mobile ipv6 (hmipv6) mobility management. RFC 5380 (2008)
36. Song, Q., Jamalipour, A.: A network selection mechanism for next generation networks. In: IEEE. ICC (2005)
37. Stewart, R.: Stream control transmission protocol (2007)
38. Stewart, R., Metz, C.: Sctp: new transport protocol for tcp/ip. IEEE Internet Comput. **5**, 64–68 (2001)
39. Stewart, R., Xie, Q., Yarroll, L., Wood, J., Poon, K., Tuexen, M.: Sockets api extensions for stream control transmission protocol (sctp) (2006)
40. Suciu, L., Bonnin, J., Guillouard, K., Stévant, B.: Towards a highly adaptable user-centric terminal architecture. In: International Symposium on WPMC (2004)
41. Teraoka, F., Ishiyama, M., Kunishi, M.: Lin6: A solution to multihoming and mobility in ipv6. draft-teraoka-multi6-lin6-00 (2003)
42. Triantaphyllou, E.: Multi-criteria decision making methods. In: Multi-criteria Decision Making Methods: A Comparative Study (2000)

43. Tsirtsis, G., Soliman, H., Montavont, N., Giaretta, G., Kuladinithi, K.: Flow bindings in mobile ipv6 and nemo basic support. RFC 6089 (2011)
44. Tuexen, M., Maruyama, S., Kozuka, M.: Network working group R. Stewart internet-draft cisco systems (2007)
45. Wakikawa, R., Devarapalli, V., Tsirtsis, G., Ernst, T., Nagami, K.: Multiple care-of addresses registration. RFC 5648 (2009)
46. Wakikawa, R., Paik, E., Ng, C., Kuladinithi, K., Noel, T.: Goals and benefits of multihoming. draft-ernst-generic-goals-and-benefits-01
47. White, C., Lewis, D., Meyer, D., Farinacci, D.: Lisp mobile node (2014)
48. Ylitalo, J., Jokikyyny, T., Kauppinen, T., Tuominen, A.J., Laine, J.: Dynamic network interface selection in multihomed mobile hosts. In: IEEE. HICSS (2003)

Mercury: Revealing Hidden Interconnections Between Access ISPs and Content Providers

Manuel Palacin[✉], Alex Bikfalvi, and Miquel Oliver

Networking Technology and Strategies (NeTS) Research Group,
Universitat Pompeu Fabra (UPF), Barcelona, Spain
{manuel.palacin,alex.bikfalvi,miquel.oliver}@upf.edu

Abstract. Knowing the detailed topology of the Internet at the Autonomous System (AS) level is extremely valuable for both researchers and industry when making network policies. Although there are many measurement projects and databases that provide this information, such as ARK, RETRO, ONO and PeeringDB, they only offer a partial view for analyzing end-to-end Internet routing paths and they do not focus on the hidden direct interconnections between Access ISPs and Content Providers. In order to address these shortcomings, we present Mercury, a web platform focused on the AS-level interconnection between content providers and content consumers. Mercury enables users to visualize the AS topology, aggregating data from traceroute measurements of participants and AS information from several databases. The advantage of Mercury is that it discovers how operators connect to other organizations and how content providers organize their server's infrastructure (CDN) to reach their target audience. To this end, Mercury identifies Internet Exchange Points (IXPs) and AS relationships along an Internet path and presents this information via a web site and a built-in API. We evaluate its potential probing a dataset of 100 popular web URLs from the major Spanish ISPs and we successfully identify many direct interconnections that were hidden for other methodologies.

1 Introduction

Discovering the hidden interconnections between access Internet Service Providers (ISPs) and Content Providers (CPs) is a challenge for engineers due to the lack of data available to the general public and due to the several weaknesses of the existing tools and methodologies to extract it. From the perspective of the ISP business relationships, these direct interconnections are critical because of the increasing demand for multimedia content requiring an optimal quality of experience (QoE) for the end users. These interconnections are elusive because they are usually based on peering agreements where the BGP announcements are only visible between peers and their customers. We also focus on another type of hidden interconnection between access ISPs and CPs, where the CP servers infrastructure is placed within the ISP.

Several efforts have been made to discover the Internet topology at the Autonomous System (AS) level. Historically, two approaches have been used: the

© Springer International Publishing Switzerland 2014
Y. Kermarrec (Ed.): EUNICE 2014, LNCS 8846, pp. 147–159, 2014.
DOI: 10.1007/978-3-319-13488-8_14

analysis of BGP paths and the *traceroute* traces. The BGP approach discovers the AS topology using a set of distributed monitors that sniff the BGP messages. This methodology uses the AS paths included in the BGP messages to infer the interconnections between the different ASes. However, BGP announcements describe the control plane which does not necessary correspond to the real path of the Internet traffic. Also, it is not effective for discovering the hidden interconnection and requires much more monitors to obtain a global topology. In contrast, the traceroute approach has the advantage that can discover the real path of the Internet traffic between two end points. As a disadvantage, the traceroute tool works at the IP level and is affected by the multi-path diversity of the IP protocol and requires an IP-to-AS mapping to infer the traversed ASes.

Toward this end we introduce *Mercury*[1], a platform for discovering the AS-level interconnections between content providers and content consumers. Mercury enables users to visualize the AS topology of access ISPs when they connect to other organizations and to identify how CPs organize their server infrastructure. To perform this, Mercury combines the two approaches presented previously. On one hand, a desktop client collects traceroute measurements from project participants. We have extended a version of traceroute, called Paris traceroute [4], which attempts to mitigate the multi-path problem for routers that implement per-flow load balancing. We rely on our own BGP datasets, collected from several data sources, to perform the IP-to-AS translation. The client uploads the measurements to the Mercury platform which presents all this information and statistics using a web site.

By leveraging this data, Mercury discovers the AS paths and interconnection relationships, while putting a special emphasis on the detection of interconnections between CPs and access ISPs. Mercury offers information about the number of AS hops to reach selected CPs, the type of AS relationships and the existence of IXPs in the path. Furthermore, Mercury allows researchers to consult aggregated statistics of different AS paths from multiple geographical locations to the same destination. This analysis is particularly useful for the identification of the server infrastructure used by Content Distribution Networks (CDNs). In addition, the platform provides a built-in API for expert users. In the following, we present several of the motivating scenarios.

Identification of the hidden interconnections: Mercury discovers many direct interconnections between CPs and access ISPs as the traceroute measurements are mostly done from commercial access ISPs with destination the most popular web sites. This information could be very useful to demonstrate that CPs are getting closer to the access ISPs.

Identify the architecture of CDNs: We identify the interconnection for CDNs, by revealing different paths to the same web resource from many points of origin. This helps researchers to analyze and classify existing CDN deployments, and to propose novel caching techniques. At the same time, CPs can evaluate the optimal strategies for reaching their target customers.

---

[1] A work-in-progress version is available at http://mercury.upf.edu/mercury.

Modeling the AS topology and the taxonomy of AS interconnections:
Mercury aggregates data of Internet paths, facilitating the generation of AS
graphs. The interconnection degree increases with the addition of new measurements. Such a dataset can serve for the evaluation of interconnection models of
commercial networks.

Network economics: Mercury provides information about the AS relationships. Network operators can use this to optimize their traffic routing policies
based on the observation of other AS topologies. Thanks to this data, an ISP
can discover peering partners and avoid using transit connections.

Although Mercury was implemented to collect data from participants around
the world, this paper only focuses on the Spanish interconnection market to
facilitate the evaluation of the system. Our objective is to answer the following
research questions: (i) how common are the direct interconnections between CPs
and access ISPs and (ii) what are the most common content delivery solutions
for CPs.

2   Related Work

Improving the accuracy of the Internet AS topology through measurements has
been a major objective for researchers for many years. The Route-Views project
provided one of the first datasets expressing the AS topology of the Internet,
based on BGP measurements [13]. Despite their pioneering work, researchers
realized that measuring the Internet topology from few vantage points leads
to partial results [7]. To address this, Mao et al. developed an AS-level traceroute tool, creating a database of IP-to-AS mappings based on the observation
of both BGP announcements in combination with IP traceroute measurements
[11]. However, the authors noticed the difficulty of detecting IXPs and sibling
relationships, as well as mapping mismatches due to measurements in a limited
geographic region.

Recognizing the benefit of measuring the Internet from the edge, Shavitt et al.
propose DIMES, a measurement infrastructure using a large number of clients
[17]. Although the project is open and its data is freely available, the information
does not include the relationship between ASes. In parallel, Dimitropoulos et al.
focused on this issue. Their work started initially as an effort to model and generate synthetic but realistic AS topologies [9]. Subsequently, they attempted a
classification of the Internet ASes using data collected from the Internet Routing
Registries and RouteViews. Their data in combination with the active measurements of the Ark project sponsored by CAIDA has contributed to the improvement in the knowledge of the AS Relationships [5].

In parallel, other projects such as PeeringDB, PCH and EuroIX were developed to facilitate the AS interconnection. They put a special emphasis on peering interconnections, such that participant ASes can register their IP prefixes.
Based on this data, there have been many new contributions augmenting the
AS topology with relationship information [14]. He et al. merge both data from

these databases with their own traceroute tool, called RETRO, to identify IXP participants [10]. While they collect data using public traceroute servers, Chen et al. increase the number of traceroute sources by developing a measurement add-on, called ONO, for a popular BitTorrent client [8]. In parallel, Augustin et al. provided a new approach for detecting IXPs and inspecting their AS participants based on various databases and traceroute measurements [3]. They detected 223 out of 278 IXPs and demonstrated that most of the remaining IXPs are invisible to tracerouting.

Almost all of these works point to discover the Internet topology in a global way, not focusing in any specific player. Ager et al. [1] proposed a new methodology for detecting web content infrastructure based on the evaluation of BGP snapshots and DNS queries to the most popular and long-tail web sites. Their results revealed what ASes have the content and where are they located. Our work, although uses a similar methodology to these previous efforts, differs in that we focus on identifying a specific type of interconnection, the CP to access ISP interconnection.

3   Objectives and Methodology

Mercury is a measurement platform dedicated to discovering the interconnection between content providers and content consumers. Figure 1 illustrates the AS information that one can discover using Mercury. On the consumer's side, Mercury illustrates how access ISPs reach the CPs. This result should reveal whether access ISPs use different interconnections strategies depending on their size. On the provider's side, Mercury facilitates the identification of content distribution architectures, depending on the determined geographical, IP or AS destinations.

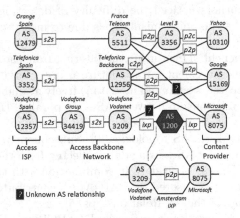

Fig. 1. Example of AS interconnections.

Our objective is transform Mercury into a comprehensive public dataset of end-to-end Internet paths. In addition to accessing the data, users can contribute, sending their own traceroute measurements using a desktop client. Although we evaluated the option of implementing a web-browser plugin, we discarded this option due to the inability of accessing to certain restricted functions of the operating system such as opening raw sockets. Therefore we finally implemented a stand-alone application inspired by the DIMES and ONO projects.

Mercury features a user-friendly web environment to navigate through the available datasets, query for certain data entries and to visualize interactive plots. Expert users can alternatively use the provided API to query for stored information. The API is open and based on the REST-WS protocol.

3.1   Measurement Methodology

As illustrated in Fig. 2, Mercury collects topology data from two main sources: (i) traceroutes from end-points clients across the Internet, and (ii) Internet topology information from several trusted databases. The measurement methodology is the following.

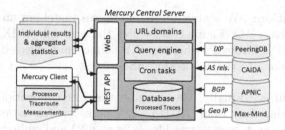

Fig. 2. The Mercury architecture.

Content Destination Selection: We selected the top 100 web site destinations from Alexa Top Sites [2] for 18 different countries. Once, we have the top 100 destinations for each country, we parse each web site in order to extract all the URL resources. With this step we determine all web servers that contribute content to the rendering of an individual web page, a step of particular importance when embedded content is hosted by a CDN. Finally, we obtain between 700 and 800 unique URLs per country that we store in the Mercury main server and the clients download their URL list according to their country.

Traceroute Collection: Mercury platform receives IP traceroute paths from the desktop clients and stores them into a database. Our client extends and implements Paris *traceroute* [4] in order to prevent multi-path anomalies across routers that perform load balancing. Because the correctness of traceroute data is paramount to the inference of real AS relationships, we resort to multiple tests per destination, at least 50 in most cases, which helps us to filter correct traceroutes. Using a desktop client, as opposed to a specially deployed traceroute servers in vantage points, guarantees a greater topological and geographical diversity [8]. Processed traceroute information is uploaded via the API to the Mercury platform. Clients probe a set of web destinations provided according to the geographical region. The rationale for this approach rests on the belief that access ISPs and CPs have incentives to directly connect when the corresponding content is popular in their country.

AS Resolution: Upon executed a traceroute measurement, the client translates the IP addresses to the equivalent AS number requesting mapping data to the Mercury platform. A scheduled task in the Mercury platform collects every 24 h IP prefixes from the APNIC/RouteViews from BGP announcements [16] and updates its own database with the new IP-to-AS mappings.

Geolocation: In parallel to the AS resolution, the Mercury client obtains, when it is available, the geographical location of IP addresses. The Mercury platform has a scheduled task that requests the IP-to-geo dataset from the MaxMind service [12]. Although we offer this information, we have to note that sometimes these mappings are not precise, specially those related to IP address that belong to large CPs or CDNs.

IXP Identification: We search the IP addresses matching an IXP from the PeeringDB database [15]. Figure 1 illustrates the principle of IXP interconnection, where the IP addresses within the IXP subnet and revealed by the traceroute, actually belong to the connecting ASes.

AS Relationships: Finally, we examine the interconnection relationships between ASes using data from CAIDA [5]. Thanks to this dataset, we identify the peering ($p2p$), customer-to-provider ($c2p$ or $p2c$) and sibling ($s2s$) relationships (see Fig. 1). In addition to this, we provide an extra dataset with ($s2s$) relationships extracted from analyzing the ISPs owners.

3.2 Implementation Internals

Mercury is formed by two main software instances: (i) the *desktop clients*, geographically distributed around the world and used by the participants, and (ii) the *Mercury Central Server* or *MCS*. The MCS is the responsible of formatting and storing the information from the external datasets and the responsible of storing and publishing the processed measurements sent by the clients. The client performs the traceroute probes and processes the results for obtaining the IP-to-AS translation, the IXP detection and the AS relationships of the end-to-end path.

The MCS obtains the IP-to-AS mappings from the BGP monitors through the Routing Report project [16]. We download daily the BGP report that contains the AS origin of the running IP prefixes. This information is structured and stored in a database and combined with IXP mappings from PeeringDB. In addition, we obtain the relationship type of each interconnected AS pair from the CAIDA AS relationships table [5] and the geolocation of the IPs from MaxMind [12]. Finally the central server has the list of URLs to be examined for each country. All these datasets are stored in the MCS and the clients can download them using the REST-API.

The Mercury client is a Desktop application written in C# that automatically downloads the list of URLs and executes the traceroute probes. Before tracerouting, the client executes a *nslookup* query for each URL in order to obtain the corresponding IP address. Sometimes it obtains multiple IPs for a same URL. This denotes the existence of load-balancing which is a technique of CDN architectures. Then, the client execute the traceroute measurements for the set of IPs of each URL.

The traceroute is performed using a modified version of Paris traceroute [4] to minimize the effect of multiple paths during IP routing. That is, using Paris traceroute we modify the IP packets for generating traffic flows that follow the same paths across routers that implement per-packet load balancing. In our implementation, for each destination IP address we generate 5 different flows with 5 attempts per flow, for both ICMP and UDP traffic, respectively. Therefore, we generate 50 different traceroutes for each destination. The client translates each IP address from each IP hop to an AS number using the MCS-API. We are mostly interested in the AS level of a traffic path. This means that we are mostly concerned about detecting and correcting inconsistencies at edge routers between different ASes. This step is crucial because it aggregates flows and detects, corrects (if possible) and discards multi-path behaviours that lead us to obtain loops and missing ASes. To solve these anomalies we use an algorithm that detects AS hop inconsistencies and corrects them based on the analysis of the previous and next AS hops (see Fig. 3). We also assume a hot potato policy at the AS level. Therefore, the combination of Paris traceroute with this algorithm minimizes the number of incorrect traces.

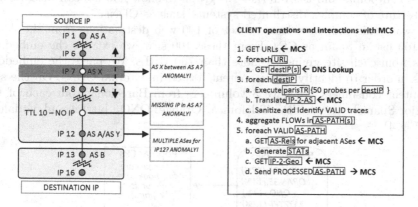

Fig. 3. Processing AS paths.

Once the traceroutes are executed, the client adds extra information from the external datasets of the MCS. In this step it includes to the traces the AS relationships between adjacent ASes, the geolocation of the end-points and it generates an statistical summary. The client is the responsible of processing all the information releasing the MCS for doing only searching and publication tasks. Finally, when the client ends processing, all the data is sent to the MCS.

All the stored measurements are publicly available using the Web interface and the REST API. Researchers can obtain aggregated statistics for a set of paths. For example one can aggregate paths filtering by destination URL, AS number or geographic location. These statistics include average, mean and standard deviation about the number of AS hops and the type of the AS relationships but also other network indicators like the number of destinations IPs and ASes that host a destination URL, e.g. http://www.20minutos.es is in average at 0.88 AS hops, points to two different IPs (193.148.34.26 and 89.140.253.190) and is hosted in two different ASes (AS3324 and AS6739).

4   Case Studies

We conducted an experiment using a set of traceroute measurements from various end-points located in the major Spanish access ISPs. We select Spain because is a typical post-monopoly market and we expect that this experiment will obtain similar results in the larger European countries. This experiment does not require too many participants as we consider that most of the users of a certain access ISP will be routed, at the AS-level, using the same policy. Hence, at least one participant in each one of the five major Spanish access ISPs will be enough to draw conclusions on their interconnections. The objective of this experiment is twofold. Firstly, we test the detection and aggregation of interconnection relationships for a set of given URL destinations, showing the types of connectivity for a given end-point. Secondly, we leverage the known relationships etween end-points and the Internet AS graph to show how we can discover the architecture of complex distributed systems, such as CDNs.

Toward this end, we selected a set of 100 web destinations from the Alexa Top 100 list in Spain as CPs. From these 100 sites we extract the embedded URLs from each site giving us more than 700 URLs. We parse the embedded URLs in order to identify media content hosted in external CDNs. On the side of content consumers, we have 5 volunteers from Barcelona from each of the 5 major Spanish access ISPs: Telefonica, Orange, ONO, Jazztel and Vodafone (see Fig. 4).

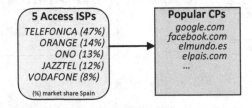

Fig. 4. Major access ISPs probing popular CPs

Each participant uses the client for tracerouting the set of destinations, and uploading the results to the MCS. We require clients located at commercial access

ISPs in order to see how these ISPs interconnect with the CPs. Upon receiving the measurement data, Mercury distinguishes between *completed* and *inconsistent* traceroutes. Then it stores the measurements with a flag that identifies the different inconsistences of a path.

4.1   Revealing Hidden Interconnections

We use Mercury to discover direct interconnections between CPs and access ISPs without intermediaries and CPs that place their servers within the access ISP network. Table 1 shows the identification of direct interconnections for a subset of popular web sites that include global and local CPs. It compares the existence of direct interconnection relationships, either physically direct or across a sibling AS of the same organization, with the AS relationships from the CAIDA dataset [5]. In these results, we use checkmarks to emphasize the matches between Mercury and CAIDA, crossings to indicate relationships not found in CAIDA, and dashes represents the non-existance of direct interconnections.

Table 1. Identification of direct interconnections.

	Google	Facebook	Yahoo	Twitter	Amazon	MSN	Wikipedia
Telefonica	Sibling ✗	Sibling ✓	Sibling ✓	No –	Sibling ✓	Sibling ✓	Sibling ✓
Orange	Sibling ✗	Sibling ✓	No –	No –	No –	Sibling ✗	Sibling ✓
ONO	Direct ✗	No –	No –	No –	No –	No –	No –
Jazztel	Direct ✗	Direct ✗	Direct ✗	IXP ✗	IXP ✗	IXP ✗	No –
Vodafone	Sibling ✓	Sibling ✓	Sibling ✓	IXP* ✓	IXP* ✓	Sibling ✗	Sibling ✓

Note: IXP* is a relationship where a sibling AS is connected to an IXP

Mercury identifies more links than CAIDA dataset when we focus on detecting direct interconnections. Although Mercury sometimes is not capable to identify the AS relationship type of a direct interconnection, it at least detects it, making possible to focus on this link in future studies in order to detect the relationship type. However, we conjecture that most of the direct interconnections are based on peering or paid-peering relationships according to the peering policies of both access ISPs and CPs. One can observe that access ISPs and large CPs find more attractive this formula than using an intermediary AS (see Google and MSN with Jazztel). They find the direct interconnection mutually beneficial, i.e. the content provider can be closer to the users and can offer a better QoE while the access ISP obtains an economic compensation from the paid-peering agreement.

Mercury shows us that Google has direct connections with all the major spanish ISPs. We also observe that not all CPs have direct interconnections to all access ISPs. This could be for different reasons: there are some CPs that only allocate the cacheable content using direct interconnections and there are also some CPs that have only agreed direct interconnections with some certain access ISP's and require an intermediary to reach the rest of access ISPs. This can be seen in Fig. 5, where one of the major Spanish press groups (ElMundo.es) maintain its own AS, but they contract a third party for delivering their cached content.

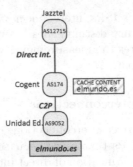

Fig. 5. Multiple content delivery strategies for web sites.

4.2 Revealing Interconnections Inside the Access ISP: The CDN

When seeking evidence of whether a content provider uses a CDN solution, Mercury provides a number of statistical indicators that are adequate to this task: (i) the number of AS hops to reach a server, (ii) the list of destination countries, and the list of (iii) IPs and (iv) ASes for a same URL. The number of AS hops to reach a CDN destination is a weak parameter of CDN existence, but it reveals the location of the content server relative to the user (when zero, the server is insider the user ISP). The list of destination countries is a better indicator of CDNs when the geolocation service is accurate, giving us the distribution of the server infrastructure. However, in practice, we must be careful because global CPs do not publish the location of their servers. For example Google servers are geolocated only in the USA, based on the registration of their AS. Currently, a lot of research effort is invested into improving the geolocation of IP addresses [1,6]. The list of destination IPs and ASes are the strongest indicators of a CDN. They show that a web site is deployed along multiple distributed servers, confirming the existence of some type of load balancing or caching technique, which are intrinsic to the use of CDN solutions. In addition, we can use them to determine the taxonomy of CDN strategies. As illustrated in Fig. 6, we can distinguish between two main types: (i) CDNs that host their cache servers inside the Tier 3 ISPs (Akamai and Google strategy) and (ii) CDNs that locate their

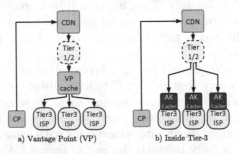

Fig. 6. Types of CDN architectures.

cache servers in vantage points (VPs), near to the access operator (Cogent or Level3 strategies).

Table 2 summarizes the Mercury data for several CDN destinations. Our results indicates that most of the web sites we analyzed resort to some type of CDN. We observe that many global CPs like Facebook or Microsoft use Akamai, which deploys servers in both access ISPs and Tier 1 carriers, in addition to their own VPs. Furthermore it is also interesting that Elpais, the second major press group in Spain, also uses Akamai. The number of servers deployed by Akamai in other ASes stands well above the other CDNs, something observed by previous research publications [18]. Google uses a similar strategy and has direct interconnections with most of the access ISPs and has servers inside some access ISPs (Fig. 7 shows that Google has cache servers pointing to Jazztel IP addresses).

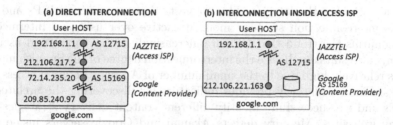

Fig. 7. Google places cache servers in vantage points and within the access ISP network

The remaining CPs use VPs to host their cache servers, based on different strategies. LinkedIn uses a multi-vendor CDN solution formed by Level3, LimeLight and others. This case is quite interesting because LinkedIn diversifies the spending in content delivery services. Similarly, the Spanish press groups ElMundo and 20Minutos use a similar multi-vendor strategy. For Amazon CDN,

Table 2. CDN strategies for differentcontent providers.

CP	Google	Facebook	Yahoo	Amazon	MSN	Instagram
CDN	Google	Akamai	Yahoo	Amazon	Akamai	Amazon
# servers	43	5	4	85	4	12
Inside ISP	✓	✓	–	–	✓	–
VP	✓	✓	✓	✓	✓	✓
Multi-vendor	–	–	–	–	–	–

CP	Elmundo	Elpais	LinkedIn	20minutos	Wikipedia
CDN	Cogent Interroute	Akamai	Limelight Level3	Level3 Fujitsu ... ONO	Wikipedia
# servers	41	12	4	4	1
Inside ISP	–	✓	–	–	–
VP	–	✓	–	–	✓
Multi-vendor	✓	–	✓	✓	–

we highlight the large number of servers and that it resells CDN services to other web sites like Instagram.

5 Conclusions

In this paper we introduced Mercury, an Internet measurement platform that aggregates traceroute measurements from multiple locations and analyzes the AS interconnection relationships along a network path. Mercury stands-out over other solutions because it discovers the end-to-end network path at the AS-level, while including information about the AS relationships, detecting IXPs and adding geolocation. We evaluate Mercury for a set of web sites using clients located at major Spanish access ISPs. Our results reveal the existence of many direct AS interconnections between access ISPs and content providers that are hidden for other methodologies. This suggests that some access ISPs and CPs find this interconnection strategy more attractive over using an intermediary and it confirms the trend that CPs are increasingly closer to the end users. In addition, our results emphasize the interconnection degree of the Spanish market, which is relatively high due to the small number of AS hops between access ISPs and CPs. Finally, Mercury provides indicators for discovering the architecture of CDNs and we successfully identify different content delivery strategies used by many web sites. Mercury detects Akamai and Google servers inside some Spanish ISPs which demonstrates the interest of these companies in offering a high quality content delivery.

Acknowledgments. This work was partially supported by the Spanish government, through the project CISNETS (TEC2012-32354).

References

1. Ager, B., Mühlbauer, W., Smaragdakis, G., Uhlig, S.: Web content cartography. In: Proceedings of the 2011 ACM SIGCOMM Conference on Internet Measurement Conference, IMC '11, pp. 585–600. ACM, New York (2011)
2. Alexa: Alexa top sites. http://www.alexa.com/topsites
3. Augustin, B., Krishnamurthy, B., Willinger, W.: IXPs: mapped? In: Proceedings of the 9th ACM SIGCOMM Internet Measurement Conference (IMC) (2009)
4. Augustin, B., Cuvellier, X., Orgogozo, B., Viger, F., Friedman, T., Latapy, M., Magnien, C., Teixeira, R.: Paris traceroute. http://www.paris-traceroute.net/
5. CAIDA: The CAIDA AS relationships dataset (2012). http://www.caida.org/data/active/as-relationships/
6. Calder, M., Fan, X., Hu, Z., Katz-Bassett, E., Heidemann, J., Govindan, R.: Mapping the expansion of google's serving infrastructure. In: Proceedings of the 2013 Conference on Internet Measurement Conference, IMC (2013)
7. Chang, H., Govindan, R., Jamin, S., Shenker, S.J., Willinger, W.: Towards capturing representative AS-level internet topologies. In: Proceedings of ACM SIGMETRICS, pp. 280–281. ACM (2002)

8. Chen, K., Choffnes, D.R., Potharaju, R., Chen, Y., Bustamante, F.E., Pei, D., Zhao, Y.: Where the sidewalk ends: extending the Internet AS graph using traceroutes from P2P users. In: Proceedings of the 5th International Conference on Emerging Networking Experiments and Technologies (2009)
9. Dimitropoulos, X., Riley, G.: Modeling autonomous-system relationships. In: Proceedings of the 20th Workshop on Principles of Advanced and Distributed Simulation (PADS), pp. 143–149. IEEE Computer Society (2006)
10. He, Y., Siganos, G., Faloutsos, M., Krishnamurthy, S.: A systematic framework for unearthing the missing links: measurements and impact. In: Proceedings of 4th USENIX Symposium on Networked Systems Design and Implementation (NSDI), pp. 187–200. USENIX (2007)
11. Mao, Z.M., Rexford, J., Wang, J., Katz, R.H.: Towards an accurate AS-level traceroute tool. In: Proceedings of ACM SIGCOMM (2003)
12. MaxMind: GeoLite databases. http://dev.maxmind.com/geoip/legacy/geolite
13. Meyer, D.: University of Oregon Route Views. http://www.routeviews.org/
14. Oliveira, R.V., Zhang, B.: Observing the evolution of Internet AS topology. ACM SIGCOMM Comput. Commun. Rev. **37**(4), 313–324 (2007)
15. PeeringDB. https://www.peeringdb.com/
16. Smith, P., Cisco Systems: BGP routing table. http://thyme.apnic.net/
17. Shavitt, Y., Shir, E.: DIMES: let the internet measure itself. ACM SIGCOMM Comput. Commun. Rev. **35**(5), 71–74 (2005)
18. Su, A.-J., Choffnes, D.R., Kuzmanovic, A., Bustamante, F.E.: Drafting behind Akamai: inferring network conditions based on CDN redirections. IEEE/ACM Trans. Network (TON) **17**(6), 1752–1765 (2009)

Malleability Resilient Concealed Data Aggregation

Keyur Parmar$^{(\boxtimes)}$ and Devesh C. Jinwala$^{(\boxtimes)}$

S. V. National Institute of Technology, Surat, India
{keyur.mtech,dcjinwala}@gmail.com

Abstract. Concealed data aggregation protects against passive attackers and ensures privacy of sensor readings at intermediate nodes. However, the use of inherently malleable privacy homomorphism makes it susceptible to active attackers. In addition, it is a well-known fact that encrypted data processing is vulnerable to pollution attacks where a single malicious node can flood the network by fake readings. Hence, there exists a need to authenticate the processed readings. Traditional authentication mechanisms are not viable due to the conflicting requirements like in-network processing and encrypted data processing. The need for en route aggregation of sensor readings, the need for encrypted data processing and the need for message authentication both at the base station and at aggregator nodes, make message authentication a formidable challenge. Homomorphic Message Authentication Codes (H-MACs) help to verify the integrity of processed sensor readings. However, the need to verify the integrity of sensor readings both at intermediate node(s) and at the base station cannot be realized simultaneously through the currently available techniques. In this paper, we combine the benefits of privacy homomorphism and H-MACs to provide malleability resilient concealed data aggregation in the presence of both insider and outsider adversaries. As per our knowledge, our solution is the first to achieve integrity protecting concealed data aggregation in the presence of both insider and outsider adversaries.

Keywords: Wireless sensor networks · Concealed data aggregation · Privacy homomorphism · Homomorphic MAC · Malleability resilience

1 Introduction

The resource constrained nature of tiny sensor devices has a profound effect on the design and development of wireless sensor network (WSN) protocols. Amongst limited resources like memory, processor, battery power, bandwidth, etc. [3], the battery power has a severe impact on the lifetime of WSNs. Although both computation and communication require power to operate, the significant amount of power consumption is due to the communication [11]. Thus, different techniques have been employed to reduce the communication traffic; one such technique is in-network processing or data aggregation [8]. Instead of

© Springer International Publishing Switzerland 2014
Y. Kermarrec (Ed.): EUNICE 2014, LNCS 8846, pp. 160–172, 2014.
DOI: 10.1007/978-3-319-13488-8_15

transmitting redundant sensor readings over the network, in-network processing processes them near to their sources and transmits the results. Hence, it reduces the communication traffic.

Security in WSNs becomes essential due to unreliable communication environment and hostile deployment. In addition, different application areas, like military environments, require security as their primary goal. However, requirements like data aggregation and security are in sharp contrast with each other; the goal of data aggregation is to reduce the number of bits required for communication while the goal of security is to add extra bits to provide security. This leads to the development of secure data aggregation protocols that simultaneously provide security and en route aggregation.

Initial secure data aggregation protocols tend to provide the security per hop basis and require raw sensor readings to operate upon. They decrypt the data at each hop, perform aggregation and re-encrypt them before forwarding them to the next hop. Although such approaches handle security and aggregation requirements, they introduce extra computation and communication cost, latency and security vulnerabilities at compromised intermediate nodes. Hence, end-to-end secure data aggregation a.k.a. concealed data aggregation has been proposed by Girao et al. [9] to protect the privacy of sensor readings at intermediate nodes.

The goal of concealed data aggregation is to provide the end-to-end privacy of sensor readings. Hence, it needs to process the encrypted data at intermediate nodes. Privacy homomorphism [18] helps to process the encrypted data which yields same result as encrypting the processed (raw) data. Although privacy homomorphism based techniques support different operations like addition, multiplication, X-OR etc., majority of WSNs applications require a support for only additive aggregation. Additive privacy homomorphism supports aggregation operations like SUM, MIN, MAX, AVG, movement detection.

Although privacy homomorphism protects the sensor readings from passive attackers, it makes the system more vulnerable to active attackers. Encrypted data processing not only allows genuine sensor nodes to process the encrypted data, it also allows adversaries to process the encrypted data. Any adversary or compromised intermediate node with public parameters to perform encrypted data processing can manipulate the sensor readings. Hence, the need to protect the data from unauthorized manipulation arises; traditional networks handle this issue by providing message authentication. However, the message authentication becomes challenging in a concealed data aggregation due to the following reasons. (1) Unlike traditional networks, concealed data aggregation modifies data at intermediate hops. Thus, traditional mechanisms used to protect the end-to-end integrity can only provide the hop-by-hop integrity. (2) Concealed data aggregation uses the privacy homomorphism to protect privacy of sensor readings at intermediate nodes. However, the privacy homomorphism is inherently malleable; it allows the modification of a ciphertext without the need for a decryption key. Hence, any malicious node with public parameters, can manipulate the encrypted data. Traditional networks protect against such malicious nodes through source authentication. However in concealed data aggregation, only the base station possesses a decryption key. Hence the data and source information cannot be bound together like traditional networks. (3) Unreliable wireless communication environment and lack of physical security make encrypted data processing extremely vulnerable. In addition, capturing the genuine sensor nodes to access their public parameters or eavesdropping the communication to capture the ciphertexts is relatively easy in sensor networks.

Message authentication in end-to-end secure data aggregation requires verification of sensor readings at two levels; (1) The base station (2) Intermediate nodes. Although traditional authentication mechanisms like hash functions, message authentication codes (MACs) or digital signatures provide authentication per hop basis, they cannot be used to provide the end-to-end authentication in data centric networking. Hence, Agrawal et al. [2] introduce homomorphic MAC to support the need of data centric networking in resource constrained environments. Westhoff et al. [21] use the homomorphic MAC to protect the network from outsider adversaries. In their technique, the base station protects the integrity of sensor readings only against outsider adversaries. Therefore, it leaves sensor network vulnerable to active insider adversaries. In addition, the omnipresent threat of denial of service attacks in WSNs requires the verification of sensor readings as close to their sources as possible. However, it verifies the sensor readings only at the base station that limits its usage in resource constrained environments.

In this paper, we propose non-malleable concealed data aggregation that protects against both insider and outsider adversaries. The major contribution of this work is to protect the sensor readings from both passive and active adversaries as well as insider and outsider adversaries. Although the proposed approach supports encrypted data processing using inherently malleable privacy homomorphism, its design makes it non-malleable against both insider and outsider adversaries. As per our knowledge, our solution is the first to provide the privacy and the authenticity against both insider and outsider adversary for reverse multicast traffic.

The rest of the paper is organized as follows. In Sect. 2, we present a survey of relevant literature. In Sect. 3, we provide a brief overview of homomorphic primitives required for the proposed protocol. Section 4 discusses the proposed protocol for malleability resilient concealed data aggregation. We analyze the security of the proposed protocol in Sect. 5 and analyze the resource overhead in Sect. 6. Section 7 concludes the paper by emphasizing our contributions.

2   Related Work

Girao et al. [9] explored the need to protect the privacy of sensor readings at intermediate nodes and coined a term concealed data aggregation to refer the encrypted data processing at intermediate nodes in WSNs. They propose to use Domingo-Ferrer's privacy homomorphism [7]. In addition, Castelluccia et al. [5] proposed a symmetric key based cryptosystem with the support for additive privacy homomorphism. Although symmetric key based privacy homomorphisms are cost effective in terms of ciphertext expansion, computation cost, etc., the physical vulnerability of sensor nodes increases the difficulty in utilizing such schemes in practical. A single compromised node can reveal the group key which might have catastrophic effects on the security of large number of sensor nodes.

Asymmetric key based cryptosystems mitigate the threat of exposing keys to attackers by using different keys for senders and receivers. In addition, elliptic curve based asymmetric key cryptosystems [14] provide the same level of security with reduced key size. Thus, they are more suitable for resource constrained devices like sensor nodes. Gura et al. [10] investigate the need to implement public key cryptography over 8-bit micro-controllers, generally used for sensor platforms. They have implemented RSA and elliptic curve cryptography over 8-bit micro-controllers to show the viability of public key infrastructure without any specialized hardware devices. Malan et al. [15] first implemented elliptic curve cryptography over $\mathbb{F}_{2^p}$ to check the viability of ECC over MICA2 mote. Mykletun et al. [16] comparatively analyze the public key based additively homomorphic algorithms for concealed data aggregation in WSNs. As per their analysis, EC-ElGamal [14] and Okamoto-Uchiyama [17] are preferable for resource constrained devices.

Existing literature work in concealed data aggregation [9, 20] inclines towards privacy protection. Although, numerous solutions [4, 6] claim to provide the message authentication in WSNs, very few of them [21] claim to provide the end-to-end message authentication. Hop-by-hop message authentication is not effective when there exist insider adversaries. The end-to-end message authentication in the presence of insider adversaries is considered to be an open problem. Traditional authentication mechanisms like hash functions, digital signatures or message authentication codes cannot adequately deal with the requirement of en route aggregation and encrypted data processing. However, authentication based on homomorphic primitives can help to authenticate the encrypted and aggregated data. Agrawal et al. [2] proposed a solution to provide homomorphic MAC. Recently, Homomorphic MAC based solutions [4, 21] are proposed to provide the integrity protection for WSNs.

3   Preliminaries

In this section, we describe the homomorphic primitives used to provide the encrypted data processing and end-to-end message authentication. The EC-ElGamal [14] is an elliptic curve based public key cryptosystem with the support for additive privacy homomorphism. The EC-ElGamal is used to protect the privacy, while the Homomorphic MAC [2] is used to verify the authenticity of aggregated ciphertext.

3.1   Elliptic Curve ElGamal Cryptosystem

Here we describe the ElGamal cryptosystem adapted for use with elliptic curves [14]. Let E be an elliptic curve defined over a finite field $\mathbb{F}_p$ such that the discrete log problem is hard for $E(\mathbb{F}_p)$. Choose a point, P, on E (such that the order of P is a large prime). Now choose a secret integer x and compute $Q = xP$. The public key consists of E, $\mathbb{F}_p$, and the points P and Q, while the integer x is kept private.

- Encodes a message as a point, $M \in E(\mathbb{F}_p)$.
- Choose a secret random integer r and compute,

$$C_1 = rP \quad \text{and} \quad C_2 = M + rQ$$

- Decryption is done by calculating $C_2 - x\,C_1$.

In principle, the EC-ElGamal cryptosystem works fine, but there are some practical difficulties.

- It is not easy to map values (e.g. plaintexts) to points (e.g. ciphertexts) in $E(\mathbb{F}_p)$, and vice versa. As the operands of elliptic curve operations are points on elliptic curves, this requirement is considered to be the base requirement. In addition, such mapping function should be deterministic and efficient. There exists a number of mapping functions that maps plaintext values to elliptic curve points. However, our requirement is to choose a mapping function that is homomorphic, i.e. $\text{map}(m_1 + m_2) = \text{map}(m_1) + \text{map}(m_2)$, as suggested in [1,19].
- The EC-ElGamal cryptosystem has 4-to-1 message expansion, as compared to the 2-to-1 expansion ratio of ElGamal using $\mathbb{F}_p$. The plaintext M is a single point in $E(\mathbb{F}_p)$ while the ciphertext (C_1, C_2) consists of two point in $E(\mathbb{F}_p)$ and each point in $E(\mathbb{F}_p)$ has two coordinate values. However, the use of point compression techniques, as mentioned in [12], can significantly reduce the ciphertext size.

In [16], Mykletun et al. studied different public key based homomorphic cryptosystems and conclude that the use of EC-Elgamal is the best choice due to its comparatively smaller ciphertext size. However, it is only preferable in a situation where the expensive decryption is carried out at the base station.

3.2   Homomorphic MAC

In WSNs, intermediate nodes aggregate packets en route. Hence, traditional solutions like MAC or hash cannot provide the sufficient (end-to-end) integrity protection. A single malicious node can harm WSNs by flooding bad packets. In addition, due to the encrypted data processing, such packets are aggregated with genuine packets and affect the results of entire WSNs. In this section, we briefly discuss the homomorphic MAC [2] used to protect the integrity in such scenarios and its detail description with security proofs can be found in [2].

Homomorphic MAC Construction: To construct a homomorphic MAC, we need a pseudo random generator $G : \mathcal{K}_G \to \mathbb{F}_q^{n+m}$ and a pseudo random function $F : \mathcal{K}_F \times (\mathcal{I} \times [m]) \to \mathbb{F}_q$. Keys for homomorphic MAC consist of pairs (k_1, k_2) where $k_1 \in \mathcal{K}_G$ and $k_2 \in \mathcal{K}_F$. The homomorphic MAC works as follows:

- To generate a MAC tag $\mathcal{T} \in \mathbb{F}_q$, for a vector $v \in \mathbb{F}_q^{n+m}$, using key $k = (k_1, k_2)$, compute:
  - $u \leftarrow G(k_1) \in \mathbb{F}_q^{n+m}$
  - $b \leftarrow F(k_2, (id, i)) \in \mathbb{F}_q$
  - $\mathcal{T} \leftarrow (u \cdot v) + b \in \mathbb{F}_q$
- To aggregate MAC tags $\mathcal{T}_1, \mathcal{T}_2, \cdots \mathcal{T}_m$,

$$\mathcal{T} \leftarrow \sum_{j=1}^{m} \alpha_j \mathcal{T}_j \in \mathbb{F}_q \tag{1}$$

- Given a secret key $k = (k_1, k_2)$ and $y = (y_1, \cdots, y_{n+m}) \in \mathbb{F}_q^{n+m}$, verify a tag $\mathcal{T}$ as follows.
  - $u \leftarrow G(k_1) \in \mathbb{F}_q^{n+m}$ and $a \leftarrow (u \cdot y) \in \mathbb{F}_q$
  - $b \leftarrow \sum_{i=1}^{m} [y_{n+i} \cdot F(k_2, (id, i))] \in \mathbb{F}_q$
  - If $a + b = \mathcal{T}$ then output 1; otherwise output 0.

4 The Proposed Protocol

In this section, we present the proposed protocol for malleability resilient concealed data aggregation in the presence of both insider and outsider adversaries. The proposed protocol is based on the EC-ElGamal cryptosystem [14]

Table 1. Notations used in the proposed protocol

Symbol	Description
i	Sensor node ID
n	Total number of nodes in the network
S_i	Plaintext value sensed by a sensor node i
C_i	Ciphertext value computed by a sensor node i
E_{BS}	Encryption using the base station's public key (EC-ElGamal Algorithm)
D_{BS}	Decryption using the base station's private key (EC-ElGamal Algorithm)
MAC	MAC generated using a key shared between the base station and sensors
$\mathcal{T}_i$	MAC tag produced on ciphertext of node i
m	Distance in terms of hops from a node to its parent node
j_m	Parent node of node i at a distance of m hops
t	Distance in terms of hops between a node and the base station
E_{i,j_m}	Encryption using a symmetric key cipher and a shared key of a node i and its parent node j_m
D_{i,j_m}	Decryption using a symmetric key cipher and a shared key of a node i and its parent node j_m
x	Number of child nodes of a node
$\oplus$	Operator used to perform homomorphic operation (Encryption and MAC)

and homomorphic MAC [2]. The notations used in the proposed protocol are as shown in Table 1. Here, we assume a tree topology as shown in [5]. We also assume that the network is deployed with the secret key shared between the base station and all sensor nodes. In addition, the public key of the base station is available on all sensor nodes. In addition, we assume that during the bootstrapping phase, a node shares a symmetric key with its parent node upto m hops. Here, m must always be greater than 2 to protect the network against insider adversaries.

4.1   The Proposed Protocol for Malleability Resilient Concealed Data Aggregation

1. Each leaf (sensor) node i senses a value S_i and encrypts it with the public key generated by the base station using EC-ElGamal cryptosystem.

$$C_i = E_{BS}(S_i) \qquad \forall i \in \{1, 2, \cdots, n\}$$

2. Node i computes a MAC tag: $T_i \leftarrow MAC(C_i)$. It is generated with a secret key k shared between the base station and sensor nodes. Here, a MAC is generated on ciphertext unlike traditional networks.
3. Node i encrypts a MAC tag using a key shared with node j_m which is m^{th}-hop parent for node i. Here, an encryption algorithm can be any symmetric key based algorithm like AES, RC5, etc. The privacy homomorphism property is not required for this algorithm.

$$E_{i,j_m}(T_i) \qquad \forall i, j_m \in \{1, 2, \cdots, n\}, i \neq j_m, \forall m \in \{1, 2, \cdots, t\}$$

Here, t is a number of hop distance between a leaf node and the base station.
4. Node i transmits,
   - $C_i \qquad \forall i \in \{1, 2, \cdots, n\}$
   - $E_{i,j_m}(T_i) \qquad \forall i, j_m \in \{1, 2, \cdots, n\}, i \neq j_m, \forall m \in \{1, 2, \cdots, t\}$
5. Each intermediate node j receives,
   - $C_i \qquad \forall i \in \{1, 2, \cdots, n\}$
   - $E_{i,j_m}(T_i) \qquad \forall i, j_m \in \{1, 2, \cdots, n\}, i \neq j_m, \forall m \in \{1, 2, \cdots, t\}$
6. Node j_m, m-hops away from node i, decrypts $E_{i,j_m}(T_i)$ using its shared secret key with node i. Number of child nodes of node j is denoted by x, where $1 \leq x \leq n - 1$.

$$D_{i,j_m}(\oplus_{i=1}^{x} T_i)$$

Here, $\forall i, j_m \in \{1, 2, \cdots, n\}, i \neq j_m, \forall m \in \{1, 2, \cdots, t\}, 1 \leq x \leq n - 1$
7. Node j_m generates a MAC tag of ciphertext C_i using its shared secret key with node i and compares it with the decrypted MAC tag of previous step.

$$D_{i,j_m}(T_i) \stackrel{?}{=} MAC(C_i)$$

Here, $\forall i, j_m \in \{1, 2, \cdots, n\}, i \neq j_m, \forall m \in \{1, 2, \cdots, t\}, 1 \leq x \leq n - 1$. If it holds, it accepts the ciphertext C_i.

8. If all the ciphertexts, $(1, 2, \cdots, x)$, coming from child nodes are valid, node j_m uses EC-ElGamal cryptosystem and Homomorphic MAC to aggregate the ciphertexts of its child nodes and their corresponding MACs.

$$C_{j_m} = \oplus_{i=1}^{x} C_i \quad 1 \leq x \leq n - 1$$

$$T_{j_m} = \oplus_{i=1}^{x} T_i \quad 1 \leq x \leq n - 1$$

9. Node j_m encrypts the newly generated MAC with a key shared with its parent node(s) which is/are upto m-hops away and repeats the steps 4–9.
10. The base station follows the steps 5, 6 and 7. After verifying the homomorphic MAC and its corresponding ciphertext, it decrypts the ciphertext.

$$D_{BS}(\oplus_{i=1}^{n-1} C_i) = \oplus_{i=1}^{n-1} S_i \tag{2}$$

4.2 Example

As shown in Fig. 1, for m = 2, each sensor node shares a secret key with its parent node and its grand-parent node. For ease of discussion, we assume that only leaf nodes are the sensors, while intermediate nodes are either forwarders or aggregators. If m = 3, a node shares a secret key with its 1-hop, 2-hop and 3-hop parent node(s). Here, keys shared between each pair of nodes are different.

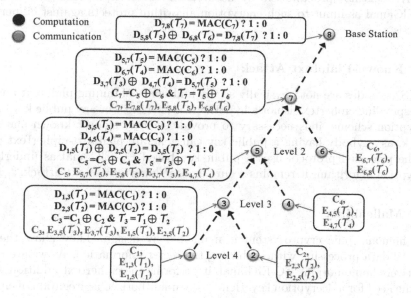

Fig. 1. Malleability resilient concealed data aggregation (m = 2)

Sensor readings that are encrypted at leaf nodes are aggregated en route using EC-ElGamal cryptosystem [14] and their corresponding MACs are aggregated using homomorphic MAC [2]. Intermediate nodes verify the ciphertext by generating its MAC and comparing it with the MAC generated by its child node. In addition, intermediate nodes can verify the aggregated ciphertext using the encrypted MACs transmitted by their grand-child nodes. Hence,any malicious activity of child node is detected by comparing the MAC with its grand-children's MACs. Finally, the base station can verify the ciphertext and aggregated MAC and if they are correct, it can decrypt the ciphertext using its private key.

5   Security Analysis

In this section, we evaluate the possible attack scenarios and measure the resilience of the proposed protocol against known attacks.

5.1   Ciphertext Analysis

In a ciphertext only attack, an attacker eavesdrops the ciphertexts and analyses them to deduce the key. Any probabilistic cryptosystem that generates a different ciphertext for a same plaintext is secure against such attack. In the proposed protocol we used EC-ElGamal cryptosystem, which is probabilistic and hence secure against ciphertext analysis. In addition, we use symmetric key based encryption scheme to encrypt the MACs. Although, symmetric key based scheme (i.e. AES) is not probabilistic by nature, the use of ciphertext generated by EC-ElGamal as input to such encryption algorithm protects against cihpertext analysis.

5.2   Known-Plaintext Attack

In WSNs, nodes are not physically secure and hence obtaining plaintext and its corresponding ciphertext is not a hypothetical scenario. For any public key based encryption scheme, it is necessary to provide security against known-plaintext attack, as anybody having a public key can generate plaintext-ciphertext pair. As the proposed protocol uses a public-key based EC-ElGamal as underlying encryption algorithm, it remains secure against known-plaintext attack.

5.3   Malleability

Any homomorphic cryptosystem is malleable by design. They allow the encrypted data processing without having the secret information. As we are using additively homomorphic EC-ElGamal, it performs the ciphertext addition without the need for a decryption key. Hence, any unauthorized aggregation of ciphertext must be prevented to ensure the correctness of aggregated ciphertext. The proposed protocol protects against such malleablity by using dual authentication mechanism. The homomorphic property of a MAC verifies the validity of aggregated ciphertext at the base station. In addition, encryption of a MAC using a pairwise key ensures that no outsider adversary can use the base station's key to generate a MAC corresponding to the forged ciphertext. In addition, each parent node at a distance of m hops can verify the aggregated ciphertext, forwarded by its child nodes, using the MACs generated by its child node at a distance of m hop. Hence, the dual authentication mechanism used in the proposed protocol ensures that no active insider adversary or outsider adversary can successfully manipulate the ciphertext without compromising m consecutive nodes.

6 Overhead Analysis

Elliptic curve cryptosystems achieve the same level of security as public key based cryptosystems using smaller parameter sizes. However, there exist some practical difficulties to use elliptic curve based cryptosystems like EC-ElGamal. (1) There is no efficient way to map plaintext values to elliptic curve points. In addition, the mapping function needs to be deterministic such that it can uniquely associate each plaintext value to an elliptic curve point, and vice versa. Moreover, the mapping function needs to be homomorphic such that aggregated plaintext values can be uniquely mapped to the corresponding elliptic curve points representing aggregated ciphertext. (2) The original ElGamal cryptosystem has 2-to-1 message expansion ratio. However, the EC-ElGamal cryptosystem has 4-to-1 message expansion ratio. The reason behind this is due to the fact that each elliptic curve point is represented by two co-ordinate values. Such increased overhead can be efficiently reduced by point compression techniques as mentioned in [12]. By using a point compression technique [12], we can efficiently compute a value of y-coordinate from an x-coordinate value and an additional sign bit. To compute the overhead analysis, we consider an elliptic curve E over $\mathbb{F}_{163}$, as recommended by the NIST standards.

Communication Cost: As EC-ElGamal generates two ciphertexts and each ciphertext is represented by a curve point having two coordinates, the message expansion of EC-ElGamal becomes 4-to-1. However, the elliptic curve cryptography requires only 160-bit parameter size to achieve the same security level as provided by 1024-bit RSA. Hence, although having the message expansion ratio of 4-to-1, the ciphertexts of EC-ElGamal require fewer bits compared to the ciphertext(s) of public key based cryptosystems. In addition, ciphertext size of EC-ElGamal can also be reduced through the point compression techniques mentioned in [12] which require a single bit instead of a y-coordinate value. In the proposed protocol, we consider $E(\mathbb{F}_{163})$. Hence, the number of bits required by both ciphertexts is, $2 * 163 + 2 = 328$. As the proposed protocol aggregates the ciphertexts at each intermediate node, the total number of bits required to be transmitted, remains constant.

In addition, each sensor node forwards m number of MACs to its parent node. The choice of m depends on the level of security required by an application. If $m = 1$, the proposed protocol transmits the same number of bits as in [21]. If we assume, k-ary tree like topology, each intermediate node transmits $m * k$ MACs. TinySec [13], the first security architecture for wireless sensor networks uses a 4-byte MAC to provide the sufficient security. As the proposed protocol encrypts each MAC with the pairwise (symmetric) key shared with its parent nodes, we can reduce the MAC size without affecting its security strength. As shown in Fig. 1, each intermediate node has to transmit 4 MACs. However, as we are transmitting the encrypted MAC, we can reduce its size to compensate the cost increased due to multiple MACs without affecting its security.

Although we have considered only communication cost, computation also consumes the sensor node's limited resources. However, the energy consumption for CPU processing is negligible compared to RF operations. As shown in [11], transmitting a single bit requires the same amount of energy as computing 1000 CPU instructions. Hence, we neglect the computation cost which is negligible compared to communication cost.

7   Conclusion

Data aggregation changes the data en route and hence protecting the privacy and integrity in end-to-end secure data aggregation become a formidable challenge. Although privacy homomorphism protects the data from passive adversaries, it makes them more vulnerable to active adversaries. In this paper, we present a solution to protect the network from passive and active adversaries, as well as insider and outsider adversaries. The proposed solution ensures the privacy and message authentication while allowing en route data aggregation. In addition, we use symmetric key based message authentication that further reduces the communication/computation overhead compared to asymmetric key based solutions. The proposed protocol authenticates the data at intermediate nodes as well as at the base station. Hence, it restricts the pollution attacks and denial of service attacks caused by maliciously aggregated packets. Future work should focus on restricting the communication cost incurred by different security attributes. In addition, exploring the symmetric key based solutions having resilience toward node capture attacks would be an interesting research problem.

Acknowledgments. This research was a part of a project "A Secure Data Aggregation System and An Intrusion Detection System for Wireless Sensor Networks". It was supported by the Department of Electronics and Information Technology, Ministry of Communications and Information Technology, Government of India.

References

1. Adler, J., Dai, W., Green, R., Neff, C.: Computational details of the votehere homomorphic election system. In: VoteHere. Inc. (2000)
2. Agrawal, S., Boneh, D.: Homomorphic MACs: MAC-Based Integrity for Network Coding. In: Abdalla, M., Pointcheval, D., Fouque, P.-A., Vergnaud, D. (eds.) ACNS 2009. LNCS, vol. 5536, pp. 292–305. Springer, Heidelberg (2009)
3. Akyildiz, I.F., Su, W., Sankarasubramaniam, Y., Cayirci, E.: Wireless sensor networks: a survey. Comput. Netw.: Int. J. Comput. Telecommun. Netw. **38**, 393–422 (2002)

4. Apavatjrut, A., Znaidi, W., Fraboulet, A., Goursaud, C., Lauradoux, C., Minier, M.: Energy friendly integrity for network coding in wireless sensor networks. In: Proceedings of the 2010 Fourth International Conference on Network and System Security. pp. 223–230. NSS '10, IEEE Computer Society, Washington, DC, USA (2010)
5. Castelluccia, C., Chan, A.C.F., Mykletun, E., Tsudik, G.: Efficient and provably secure aggregation of encrypted data in wireless sensor networks. ACM Trans. Sens. Netw. (TOSN) 5(3), 20:1–20:36 (2009)
6. Chan, A.C.F., Castelluccia, C.: On the (im)possibility of aggregate message authentication codes. In: ISIT. pp. 235–239. IEEE (2008)
7. Domingo-Ferrer, J.: A provably secure additive and multiplicative privacy homomorphism. In: Chan, A.H., Gligor, V.D. (eds.) ISC 2002. LNCS, vol. 2433, pp. 471–483. Springer, Heidelberg (2002)
8. Fasolo, E., Rossi, M., Widmer, J., Zorzi, M.: In-network aggregation techniques for wireless sensor networks: a survey. Wireless. Commun. IEEE 14, 70–87 (2007)
9. Girao, J., Westhoff, D., Schneider, M.: CDA: concealed data aggregation for reverse multicast traffic in wireless sensor networks. In: 40th International Conference on Communications, IEEE ICC 2005 pp. 3044–3049 (May 2005)
10. Gura, N., Patel, A., Wander, A., Eberle, H., Shantz, S.C.: Comparing Elliptic Curve Cryptography and RSA on 8-bit CPUs. In: Joye, M., Quisquater, J.-J. (eds.) CHES 2004. LNCS, vol. 3156, pp. 119–132. Springer, Heidelberg (2004)
11. Hill, J., Szewczyk, R., Woo, A., Hollar, S., Culler, D., Pister, K.: System architecture directions for networked sensors. ACM. SIGPLAN. Not. 35(11), 93–104 (2000)
12. Hoffstein, J., Pipher, J., Silverman, J.: An Introduction to Mathematical Cryptography, 1st edn., New York, Incorporated (2008)
13. Karlof, C., Sastry, N., Wagner, D.: Tinysec: A link layer security architecture for wireless sensor networks. In: Proceedings of the 2Nd International Conference on Embedded Networked Sensor Systems pp. 162–175. SenSys '04, ACM, New York, (2004)
14. Koblitz, N.: Elliptic curve cryptosystems. Math. Comput. 48(177), 203–209 (1987)
15. Malan, D.J., Welsh, M., Smith, M.D.: A public-key infrastructure for key distribution in tinyos based on elliptic curve cryptography. In: First IEEE International Conference on Sensor and Ad Hoc Communications and Network (IEEE SECON 2004), pp. 71–80 (Oct 2004)
16. Mykletun, E., Girao, J., Westhoff, D.: Public key based cryptoschemes for data concealment in wireless sensor networks. In: IEEE International Conference on Communications. ICC-2006, Istanbul, Turkey (June 2006)
17. Okamoto, T., Uchiyama, S.: A New Public-Key Cryptosystem as Secure as Factoring. In: Nyberg, K. (ed.) EUROCRYPT 1998. LNCS, vol. 1403, pp. 308–318. Springer, Heidelberg (1998)
18. Rivest, R., Adleman, L., Dertouzos, M.: On data banks and privacy homomorphisms. In: Foundations of Secure Computation, pp. 169–177 (1978)

19. Ugus, O.: Asymmetric Homomorphic Encryption Transformation for Securing Distributed Data Storage in Wireless Sensor Networks (in cooperation with NEC Heidelberg). Master's thesis, Technische Universität Darmstadt (2007)
20. Westhoff, D., Girao, J., Acharya, M.: Concealed data aggregation for reverse multicast traffic in sensor networks: encryption, key distribution, and routing adaptation. IEEE. Trans. Mob. Comput. **5**(10), 1417–1431 (2006)
21. Westhoff, D., Ugus, O.: Malleability resilient (premium) concealed data aggregation. In: Proceedings of the 4th IEEE International Workshop on Data Security and Privacy in Wireless Networks (D-SPAN'13). IEEE Press, Madrid Spain (2013)

Aligned Beacon Transmissions to Increase IEEE 802.11s Light Sleep Mode Scalability

Marco Porsch and Thomas Bauschert[✉]

Technische Universität Chemnitz, Reichenhainer Str. 70,
09126 Chemnitz, Germany
{marco.porsch, thomas.bauschert}@etit.tu-chemnitz.de

Abstract. In wireless mesh networks battery-powered devices rely on a sophisticated power save scheme to provide enduring network connectivity. Therefore, IEEE 802.11s defines different power save modes to reduce the energy consumption of Wi-Fi mesh nodes. The most common of these modes, light sleep mode, aims at conserving energy while maintaining mesh link performance. To achieve this, it relies on periodic receipts of corresponding peer nodes' beacons. This approach makes it unsuitable for dense topologies where an increasing number of peer links leads to frequent wakeups and higher energy consumption. To overcome this issue we introduce a novel synchronization algorithm to minimize the overhead of scheduled beacon receipts. We evaluate the effectiveness of the algorithm using testbed measurements and a state model-based approach, in which we compare its performance with respect to energy efficiency with that of the standard's synchronization algorithm.

Keywords: Wireless mesh networks · IEEE 802.11s · Power save · Synchronization · Green networking · Energy efficiency

1 Introduction

Wireless mesh networks are well-known in industry and academia but have not yet made their breakthrough in consumer electronics. Actually, wireless mesh networking would be a promising addition to today's Wi-Fi devices as it provides increased flexibility and robustness. For example in a smart home there is no need for additional access points to increase the network coverage if e.g. the Wi-Fi-equipped TV serves as a mesh access point to other mesh and legacy devices. Another example are smartphone users who exchange multimedia content in a Wi-Fi hotspot; in case the hotspot and phones are mesh-enabled, the users may freely roam out of the access point coverage without losing their connection. In its 2012 revision the IEEE 802.11 standard includes the former 802.11s amendments. Note that 802.11s mesh uses regular Wi-Fi hardware as commonly found in almost any of today's smart consumer electronics. Of course, for use on battery-driven user devices there are high requirements concerning energy efficiency. Therefore, 802.11s introduces different power modes which, in the meshed environment, are set per neighbor link. Light sleep power mode promises high energy savings on sporadically used links while still maintaining proper connectivity with the corresponding neighbors. As we have shown in [4], light sleep mode scales

© Springer International Publishing Switzerland 2014
Y. Kermarrec (Ed.): EUNICE 2014, LNCS 8846, pp. 173–184, 2014.
DOI: 10.1007/978-3-319-13488-8_16

poorly with the number of peer nodes since the energy consumption can even increase linearly in the worst-case scenario. Therefore, this paper proposes an 802.11 standard-compliant synchronization algorithm that reduces the effects of an increasing number of light sleep peers on a node's energy consumption. We focus on the case of an idle network with almost no user data being sent or received. For typical user devices this case is relevant as, for example, a smartphone rests in standby state most of the time and just periodically checks for incoming mails. Similarly, a laptop or tablet does not send or receive data while the user is reading a web page. Conserving energy in these situations is most crucial for proper battery runtime.

This paper refers to the rules and definitions of the IEEE 802.11 standard for wireless LAN in its 2012 revision [1]. Previously, in [2] we focused on the effects of power save on user data forwarding on a 802.11s mesh link. Similar research has been conducted by Alam et al. in [3] using ns-2 simulations. In [4] we used testbed measurements to quantify the scalability properties of 802.11s light sleep mode. The authors of [5] highlight the importance of information disseminated in 802.11s beacon frames and why legacy beaconing, as in ad hoc networks, is not suitable here. For synchronization numerous algorithms have been proposed in the literature for mobile ad hoc networks and wireless mesh networks. For example, in [6] Tyrrell et al. derive an algorithm inspired from nature where fireflies synchronize their flashing.

Key contributions of this paper are testbed measurements and modelling of IEEE 802.11s power save mode with respect to an increasing number of peers and the proposal of a standard-compliant synchronization algorithm for improved scalability. The paper is structured as follows: Sect. 2 gives an introduction to IEEE 802.11s synchronization and power save mode. Section 3 explains our novel beacon alignment synchronization algorithm before we assess its performance in Sect. 4, where we use results from our mesh testbed to create a model to prove the algorithm's performance. Section 5 concludes and summarizes the paper.

2 IEEE 802.11s Synchronization and Power Save

All 802.11 family protocols have a common approach to power save: for saving energy the radio is suspended in times of no activity. With the complex receiver baseband processing disabled, the device power consumption is reduced drastically. This makes it more useful than sole transmission power control as it especially allows idle nodes to conserve energy. Also, without any receiver interrupts, the CPU may spend more time in low power sleep states. The radio will be reactivated for frame transmission or for a scheduled receipt, e.g. of a neighbor beacon.

To reliably schedule doze and wakeups in any of the 802.11 family power save schemes, a tight synchronization is required. The time reference is maintained by a local TSF (timing synchronization function) and by sending out beacon frames with a fixed beacon interval. The TSF timer is a 64 bit counter incrementing in one microsecond intervals. It determines the TBTT (target beacon transmission time) when the counter value is a multiple of the beacon interval. At each TBTT the node schedules the beacon transmission and subsequently transmits according to the general CSMA/CA channel access rules. A beacon frame contains a timestamp of the transmitter's TSF at

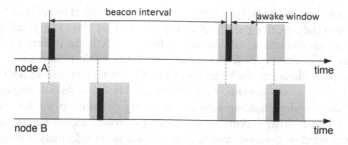

Fig. 1. Doze/wakeup scheduling of two peers in light sleep mode towards each other

the time of transmission. It should be mentioned that, although the beacon frames are transmitted using CSMA/CA, the transmitter sets the TSF timestamp just once the transmission actually begins. Thus, the channel access delay does not influence the accuracy of the synchronization algorithms. Apart from these similarities, the synchronization and beaconing algorithm of IEEE 802.11s mesh networks differs from that of IEEE 802.11 managed mode or ad hoc networks. First of all, in mesh mode each node has to send its own beacon. This is necessary, since in mesh mode the beacon frame carries many information elements with time-critical content that makes the mesh beacon highly dynamic compared to that of ad hoc mode [7]. In mesh mode the algorithm used in synchronization is not strictly defined. To adapt to the different use cases of wireless mesh networks, IEEE 802.11s defines an extensible synchronization framework that allows implementing application-specific synchronization algorithms. 802.11s networks announce the use of such algorithm in beacon and probe response frames and only nodes supporting this method may join the MBSS (mesh basic service set). As a common fallback IEEE 802.11s defines a default synchronization method in [1] Sect. 13.13.2.2, called neighbor offset synchronization. This method does not shift the TBTT to a common time; instead, it focuses on keeping the arbitrary offsets between the TSF and TBTT of neighboring nodes constant. Upon receipt of a beacon or probe response frame nodes will evaluate the contained peer's TSF at transmission time T_t and their own TSF at the time of receipt T_r to calculate the TSF offset to the respective peer. By periodically monitoring these values, nodes can determine the maximum clock drift within the MBSS. Subsequently, all peers adjust their own TSF increments to the slowest clock to mitigate further clock drift. IEEE 802.11s defines that this adjustment may only be performed with a maximum speed of 0.04 % of the beacon interval per beacon period to avoid that power-saving nodes lose sync with the nodes shifting their TBTT.

With the time references synchronized, a doze/wakeup schedule can be set up according to the TBTTs of the neighbors towards which a node is in light sleep mode. Again, the IEEE 802.11s schemes differ from those of legacy Wi-Fi, as there are multiple wakeup events determined by multiple peer TBTTs and the own beacon transmission. Furthermore, in IEEE 802.11s the power mode is set for each peer link individually for each direction by the respective party. Furthermore, this power mode is not just a binary value representing power save on or off; instead, three power modes are defined: active, light sleep and deep sleep mode. A link in active mode may receive packets anytime and therefore the radio cannot be suspended at all. A peer link in light sleep mode will only receive packets at certain times. This allows suspending the radio while there are no receipts scheduled on any link. A link in deep sleep mode behaves similarly but the amount of wakeups—and also the possible performance—is further reduced. Figure 1 illustrates the behavior of links in light sleep mode; here both peers are in light sleep mode towards each other. In this example no further links are established and the doze/wakeup schedule is solely determined by the own and the single peer's TBTT. After waking up to transmit its own beacon, a node stays awake for the awake window duration, which is advertised in an information element within the beacon. During this time interval it can receive frames from other peers. After the awake window passed, the node resumes its doze. Mesh nodes wake up just before the TBTT of their light sleep peers to receive their beacon frames and resume doze afterwards. This process is repeated periodically with the beacon interval. With a link in deep sleep mode on the other hand, a node will not wake up for the TBTT of the respective peer. This increases delay on that link further and requires special routines to maintain synchronization and for the forwarding of broadcast frames which are, for example, required for path discovery. As the standard leaves many parts of the behavior in deep sleep mode undefined and as the performance on these links might be severely degraded, we will focus solely on light sleep mode in the remainder of this paper.

3 Beacon Alignment Synchronization Algorithm

An issue of the IEEE 802.11s power save algorithm is its scalability concerning the number of peers; with more peers more wakeups are necessary when links are in light sleep mode [4]. Theoretically, this should not be a big issue, as the time needed to receive a mesh beacon frame is typically very low compared to the beacon interval. But besides the actual receive time there are additional delays due to the CSMA/CA channel access mechanism and the time for powering up the receiver's radio, processing the beacon and resuming doze. To minimize these wakeup overheads we propose an algorithm subsequently called *beacon alignment synchronization*. Via this synchronization algorithm we align the TBTT of all MBSS members in a narrow time range to benefit from overlapping awake phases, hence keeping the number of wakeups per beacon interval minimal. In the case that all MBSS members are in direct range of one another and use a common beacon interval, subsequently only a single wakeup is required for all light sleep peers. Our synchronization algorithm fits into the extensible synchronization framework that IEEE 802.11s provides as explained in Sect. 2. Thus, it is fully standard-compliant.

The algorithm consists of three steps; the first step is to determine the TBTT offsets between all peers. With this information then the "steady node" can be determined, which will furthermore not shift its TBTT. In the third step all but the steady node will gradually shift their TBTTs until they are aligned with their peers. The algorithm's behavior is illustrated for an example MBSS in Fig. 2. Here in the upper part the TBTT timing of the MBSS is given before the beacon alignment algorithm starts, while the lower part shows the situation after the alignment procedure is finished. The beacon

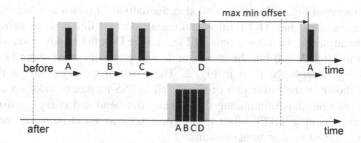

Fig. 2. Behavior of beacon alignment synchronization for common beacon interval values

transmissions at TBTT are indicated in black while the awake phases are marked in grey. In the following we will look at the individual steps in more detail.

The first step for each node is to calculate the TBTT offsets among all peers. To determine these, only two values are required, which can both be determined on receipt of a beacon or probe response frame. This makes the approach equally applicable to active or passive scanning before joining the MBSS. The first value is the beacon interval T_{BI} of the neighbor in microsecond units calculated from the corresponding frame field. The second value is the TSF offset T_{offset} of the local node towards the peer node in microsecond units as described in the IEEE standard [1] for neighbor offset synchronization: T_{offset} is calculated from the TSF timestamp set by the transmitter T_t and the TSF timestamp T_r set by the receiver. The T_{offset} determined by a node A towards a node B, $T_{offset,AB} = T_{t,B} - T_{r,A}$, represents the absolute TSF difference between the two nodes and allows to determine the peer's TSF from the local TSF. Based on T_{BI} and T_{offset}, node A is able to determine the TBTT offset towards node B as follows:

$$T_{TBTToffset,AB} = T_{offset,AB} \bmod \min(T_{BI,A}, T_{BI,B})$$

As we look for offsets towards later TBTT, which generally correspond to negative values, it is sometimes necessary to get the complementary offset value to the next later TBTT:

$$T^*_{TBTToffset,AB} = T_{TBTToffset,AB} - \min(T_{BI,A}, T_{BI,B})$$

To determine the TBTT offset between two peers B and C, node A applies the following equation:

$$T_{TBTToffset,BC} = (T_{offset,AC} - T_{offset,AB}) \bmod \min(T_{BI,B}, T_{BI,C})$$

In the previous step we calculated all peer's TBTT offsets towards all other peers. Out of these only the offsets between TBTTs that directly follow one another are of interest, e.g. in the example of Fig. 2 $T_{TBTToffset,AB}$ and $T_{TBTToffset,BC}$. These are the per-peer minimum TBTT offsets. Notice that offsets to TBTT later than the own are negative values. Hence, when comparing offsets we speak in absolute terms. With this information gathered, the node is aware of its peer's TBTT timing as depicted in the upper illustration of Fig. 2. In the second step the individual nodes determine the node with the largest minimum TBTT offset among all peers – this node is subsequently called the steady node. In the example of Fig. 2 node D is the steady node, due to its large offset towards A. All but the steady node will gradually delay their TBTT, thus slowly shifting towards the right in Fig. 2. The result of the algorithm in the given example is shown in the lower part of Fig. 2: all MBSS members wake up only once per beacon interval, thus minimizing the wakeup overhead and energy consumption. A minimum remaining TBTT offset is pre-configured to avoid increased contention between the aligned beacon transmissions.

The key criterion for our algorithm is to minimize the time until all peer TBTTs are aligned. Our algorithm avoids moving the longest TBTT offset while all other node's TBTT move concurrently. Thus the time until all beacons are aligned is minimal. For neighbor offset synchronization, IEEE 802.11 mandates shifting TBTT with a maximum of 0.04 % of the beacon interval per beacon period. For our algorithm the maximum time to termination would be experienced in the case of an infinite number of peers with common beacon interval and TBTTs distributed evenly. In this case the maximum distance shifted would be one full beacon interval. In this worst case scenario the beacon alignment synchronization would require 2500 beacon periods until termination which translates to 512 s for a beacon interval of 200TU (time units of 1024 μs). This may not be suitable for a short-lived mesh network of mobile nodes. To avoid this issue, our algorithm might as well be implemented as part of the mesh joining procedure. In this case all required input values are acquired through active or passive scanning before the node starts beaconing itself. Based on this information the node may then choose a suitable TBTT. The algorithm performs similar in an MBSS of peers with different beacon interval values. IEEE 802.11 mandates that the beacon intervals of MBSS members do not have to be equal, but only values to the power of two are allowed. In this case the rules formulated in this section form multiple wakeup groups depending on the minimum beacon interval. To cope with clock drift among peer nodes, the schemes from neighbor offset synchronization may be used once the alignment procedure is finished. Node movement or limited visibility may result in beacon losses and a differing determination of the steady node. Under most circumstances this will not cause further issues except for creating multiple wakeup groups. Under rare circumstances a circular dependency may lead to ever-following TBTT shifts. For this to happen, a quasi-circular topology is required in which the initial TBTT distribution of the neighboring peers follows one another. This issue may be avoided by implementing a timeout, where the node stops shifting its TBTT after the expected maximum algorithm runtime of 2500 beacon periods.

4   Algorithm Evaluation

In this section we evaluate the new synchronization algorithm described in Sect. 3. First, we present testbed measurements to qualitatively visualize the algorithm and to obtain real-life parameters. Second, we feed the measured values into models of the power save algorithms to quantitatively evaluate and compare their performance.

4.1 Testbed Implementation

In order to evaluate the synchronization and power saving algorithms of IEEE 802.11s and to obtain parameters from real-life Wi-Fi mesh equipment, we set up a testbed. We implemented the necessary routines in the Linux kernel's Wi-Fi stack [8] in cooperation with the original authors of the open Wi-Fi mesh implementation, *cozybit Inc.* [9]. Most of the code is made open source and included in current Linux distributions. On hardware, which employs a soft-MAC architecture where most MAC layer management functions are performed in software, the full range of the 802.11s power saving and synchronization schemes is available. Furthermore, we implemented the beacon alignment algorithm using the extensible synchronization framework, which allows us to switch between our algorithm and the standard's neighbor offset synchronization. As embedded mobile mesh devices, e.g. smartphones, are not yet available, we used off-the-shelf *Netgear WNDR3800* Wi-Fi routers that provide a suitable soft-MAC protocol stack. In our setup we measured the overall device current consumption that also includes power sinks that are not Wi-Fi related, like CPU or Ethernet controller. The measurements were processed using a Tektronix TLS-216 digital oscilloscope and logic analyzer. The oscilloscope plots were taken with a sampling rate of 1 kS/s and a scale of 50 mV/div vertical and 200 ms/div horizontal. To reduce transients and noise effects an averaging factor of 10 was used.

Figure 3 shows a measurement plot taken in a setup with seven close-by peer nodes where the beacon alignment synchronization is enabled and has just started. The highest spike in current consumption marks the device's beacon frame transmission followed by the awake window period configured to 100TU. The smaller consumption peaks are the wakeups for the peer TBTTs. The vertical bars serve as a reference to the beacon interval of 1000TU. The area under the graph between the drawn reference bars corresponds to the current consumption per beacon interval. Given that the network is idle, this curve repeats periodically for each beacon interval. The mesh router of Fig. 3 has seven established peer links and all peer nodes use an equal beacon interval of 1000TU. As all nodes are direct peers of each other they can equally determine the steady node. In the situation of Fig. 3 the steady node is the node whose TBTT is marked by the vertical reference bars. All other nodes start shifting their TBTT towards the right. The node with the highest to-shift distance is the node on the right side of the gap; it has approximately 60 % of the beacon interval to shift. Thus, in the situation of Fig. 3 the algorithm will take about 1500 s until it terminates with all beacons aligned.

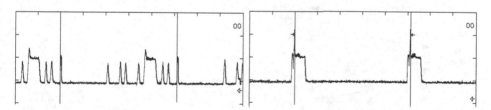

Fig. 3. Beacon alignment synchronization of seven peers with common beacon interval ongoing (50 mV/div vert., 200 ms/div hori.)

Fig. 4. Beacon alignment synchronization of seven peers with common beacon interval terminated (50 mV/div vert., 200 ms/div hori.)

Because of the gradual movement of all but the steady node's TBTT and the applied averaging, the current consumption peaks are slightly deformed to a triangular shape. Figure 4 shows the outcome of the situation of Fig. 3 after the synchronization algorithm has terminated. As all nodes use a common beacon interval, one single wakeup group is formed. The final current consumption depends on the position within the group of aligned TBTTs. This position determines whether the own awake window overlaps with the wakeups for peer TBTTs. In Fig. 4 the electrical current consumption per beacon interval is 354,69 mAs, while it had been 356.99 mAs in the situation of Fig. 3. Instead of the actual seven peers of this MBSS, this corresponds to the consumption in a scenario with only three peers. So the overall wakeup duration and energy consumption is successfully reduced by the proposed beacon alignment synchronization algorithm.

4.2   Model-Based Evaluation

In this section we evaluate our beacon alignment algorithm using a model-based approach. Therefore, we use a state model consisting of the states seen in Fig. 5: doze state, awake window and peer wakeup. The doze state corresponds to the state when both the receiver and transmitter hardware are powered down and the power consumption is minimal. The awake window state refers to the awake duration after the beacon transmission and the corresponding wakeup overhead. The peer wakeup state corresponds to the awake duration including overhead required for waking up to receive peer beacons in light sleep mode. Figure 5 illustrates the general case for IEEE 802.11s light sleep mode. Depending on the placement of the own TBTT and peer's beacon transmissions the state transitions occur. p_i corresponds to the time share of the sojourn time in the respective state i. As we assume the system to be modelled comprehensively within these three states, the sum of their time shares is one:

$$p_0 + p_1 + p_2 = 1$$

For this general case it is non-trivial to determine the time shares of the individual states. Hence, we chose to evaluate only the following three case scenarios: the worst case scenario of unaligned TBTTs without any overlap, the best and the worst case

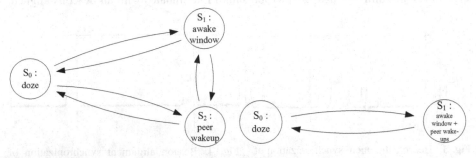

Fig. 5. General State model of mesh light sleep mode without traffic

Fig. 6. State model for the best case outcome after beacon alignment

after beacon alignment. We will subsequently use the parameters given in Table 1. The parameters for beacon interval and awake window are the ones recommended for moderate power save in [1] Annex W.3.4, while the measured values have been obtained from our lab setup of Sect. 4.1. The parameter T_{RO} describes the minimum offset that is preserved between aligned TBTTs to avoid contention between the beacon transmissions. The value has been configured according to the value given as the average beacon frame delay in [10]. We furthermore assume that all peers are configured equally and have common characteristics. Using these models and parameters we will derive performance bounds to compare the performance of our beacon alignment algorithm to that of the standard's neighbor offset synchronization.

Table 1. Model parameters

Model parameter	Value
Configured beacon interval T_{BI}	200TU
Configured awake window T_{AW}	10TU
Measured awake window duration T_{AWO}	16.24 ms
Measured peer wakeup duration T_P	12.12 ms
Configured residual TBTT offset T_{RO}	4.9 ms

Model for unaligned TBTTs, worst case. This model case refers to the situation that, due to the arbitrary TBTT placement, there are no overlapping awake phases for the current node, i.e. a peer wakeup never happens during an awake window or during another peer wakeup. For the model depicted in Fig. 5 this means that there are no state transitions between S_1 and S_2. Depending on the parameters and the number of peers N we can immediately determine the time shares of the awake window state, p_1, and peer wakeup state, p_2:

$$p_1 = \frac{T_{AWO}}{T_{BI}}$$

$$p_2(N) = \frac{N \cdot T_P}{T_{BI}}$$

The model can easily be solved to determine the time share of the doze state:

$$p_0(N) = 1 - \frac{T_{AWO} + N \cdot T_P}{T_{BI}}$$

Model for aligned TBTTs, worst case. This model case refers to the situation that the TBTTs have been aligned by our beacon alignment synchronization algorithm and we are looking at the current consumption of the steady node, i.e. the node at the end of the wakeup group. As this node has its awake window trailing the peer wakeups, it has the highest energy consumption of the group. For the model depicted in Fig. 5 this means that there is a strict order of events from S_0 to S_2 to S_1 and to S_0 again, while the transitions S_0 to S_1, S_1 to S_2 and S_2 to S_0 do not occur here. The state time shares of this model are given below. For ease of notation we use a variable time T_{PA}, which is the duration of the aligned peer wakeup. In case of a single peer, the aligned wakeup duration T_{PA} is equal to T_P, while all further aligned peers extend its duration by T_{RO}.

$$p_1 = \frac{T_{AWO}}{T_{BI}}$$

$$p_2(N) = \frac{T_{PA}}{T_{BI}}$$

$$T_{PA}(N) = \begin{cases} 0 & , \text{ for } N \le 0 \\ T_P + (N-1) \cdot T_{RO}, & \text{ for } N > 0 \end{cases}$$

The model can be solved to determine the time share of the doze state:

$$p_0(N) = 1 - \frac{T_{AWO} + T_{PA}}{T_{BI}}$$

Model for aligned TBTTs, best case. For the case that the TBTTs have been aligned and we are looking at the current consumption of first node of the group we use a different model from the one used before. This is necessary, as the aligned peer wakeup state may be omitted in case it is completely enclosed by the awake window. The corresponding model is illustrated in Fig. 6. Again, the state time shares sum up to one:

$$p_0 + p_1 = 1$$

In this model the number of peers influences whether the peer wakeups fit into the own awake window or if the wakeup period is extended due to the trailing peer wakeups. The time share of the awake state in this model is as follows:

$$p_1(N) = \frac{\max(T_{AWO}, T_{PA})}{T_{BI}}$$

The model can be solved to determine the time share of the doze state p_0:

$$p_0(N) = 1 - \frac{\max(T_{AWO}, T_{PA})}{T_{BI}}$$

Model comparison. With the doze state time share determined for the three different model cases, we can now compare the performance of the beacon alignment algorithm with the standard's neighbor offset synchronization. Figure 7 shows the doze state time share of the different models. It can be seen that the unaligned TBTTs of neighbor offset synchronization have the lowest doze state time share of the three models. The graph shows only the worst case with a linear decline of doze state time share. Since in neighbor offset synchronization the TBTT placement is completely arbitrary, there actually is a high spread of possible outcomes; with a small probability this scheme

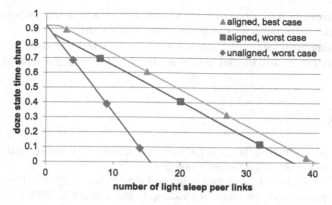

Fig. 7. Doze state time share of the different models

may perform equally well to the upper bound of beacon alignment. The worst and best case results for beacon alignment on the other hand show a higher doze state time share. Also they display a much smaller spread due to the implied ordering process of the algorithm. The best case graph starts with a constant doze state time share until the duration of aligned peer wakeups exceeds the modelled node's awake window. The graph for the worst case results of beacon alignment exhibits an initial strong decline in doze state time share for the first peer, while the slope is smaller for any further node. The performance bounds of beacon alignment may be further improved by reducing the remaining TBTT offset T_{RO}. But this in turn may increase the contention between peer's beacon and poll frame transmissions. Still, the doze state time share drops linearly with increasing number of peers. This issue can only be avoided completely by using deep sleep mode, where nodes will not wake up for peer's TBTTs anymore. This in turn reduces network performance and requires special treatment, e.g. for broadcast forwarding.

5   Conclusion

In this paper we propose a standard-compliant synchronization scheme to overcome the scalability issues of IEEE 802.11s light sleep mode. Our algorithm aligns all peer TBTTs in a narrow time range, which allows nodes in power save mode to wake up for minimum time to receive all peer beacons. Thus, we minimize the energy consumption overhead of waking up the radio for each peer individually. To evaluate our proposed algorithm we use both testbed measurements and a model-based approach. Using the testbed we provide a proof of concept and extract real-life parameters of the 802.11s power save algorithm on off-the-shelf hardware. In the models of the power save algorithms we use these parameters to get an estimation of their efficiency with respect to increasing number of peer nodes in dense scenarios. We compare the performance of our new synchronization algorithm to that of the one standardized by IEEE 802.11 with respect to its effect on the ratio of doze and awake state, which directly translates to energy consumption. The results show that, although a constant doze/awake ratio with increasing number of light sleep peer links cannot be achieved, the proposed algorithm successfully increases the power save algorithm's scalability.

In our future work we will address open issues of links in deep sleep state and design heuristics to control the link power modes depending on the network conditions.

References

1. IEEE Std. 802.11™-2012: Wireless LAN medium access control (MAC) and physical layer (PHY) specifications. IEEE Computer Society (2012)
2. Porsch, M., Bauschert, T.: A testbed analysis of the effects of IEEE 802.11s power save on mesh link performance. In: Szabó, R., Vidács, A. (eds.) EUNICE 2012. LNCS, vol. 7479, pp. 1–11. Springer, Heidelberg (2012)
3. Alam, M.N., Jäntti, R., Kneckt, J., Nieminen, J.: Performance study of IEEE 802.11s PSM in FTP-TCP. In: Vehicular Technology Conference (VTC Fall), IEEE, pp. 1–5 (2012)
4. Porsch, M., Bauschert, T.: A testbed evaluation of the scalability of IEEE 802.11s light sleep mode. In: Bauschert, T. (ed.) EUNICE 2013. LNCS, vol. 8115, pp. 292–297. Springer, Heidelberg (2013)
5. Vishnevsky, V., Lyakhov, A., Safonov, A.: New aspect of beaconing in IEEE 802.11s mesh networks. In: 12th IEEE Symposium on Computers and Communications 2007, ISCC 2007, pp. 263–268 (2007)
6. Tyrrell, A., Auer, G., Bettstetter, C.: Synchronization inspired from nature for wireless meshed networks. In: International Conference on Wireless Communications, Networking and Mobile Computing, WiCOM 2006, pp. 1–4 (2006)
7. Safonov, A., Lyakhov, A., Sharov, S.: Synchronization and beaconing in IEEE 802.11s mesh networks. In: International Conference on Telecommunications 2008, ICT 2008, pp. 1–6, 16–19 June 2008
8. Official Linux Kernel: mac80211 kernel module source code. http://git.kernel.org/cgit/linux/kernel/git/torvalds/linux.git/tree/net/mac80211
9. Cozybit Inc. www.cozybit.com
10. Mangold, S., Choi, S., May, P., Klein, O., Hiertz, G., Stibor, L.: IEEE 802.11e wireless LAN for quality of service. In: European Wireless, pp. 32–39 (2002)

Evaluation of ARED, CoDel and PIE

Jens Schwardmann, David Wagner[✉], and Mirja Kühlewind

Institute of Communication Networks and Computer Engineering (IKR),
University of Stuttgart, Stuttgart, Germany
david.wagner@ikr.uni-stuttgart.de

Abstract. In this paper we compare the three Active Queue Management (AQMs) Adaptive Random Early Detection (ARED), Controlled Delay (CoDel) and Proportional Integral controller Enhanced (PIE) in static as well as dynamic scenarios. We find significant issues when these algorithms are used for big Round Trip Times (RTTs) as well as a significant utilization decrease when used for high bandwidth links. When used for low and medium sized links, CoDel, PIE and ARED are suitable alike, but for corner scenarios clear recommendations can be given.

1 Introduction

In the recent years high delays and jitter were observed [7] in the Internet, originating from oversized network buffers; often referred to as Bufferbloat. Long lasting Transmission Control Protocol (TCP) transmissions fill up these buffers, delaying all traversing packets. Since these are a problem for delay-sensitive applications like VoIP, since 2012 new AQM schemes have been proposed aiming to keep queuing delays below a target delay, e.g. CoDel and PIE. This paper extends the research on performance of these algorithms by simulations using own AQM code of CoDel, PIE and ARED, a well known algorithm, fed by most realistic TCP traffic generated by Linux TCP stacks embedded in the simulation [14].

2 Related Work

Although CoDel and PIE date from 2012 and 2013 respectively, there already exists some research evaluating their performance. In [8] the authors present statistical simulation results targeting the same AQM algorithms only for rather low bandwidths between 400 kbps and 5 Mbps. Moreover, they just use the standard ns-2 TCP model to generate traffic which significantly differs from TCP congestion control used in today's operating systems (e.g. regarding initial window size or proportional rate reduction [11]). In contrast, the authors of [9] use testbed measurements using the Linux kernel implementation of the aforementioned three AQMs. The measurement scenarios also just cover static scenarios while dynamics, such as a newly starting flow, are the real challenge when aiming for small queues. There is another publication to appear [10] which evaluates

Y. Kermarrec (Ed.): EUNICE 2014, LNCS 8846, pp. 185–191, 2014.
DOI: 10.1007/978-3-319-13488-8_17

the overall performance of a system using not only loss-based TCP congestion control (cubic in this case) but also delay-based TCP congestion control (vegas). Nevertheless, this research only considers a bottleneck bandwidth of 1 Mbps and again uses the ns-2 TCP traffic generator.

Evaluation of AQM algorithms is currently discussed in research and also in the AQM working group of the IETF [3]. According to current discussions, the aforementioned evaluations are not exhaustive and we aim to fill some of the remaining gaps. In contrast to existing work, we use own implementations of the AQM algorithms in our simulations combined with real Linux TCP stacks embedded in the simulation [14] for most realistic traffic generation. Moreover, we evaluate not only static scenarios with long lasting TCP flows but also dynamic ones.

3   Active Queue Management Schemes

3.1   Adaptive Random Early Detection (ARED)

The original Random Early Detection (RED) [5] algorithm calculates a drop probability p from the average queue length q_{avg}, calculated as an Exponentially Weighted Moving Average (EWMA). p is zero below a minimum threshold min_th, increases linearly to max_p at a maximum threshold max_th and equals one for $q_{avg} > max\_th$. When using RED, the mentioned parameters have to be set by the operator according to the topology properties, such as the bandwidth of the outgoing link and the expected RTT.

The extension ARED [6] initially sets all parameters automatically based on the bandwidth of the outgoing link and a reference delay value. During operation, ARED periodically adopts max_p depending on the traffic load in order to keep q_{avg} between min_th and max_th. For min_th it uses a minimum value of 5 packets to guarantee a high throughput for small bandwidths. As recommended in [6] our ARED implementation used RED in gentle-mode, where not all packets are dropped when q_{avg} is greater than max_th, but instead p is increased linearly between max_th and $2 * max\_th$. When q_{avg} is greater, all incoming packets are dropped.

3.2   Controlled Delay (CoDel)

In contrast, CoDel [12] monitors the real delay for each packet and, if all packets in a configured $observationInterval$ are delayed more than the target delay, drops single selected packets. When dropping a packet, CoDel calculates the next packet drop taking into account the number of dropped packets since the first drop ($noOfDrops$) according to Eq. 1.

$$nextDropTime \leftarrow lastDropTime + \frac{observationInterval}{\sqrt{noOfDrops}} \qquad (1)$$

CoDel stops dropping when a packet's delay is below the target delay. Since CoDel actually measures the packets' queuing delays, in contrast to ARED and PIE packets are dropped at the head of the queue.

Our implementation is aligned to the Linux Kernel implementation [1].

3.3   Proportional Integral Controller Enhanced (PIE)

PIE [13] in contrast to CoDel does not measure the queue delay but estimates it using the smoothed average of the measured draining rate. PIE uses a drop probability p like ARED but in contrast updates it just every 30 ms. As shown in Eq. 2 this calculation takes into account both the current relation to the target delay as well as the trend since the last update.

$$p \leftarrow p + \alpha * (queueDelay - refDelay) + \beta * (queueDelay - lastQueueDelay) \quad (2)$$

The factors α and β increase with increasing p. Additionally, PIE avoids drops during short bursts during generally low congestion. When the estimated delay has been below half the target for two update intervals, for 100 ms PIE ignores p and enqueues all incoming packets. We decided to align our implementation to the Linux Kernel implementation [2], adopting three minor extensions not mentioned in [13]:

- When there are less than 3000 bytes in the queue, no packets are dropped.
- The drop probability p is not raised by more than 2 % points, except for queueing delays greater than 250 ms, for which it is increased by an additional 2 % points.
- If $queueDelay$ and $lastQueueDelay$ equal zero, p will be decreased nonlinearly by multiplying it by 0.98.

4   Simulative Evaluation

4.1   Simulation Setup and Scenarios

We use IKR SimLib [4] and its Linux Virtual Machine (VM) integration [14] for simulations to generate realistic TCP traffic. We use the Cubic congestion control of Linux kernel version 3.10.9. The modeled topology is depicted in Fig. 1: A greedy TCP cubic sender has always data to send and transmits packets through a bottleneck to a TCP receiver. Bandwidth and delay of this link are fixed during each simulation, but we varied each parameter in a series of simulations. The bottleneck queue is managed by one of the candidate AQMs and the buffer size is twice the Bandwidth-Delay-Product (BDP) but minimum ten packets. Since a first bottleneck shapes the overall bandwidth of all traversing flows to the bottleneck bandwidth, there is no need to examine scenarios with several queues in a row. If not otherwise stated, we use one TCP flow and 25 Mbps links with a delay of 25 ms (50 ms RTT). All simulations ran 1010 s, consisting of ten seconds start up phase ignored in statistics and 1000 s measurements. The target delay was configured to 5 ms in all experiments.

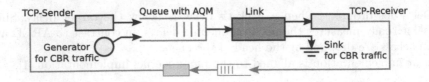

Fig. 1. Simulation scenario

Table 1. Delay d in ms and link utilization u in % in static scenarios

(a) for different bandwidths (in Mbps)

bw	CoDel d	u	PIE d	u	ARED d	u
1	22.24	99.8	16.15	99.7	94.69	100
2	12.07	99.8	7.03	97.8	45.05	100
5	2.87	96.0	5.57	96.7	16.13	99.5
10	2.59	95.9	3.34	95.7	7.01	98.2
35	1.01	93.9	1.56	94.1	1.18	92.6
100	0.90	93.8	1.31	93.7	0.71	86.7
mean	4.95	96.0	4.62	95.7	18.06	94.9

(b) for different RTTs (in ms)

RTT	CoDel d	u	PIE d	u	ARED d	u
5	4.66	100	5.00	100	4.66	100
10	3.48	100	4.70	99.8	4.51	99.8
20	2.46	99.0	3.51	98.7	3.44	99.1
50	2.23	95.9	2.21	95.1	1.91	94.1
100	0.85	90.6	1.47	89.9	1.26	81.7
200	0.75	69.6	1.26	85.1	1.30	72.6
mean	2.19	92.0	2.83	94.7	2.51	91.4

(c) for different numbers of TCP flows

No of flows	CoDel d	u	PIE d	u	ARED d	u
1	2.23	95.8	2.21	95.1	1.91	94.1
2	2.73	99.2	3.40	98.7	3.11	98.0
5	3.28	98.9	4.97	99.8	5.05	99.5
10	5.16	99.8	5.18	99.9	7.62	99.9
20	7.09	99.9	4.99	100	10.45	99.9
mean	4.45	98.9	4.30	98.9	6.18	98.6

4.2 Static Scenario

We evaluated the three AQMs in the static scenario for several values of bottleneck bandwidth, RTT and number of flows regarding average delay but also bottleneck utilization.

For varied bandwidth, the results are given in Table 1a. For low bandwidths PIE shows the smallest mean delays, while ARED results in very high delays. For bandwidths greater than 10 Mbps the delay is acceptable for all candidates. Utilization is close to the optimum for all AQMs for low bandwidths, but for high bandwidths was significantly lower with ARED than with CoDel and PIE. For our simulations with different RTTs we found decreasing link utilization and mean delay with increasing RTT for all three AQMs, see Table 1b. There is no significant difference between the algorithms for RTTs up to 100 ms, while for 200 ms PIE achieves significantly higher utilization.

When simulating with different numbers of TCP flows, ARED and CoDel could only observe the target delay for few flows, whereas PIE always satisfied the target delay, see Table 1c.

4.3   Adaptation to Newly Starting CBR Traffic

In order to evaluate the candidates' ability to adapt to changing situations, we performed simulations with five TCP flows and, starting from a random point in time, 10 Mbps of Constant Bit Rate (CBR) traffic. In such situations, two metrics can be of interest:

- the extend of the impact, i.e. the time τ the AQM needs to recover
- the severity of the impact, i.e. the maximum queuing delay occuring in consequence of such event

We measure the period τ until packet delay decreases below the reference delay for the first time after starting the CBR traffic and the maximum delay *delay_max* within that period. As the exemplary traces shown in Fig. 2 indicate, we found significant differences as shown in Table 2.

On one hand, the mean reaction time τ of ARED, 0.29 s, is lower than CoDel's, 0.41 s, and by far lower than PIE's, 0.87 s. Although we executed just

Table 2. Measured mean and standard deviation for τ and *delay_max* in milliseconds

	CoDel	PIE	ARED
τ Mean	412	869	293
τ Standard deviation	64	148	38
delay_max Mean	30.3	41.0	39.6
delay_max Standard deviation	6.0	3.8	4.0

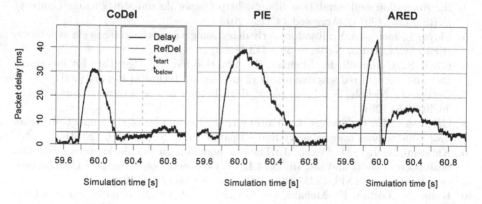

Fig. 2. Transient period with starting CBR traffic at 59.77 s simulation time.

ten runs of this simulation, the derived standard deviation suggests a statistically significant advantage of ARED and CoDel with this respect. On the other hand, the emerged discrepancy from the configured target delay, i.e. *delay_max* in that phase, is much higher for PIE and ARED than for CoDel. The average for ten runs is 41.0 ms and 39.6 ms for PIE and ARED, but 30.3 ms for CoDel. Again, the derived standard deviation indicates a statistically significant advantage of CoDel with this respect.

5   Conclusion and Outlook

We evaluated the robustness of the three AQM algorithms CoDel, PIE and ARED for various static and dynamic scenarios. For low bandwidth links, PIE achieves significantly lower delays than CoDel and ARED. For high RTTs, utilization decreases for all candidates but PIE performs clearly best. When there are many flows, only PIE still keeps the target delay. In dynamic scenarios, CoDel achieves lower maximum delay than the other candidates. Moreover, CoDel and ARED recover significantly faster from changes in the traffic offer than PIE does. Overall, CoDel, PIE and ARED are suitable alike for most scenarios, but for corner scenarios clear recommendations can be given. To show robustness and estimate performance for deployment in real Internet, it is still necessary to evaluate a broader set of scenarios, in particular including other TCP congestion control algorithms and including more traffic patterns such as web traffic.

References

1. Codel linux kernel implementation, https://git.kernel.org/cgit/linux/kernel/git/stable/linux-stable.git/tree/include/net/codel.h
2. Pie linux kernel implementation, ftp://ftpeng.cisco.com/pie/linux_code/pie_code/linux_code/pie.c
3. Charter of ietf working group active queue management and packet scheduling. http://tools.ietf.org/wg/aqm/charters (2014). Accessed 12 July 2014
4. Ikr simulation and emulation library. http://www.ikr.uni-stuttgart.de/Content/IKRSimLib/ (2014). Accessed 14 May 2014
5. Floyd, S., Jacobson, V.: Random early detection gateways for congestion avoidance. IEEE/ACM. Trans. Netw. **1**, 397–413 (1993)
6. Floyd, S., Gummadi, R., Shenker, S.: Adaptive red: An algorithm for increasing the robustness of red s active queue management. Technical Report (2001)
7. Gettys, J., Nichols, K.: Bufferbloat: dark buffers in the internet. Queue **9**(11), 40:40–40:54 (2011)
8. Grigorescu, E., Kulatunga, C., Fairhurst, G.: Evaluation of the impact of packet drops due to aqm over capacity limited paths. In: ICNP, pp. 1–6 (2013)
9. Khademi, N., Ros, D., Welzl, M.: The new aqm kids on the block: an experimental evaluation of codel and pie. In: 2014 IEEE Conference on Computer CommunicationsWorkshops (INFOCOM WKSHPS), pp. 85–90 (April 2014)
10. Kuhn, N., Lochin, E., Mehani, O.: Revisiting old friends: is codel really achieving what red cannot? In: Arvind Krishnamurthy, S.R. (ed.) CSWS 2014, ACM SIGCOMM Capacity Sharing Workshop. ACM, Chicago, (2014)

11. Mathis, M., Dukkipati, N., Cheng, Y.: Proportional Rate Reduction for TCP. RFC 6937 (Experimental) (2013), http://www.ietf.org/rfc/rfc6937.txt
12. Nichols, K., Jacobson, V.: Queue. Controlling queue delay **10**(5), 20:20–20:34 (2012)
13. Pan, R., Natarajan, P., Piglione, C., Prabhu, M.S., Subramanian, V., Baker, F., VerSteeg, B.: Pie: A lightweight control scheme to address the bufferbloat problem. In: HPSR. pp. 148–155. IEEE (2013)
14. Werthmann, T., Kaschub, M., Kühlewind, M., Scholz, S., Wagner, D.: VMSimInt: a network simulation tool supporting integration of arbitrary kernels and application. In: SIMUTools '14: Proceedings of the 7th International ICST Conference on Simulation Tools and Techniques. ACM March 2014

Analysis of the YouTube Server Selection Behavior Observed in a Large German ISP Network

Gerd Windisch[✉]

TU Chemnitz, Chemnitz, Germany
gerd.windisch@etit.tu-chemnitz.de

Abstract. This paper presents a detailed study on the YouTube server selection mechanism with respect to its long term behavior. We conducted a measurement campaign from different measurement points within a single German ISP network over a long period of time. Based on the measurement traces, the long-term temporal behavior of the server selection mechanism is investigated. The results reveal that the server selection behavior ranges from changing on a daily basis to being stable for several weeks. Besides analyzing the long term behavior, we also determined the dependency of the selection behavior on the geographic location of the client node. It appears that the server selection behavior mainly depends on the IP address currently assigned to a user connection. Finally the impact of the selection decision on the round trip time (RTT) is analyzed.

1 Introduction

Multimedia content, especially video, is responsible for the majority of IP traffic in today's networks. According to two studies [1, 2] the multimedia platform YouTube alone accounts for almost 30 % of the traffic in European ISP networks. Multimedia content mostly utilizes the HTTP protocol and is usually delivered by means of global content delivery networks (CDNs), like Akamai, Google, Limelight, etc. YouTube itself uses the CDN of Google.

CDNs usually deploy geographically disperse data centers to distribute content and to bring content closer to the user. Therefore, the same content is available at many servers in different locations. In order to utilize their distributed infrastructure, CDNs need an efficient way to select a server for a given content request. Most CDNs use a domain name system (DNS) based mechanism for this task. When a user requests a piece of content, the CDN resolves the host name of the content server to an IP address of a server, based on defined criteria. These criteria could be, for example, the load of the server or the round trip time (RTT). However, the load situation within the network is usually not taken into account. This may lead to increasing network congestion. Therefore, it is important for a network operator to better understand how the respective CDN server selection mechanism works and which parameters determine its behavior.

The main contribution of this paper is the analysis of the long term temporal behavior of the YouTube server selection mechanism and the parameters it depends on.

© Springer International Publishing Switzerland 2014
Y. Kermarrec (Ed.): EUNICE 2014, LNCS 8846, pp. 192–201, 2014.
DOI: 10.1007/978-3-319-13488-8_18

Since it is expected that the selection behavior depends on the geographic location of the requesting user, we emphasize on measurements in different regions within the ISP network.

The paper is organized as follows: Sect. 2 provides an overview of related work. In Sect. 3 our measurement approach is described and Sect. 4 presents the results of our study. Section 5 concludes the paper.

2 Related Work

Adhikari et al. published several papers (e.g. [3]) about reverse engineering the You-Tube content delivery platform. Their focus is on analyzing the global footprint of YouTube. They utilized a distributed measurement approach using PlanetLab nodes located at 271 sites worldwide. Key findings are the discovery of how the Video ID is mapped to server host names, and the redirection hierarchy used by YouTube. A second study conducted by the same research group focused on the traffic exchanged between the YouTube infrastructure and a tier-1 ISP [4]. They discovered that load is balanced proportionally to the data center size and that it is not influenced by the proximity to the user. This work had been conducted in 2008, before YouTube was acquired by Google.

Torres et al. [5] analyzed the server selection strategies of YouTube using packet traces captured at five measurement points in Europe and in the US. They discovered that most of the time a user is served by the content server location with the lowest RTT. They identified that at least 10 % of the decisions are influenced by other factors. They claim that the content server load and/or diurnal effects have an impact on the decision as well.

Plissonneau et al. [6] analyzed the impact of the server selection mechanism on the video Quality of Experience (QoE) perceived by the user. They reported that the RTT has no impact and that the QoE solely depends on the content server load and the peering agreement between ISPs. The results most relevant to our work are that the geographic proximity does not matter in Europe, while ISP-dependent policies do, and that the selection mechanism exhibits a distinct diurnal behavior.

In a previous paper [7] we analyzed the short term behavior of the server selection mechanism of YouTube. We conducted a measurement study based on proxy servers located within several European ISP networks. The main observation was that the YouTube server selection mechanism behaves quite differently. We developed a classification scheme to group specific selection patterns based on the observed temporal behavior.

The work presented in this paper differs from the mentioned contributions in several ways. Even though all papers mentioned above analyze the YouTube server selection mechanism, they do not consider its long term behavior. Furthermore, we investigate the server selection behavior observed at several measurement points within a single ISP network, during a time period of at least three months. Measuring in an ISP network, rather than at university sites or using PlanetLab nodes, provides results closer to the behavior seen from real users. This is due to the fact that these sites usually have high-bit rate connections, which might influence the server selection behavior.

3   Measurement Approach and Methodology

We developed a measurement probe system and placed such probe devices at different measurement points within a large German ISP network. These measurement probes operate as follows: A probe requests a set of videos from the YouTube CDN. The response of a video request comprises the video web site including a configuration field for the YouTube video player. This field contains the name of the video content server hosting the requested video. The location of the video server can be derived from the hostname of the video server (see [7] for further details). The IP address of the video server is resolved and the RTT to this IP address is actively measured, using ICMP Echo Requests/Replies. These steps are repeated periodically for the set of videos. It is not necessary to download the video itself, since all required information can be derived from the web site referring to that video. Thus the load on the YouTube CDN caused by our measurement approach is minimized. We placed five measurement probes at DSL-connections within the ISP network. Since DSL-connections are changing the IP addresses every 24 h, we also recorded the IP address currently assigned to a DSL connection. A measurement interval of 15 min was applied and the video set consists of 20 popular videos. Popular videos are more likely available at all data centers and will therefore not limit the cache selection behavior by mere video availability constraints. Thus, the responses of 20 popular videos were recorded every 15 min. In the following the result of one video request at one time instance is called a "data point". The associated RTT measurement of one data point contains four single measurements from which the minimum, maximum, average and standard deviation are derived. Note that in our measurement campaign we regard all YouTube content servers with the same location identifier in the hostname as being part of one data center location.

Before analyzing the traces, it is convenient to filter out the outliers in the server selection measurement results. For the filtering process we define an outlier as follows: if a data center location is only seen in one time instance and neither in the preceding nor in the next two successive time instance and its share of all video requests at this time instance is below 20 %, it is considered as an outlier. The removal of these outliers leads only to a minor reduction of data points. Across all measurement traces only 0.6 % of the data points were identified as outliers.

4   Results

4.1   Impact of the IP Prefix on the YouTube Server Selection

As mentioned earlier, a DSL-connection gets a new IP address every 24 h. However, we never observed the same IP prefix at different measurement points. For example IP prefix 5 was only observed at the measurement point in Munich and never at any other measurement point. We even found that two probes got IP addresses of two different IP prefixes. This change in the IP prefix can make a huge difference in the experienced YouTube server selection behavior. Figure 1 shows two server selection pattern examples recorded from the same probe, but with different IP prefixes. For IP prefix

1 the YouTube requests are mostly served by the data center in Amsterdam throughout the day. In case of the second IP prefix (prefix 2) the data center in Hamburg is the preferred one.

Using the IP address to determine the geographic location of a user is a common approach, since it is assumed that users with the same IP prefix are geographically close. However, as a DSL connection might be served with IP addresses of multiple IP prefixes, this hinders the derivation of the geographic location from IP addresses. Contrary to other CDNs which solve the location problem by means of DNS, YouTube is solely relying on the IP addresses (see [7] for further details). This finding also infers that an operator-wide YouTube server selection behavior analysis would require at least one measurement probe per IP prefix of an operator. Based on this knowledge, we decided to group the measurement traces by their IP prefix rather than by the physical location of the measurement probe.

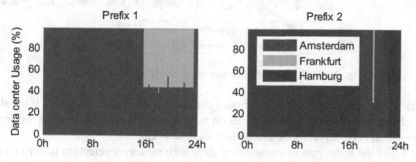

Fig. 1. Comparison of different server selection patterns for different IP prefixes (observed by the same measurement probe)

4.2   Long-Term Temporal Behavior of the Server Selection Mechanism

Figure 2 shows a 90 day trace for three different IP prefixes: IP prefix 1, IP prefix 5 and IP prefix 7. The white spaces for IP prefixes 1 and 7 are due to the prefix change of these measurement probes. The white spaces in IP prefix 5 are caused by missing data. From Fig. 2 it can be seen that the server selection behavior observed for one IP prefix is not correlated to the behavior of the other IP prefixes. The server selection behavior at IP prefix 1 is quite stable using mainly the data center in Amsterdam. For the last 4 weeks the server selection behavior of IP prefix 1 changes and also the data center in Düsseldorf is used. For prefix 5 two main server selection patterns are visible: either the data center in Munich is used exclusively or it is used only during the night until afternoon (i.e. in the low load phase) whereas the data center in Frankfurt is used in the remaining time, from afternoon to midnight (i.e. in the high load phase). IP prefix 7 is served steadily for the first 5 weeks from Frankfurt, but then the server selection pattern is only stable for short periods of time and incorporates different data centers.

Since we are interested in the effects of the server selection on the traffic distribution within an ISP network, we focus our study on the data centers used in the busy hour of the ISP network. According to [1] the busy hour is chosen to be the hour between 20 h and 21 h. A given IP prefix is served from a subset out of all possible data

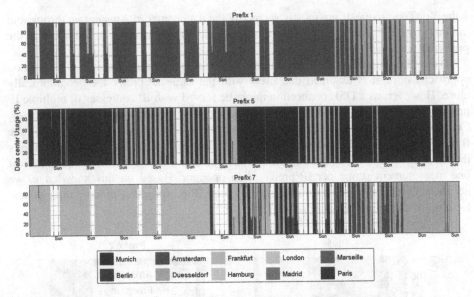

Fig. 2. 90 day server selection traces for IP prefix 1, 5 and 7

centers. Those subset elements contribute a certain share of served requests. If the share of an element changes by at least 25 % on busy hours of consecutive days we regard this as a YouTube server selection pattern change event.

In Fig. 3 the histogram of consecutive days with no server selection pattern change event is shown for IP prefixes 1, 5 and 7. The results confirm the observations from Fig. 2. Besides the 90 day trace documented in the figures of this paper, there are traces as long as 190 days available, which prove that server selection pattern change statistics also vary in the long run.

Table 1 shows how often a given data center is present in the busy and least-busy hour during the 90 day trace (relative frequency of data center occurrence). We defined the least-busy hour as the time from 5 h to 6 h. From the percentage values it can be seen that one or two dominant data centers exist per IP prefix. This holds true although the server selection behavior changes frequently for some IP prefixes.

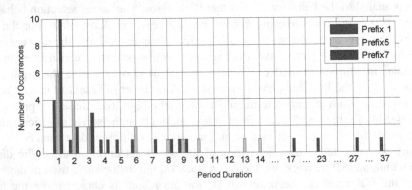

Fig. 3. Histogram of consecutive days with no server selection pattern change event

Furthermore Table 1 shows that there is a dependency between the size of the data center and its usage during the busy hour. Since there is no information published by YouTube about the size of YouTube data centers, we follow the approach from [3] and estimate the data center size by the number of/24-prefixes assigned to the data center location. For IP prefix 1 the share of the data center in Amsterdam rises from 74 % to 99 % and the share of the data center in Düsseldorf drops from 27 % to 4 %. The same holds true for IP prefix 5 with respect to the data centers in Frankfurt and Munich. For IP prefix 7 a similar behavior is observed.

Table 1. Relative usage of data centers per IP prefix (busy and least-busy hour case)

		Prefix 1		Prefix 5		Prefix 7	
	Number/24 prefixes	Busy hour	Least-busy hour	Busy hour	Least-busy hour	Busy hour	Least-busy hour
Frankfurt	15	10 %	0 %	**38 %**	2 %	**68 %**	53 %
London	12	1 %	0 %	0 %	0 %	1 %	0 %
Amsterdam	6	**99 %**	74 %	1 %	0 %	**32 %**	1 %
Paris	6	0 %	0 %	0 %	0 %	3 %	0 %
Madrid	5	0 %	0 %	0 %	0 %	9 %	0 %
Munich	2	0 %	0 %	**60 %**	98 %	0 %	18 %
Hamburg	2	0 %	0 %	0 %	0 %	4 %	0 %
Düsseldorf	1	4 %	27 %	7 %	0 %	10 %	31 %

Even some time before the busy hour begins, a data center change which then remains in the busy hour can be observed. In the following, we have a closer look at this "pre-warning" time. For that, we processed exemplarily the trace of IP prefix 5 to determine the frequency of the hours of the day at which a data center change that then remains in the busy hour occur. The results of this analysis are depicted in Fig. 4. It shows for each hour of the day the probability that in this hour a data center change which then remains in the busy hour occurs. It is significant that in most cases the change can be observed already before 17 h, i.e. there is a pre-warning time of three hours. This analysis shows that there is no fixed time schedule for the data center changes, which leads to the conjecture of a data center load dependent change policy. Unfortunately we were not able to analyze this in more detail based on our measurement traces taken from a single ISP network as the load situation of the YouTube data centers result from YouTube requests coming from several ISPs.

4.3   Locality and RTT Characteristics of YouTube Data Centers

The YouTube data center locations were extracted out of the host names of the content servers (see [7]). From that we found that 76 % of all requests (conducted from all measurement probes including all IP prefixes within the whole measurement period) were served by data centers in Germany and 24 % by data centers in Europe. Only 0.01 % of the requests were served by data centers outside of Europe.

The prefix-dependent average RTT values are between 18 ms and 28 ms for the data center in Amsterdam and between 21 ms and 37 ms for the data center in London.

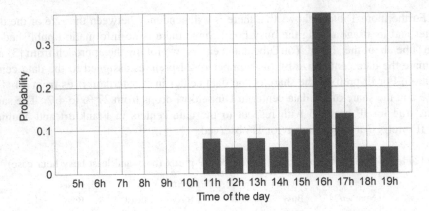

Fig. 4. Probability distribution of the hours of the day in which a server change occurs that remains in the busy hour (IP prefix 5 case)

Amsterdam and London count for 97 % of the requests served by European data centers in our traces. The RTT values for Amsterdam and London are similar to the values of the data centers located in Germany, as can be seen in Fig. 5. We found no explanation for the large RTT value measured for IP prefix 4 and the data center in Frankfurt. As for IP prefix 3, whose region is close to that of IP prefix 4, the RTT is significantly smaller (10 ms).

We also compared the RTT values in the busy hour, to the values in the least-busy hour. For this, we took the minimum RTT values of the data points, respectively. In Table 2 the mean, median and 95 % percentile of the (minimum) RTT values in the busy hour and in the least-busy hour are shown for each IP prefix. IP prefix 3 was excluded due to an insufficient number of RTT measurements. It can be seen that for IP prefixes 1, 2 and 4 the mean and the median values are almost identical in the busy

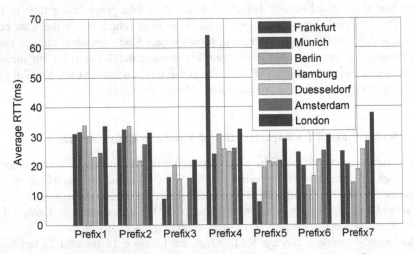

Fig. 5. Average RTTs related to selected data centers (for 7 IP prefixes)

Table 2. RTT values for 7 IP prefixes (busy and least-busy hour case)

RTT (ms)	Least-busy hour			Busy hour		
	Mean	Median	95 % per.	Mean	Median	95 % per.
Prefix 1	23.9	23.6	26.6	25.6	23.6	27.0
Prefix 2	28.2	29.6	30.4	30.1	30.0	31.4
Prefix 4	24.0	23.9	26.6	25.2	24.7	25.6
Prefix 5	8.2	6.9	13.8	10.9	9.4	15.7
Prefix 6	23.5	23.0	25.7	25.8	23.1	46.8
Prefix 7	22.9	22.5	25.3	25.9	23.0	44.0

hour and in the least-busy hour. For IP prefix 5 the RTT values increase by 35 % in the busy hour. For IP prefix 6 and 7 there is almost no difference regarding the median, but a significant increase in the 95 % percentile.

Table 3 shows the RTT values measured between selected IP prefixes and data centers, which mostly served these IP prefixes. It can be seen that there are only minor differences between the RTT values in the busy hour and in the least-busy hour. For example, the RTT related to IP prefix 5 and the data center in Munich increases only by 1 ms and for the data center in Frankfurt it does not increase at all. An explanation of this behavior might be that the load (congestion) in the ISP network is quite low even in the busy hour, so that the RTTs show no large variations. The RTT increase faced by some IP prefixes (5, 6 and 7) in the busy hour (depicted in Table 2) is caused by the selection of more distant data centers in the busy hour.

Table 3. RTT values related to selected data centers (busy and least-busy hour case)

RTT (ms)	Least-busy hour			Busy hour		
	Mean	Median	95 % per.	Mean	Median	95 % per.
Prefix 5 to Muc.	7.1	6.8	7.2	8.1	7.8	7.8
Prefix 5 to Fra.	13.4	13.3	14.2	13.4	13.4	14.2
Prefix 6 to Ams.	24.4	24.3	25.8	23.9	24.0	25.6
Prefix 6 to Fra.	22.8	22.8	24.1	22.8	22.8	24.2
Prefix 7 to Ams.	25.2	24.2	24.2	26.2	24.2	25.7
Prefix 7 to Fra.	22.9	22.7	24.2	24.5	22.8	32.4

The lower part of Fig. 6 shows the RTT values over the duration of 2 weeks for IP prefix 5. For comparison, the server selection behavior faced by IP prefix 5 is shown in the upper part of Fig. 6 (cf. Fig. 2). During the time, when requests from IP prefix 5 are only served by the data center in Munich, the RTT remains constant at 9 ms. When the data center in Frankfurt is used (in the busy hours of the second week) the RTT increases to 13 ms. In case of IP prefixes 6 and 7 the RTT increases are caused by selecting the even more distant European data centers in Madrid and Paris during the busy hour.

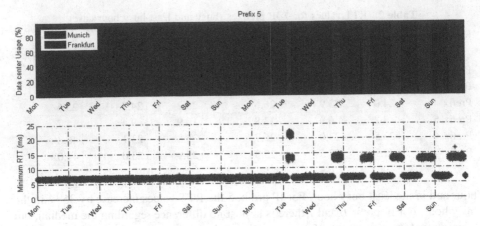

Fig. 6. Server selection behavior and corresponding RTT values for IP prefix 5 (2 week trace)

5 Summary

In this paper we report the results of a comprehensive analysis of the YouTube data center selection mechanism observed within a German ISP network. We investigated the dependency of the server selection decision on the IP prefix from which the request is sent, the long term temporal server selection pattern and the influences on the RTT. The results were obtained from a measurement campaign, where several measurement probes were placed in different regions within the ISP network and where traces were recorded over a 90-day period.

We discovered that the server selection behavior experienced by a user depends on the prefix of the IP address currently assigned to the user. No correlation between the server selection patterns faced by the different IP prefixes has been observed. Typically, only one or two dominant YouTube data centers are used per IP prefix independent of the sever selection pattern. Furthermore, it has been observed that during the busy hours the IP prefixes are more likely served by larger (and more distant) data centers. This is the main reason for the increase in RTT in the busy hours. Contrary, the traffic load in the ISP network has no significant impact on the RTT as it is quite low even in the busy hours. These results go along with the findings of [5] and [6], which already reported the general behavior patterns, but not as detailed and precise as it is documented in this paper.

References

1. Sandvine.: Global internet phenomena report 2H 2013. https://www.sandvine.com/trends/global-internet-phenomena/ (2013)
2. Finamore, A., Gehlen, V., Mellia, M., Munafò and Nicolini, M.M.: The need for an intelligent measurement plane: the example of time-variant CDN policies. In: 15th International Telecommunications Network Strategy and Planning Symposium, pp. 2–7 (2012)

3. Adhikari, V.K., Jain, S., Chen, Y., Zhang, Z.-L.: Vivisecting YouTube: an active measurement study. In: IEEE International Conference on Computer Communications: Mini-Conference, pp. 2521–2525 (2012)
4. Adhikari, V.K., Jain, S., Zhang, Z.: YouTube traffic dynamics and its interplay with a tier-1 ISP: an ISP perspective. In: Proceedings of the 10th ACM SIGCOMM Conference Internet Measurement, pp. 431–443 (2010)
5. Torres, R., Finamore, A., Kim, J.R., Mellia, M., Munafo, M.M., Rao, S.: Dissecting video server selection strategies in the YouTube CDN. In: 31st International Conference on Distributed Computing Systems, pp. 248–257, June 2011
6. Plissoneau, L., Biersack, E., Juluri, P.: Analyzing the impact of YouTube delivery policies on user experience. In: International Teletraffic Congress ITC'24 (2012)
7. Windisch, G., Knoll, T.M., Bauschert, T.: Analysis of the video server selection in the YouTube CDN. In: 2nd European Teletraffic Seminar (2013)

On the Computational Complexity
of Policy Routing

Márton Zubor[1,3]([✉]), Attila Kőrösi[1,2,4], András Gulyás[1,2,4],
and Gábor Rétvári[1,2,5]

[1] Budapest University of Technology and Economics, Budapest, Hungary
[2] Department of Telecommunication and Media Informatics,
Budapest University of Technology and Economics, Budapest, Hungary
[3] Department of Algebra, Budapest University of Technology and Economics,
Budapest, Hungary
zubor@tmit.bme.hu
[4] Hungarian Academy of Science (MTA) Information System Research Group,
Budapest, Hungary
{korosi,gulyas}@tmit.bme.hu
[5] MTA-BME Future Internet Research Group,
Budapest University of Technology and Economics, Budapest, Hungary
retvari@tmit.bme.hu

Abstract. With the advent of new network architectures, like Software
Defined Networks, the rules governing the way traffic is routed through
the network are becoming increasingly complex. In this paper, we revisit
the theoretic underpinnings of policy routing in the light of the new
requirements. We show that certain simple but plausible algebraic properties already induce intractable path selection instances, and we extend
the algebraic description of policies for which the related path selection
problem is guaranteed to be tractable with a new class, called polynomial
finite algebras, which captures many real-life application domains.

Keywords: Policy routing · Path selection · Routing algebras · Computational complexity

1 Introduction

Policy routing is the art and science of determining optimal forwarding paths
under complex operational constraints. Originally in shortest path routing the
rule was simply to pick the least cost path with respect to some additive link
weights, but network operators have increasingly turned towards more sophisticated policies like path reliability and resilience [17], bandwidth and perceived congestion [8,16], business relations and service level agreements [2], etc.
These routing policies, and the computational complexity of the path selection
problem thereof, are well-understood today, thanks to the theory of routing
algebras [4,5,14,15].

Recently, however, new routing architectures have surfaced for which today's
algebraic routing theory does not provide adequate complexity characterization.

© Springer International Publishing Switzerland 2014
Y. Kermarrec (Ed.): EUNICE 2014, LNCS 8846, pp. 202–214, 2014.
DOI: 10.1007/978-3-319-13488-8_19

Data centers, for instance, operate over starkly optimized topologies and services, defined by rules significantly more customized than allowed by classical routing policies. With the emergence of Software Defined Networks (SDN), furthermore, operators now enjoy complete freedom to shape their routing preferences [9]. A perfect example of how the seemingly simple problem of calculating the preferred path between two nodes can become surprisingly complicated is the upcoming Service Chaining paradigm [10]. Here, service functions, like intrusion detection, network address translation, or video transcoding, are realized as standalone or virtualized middleboxes scattered throughout the network, and packets must pass through these functions in specific order. In more recent deployments the particular service realized by a middlebox has become dynamically configurable, and the policy routing task involves jointly optimizing both the placement of the services *and* the forwarding paths themselves [9].

In these routing paradigms packet loops are a fairly natural consequence of the routing policy itself, something that falls completely outside the model of classical algebraic policy routing. Even our very capability to compute the preferred path is under scrutiny now, as it is no longer obvious whether what we are looking for is in fact a path or a walk. Or, in a similarly troubling scenario, a network operator might accidentally pose a service chaining rule that, even though extremely desirable from an operational perspective, happens to induce an intractable path selection problem, making that policy essentially unrealizable in practice[1]. Regrettably, conventional routing theory does not provide sufficient guidelines to identify such pathologic cases.

The goal of this paper is to take the first steps to extend the theory of policy routing into this brave new era of networking. Our main goal is to separate routing policies over which computing the preferred path/walk is "easy" from those that admit intractable path/walk selection instances. However, instead of giving piecemeal complexity characterizations for each routing policy we rather provide a *general* treatment. In particular,

(*i*) we describe the algebraic properties that are sufficient and necessary in order for the optimal walk to coincide with the optimal path;

(*ii*) we extend the "safe algebraic regime" under which path selection is guaranteed to be polynomially tractable; and

(*iii*) we identify the ensembles of simple algebraic properties that can induce NP-complete path selection instances.

As a main contribution of the paper, we provide the first ever comprehensive classification of routing algebras based on the tractability of the related path selection problem (see Fig. 1 and the discussion in Sect. 6).

The rest of the paper is organized as follows. First, we introduce the algebraic model used throughout the paper in Sect. 2. Then, in Sect. 3 we reveal the relation between the preferred walk and preferred path selection problems, in Sect. 4 we define a new algebraic property, polynomial finite algebras, that warrants a fast path selection algorithm, in Sect. 5 we discuss the reverse case, that is, algebras

---

[1] Later in Sect. 6 we shall show real-life routing policies that exhibit this problem.

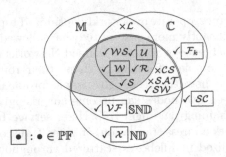

Fig. 1. A classification of routing algebras based on the algebraic properties of the corresponding path selection problem. ND denotes non-decreasing, SND strongly non-decreasing, M monotone, PF polinomial fininte and C commutative algebras. Algebras in the gray area can be solved by the Dijkstra algorithm, and algebras $\mathcal{S}$, $\mathcal{W}$, $\mathcal{WS}$, $\mathcal{SW}$, $\mathcal{R}$, $\mathcal{U}$, $\mathcal{VF}$, $\mathcal{X}$, $\mathcal{SC}$, $\mathcal{SAT}$, $\mathcal{CS}$, and $\mathcal{F}_k$, marked with ✓ (or ×), give examples for tractable (intractable, resp.) routing policies (see Sect. 6).

inducing intractable path selection instances, in Sect. 6 we highlight important practical consequences of our findings, and finally in Sect. 7 we conclude the paper.

2   An Algebraic Model for Policy Routing

The network is modeled by a finite, connected graph $G(V, E)$, $|V| = n$ and $|E| = m$. An $s - t$ *walk* is a sequence of nodes $q = (s = v_1, v_2, \ldots, v_k = t)$, where k is the length of the walk and $(v_i, v_{i+1}) \in E : \forall i = 1, \ldots, k - 1$. A *cycle* is a walk with $s = t$, a *path* p is a walk that visits a node at most once, and a *preferred walk* q^* is the one that is favored from the set of available $s - t$ walks $\mathcal{Q}_{st}$ according to some predefined policy routing rules.

A concise model for this setting is that of *routing algebras* [4,5,14,15]. In this paper, a routing algebra $\mathcal{A}$ is defined as a totally ordered monoid with a compatible infinity element. Formally, $\mathcal{A} = (W, \oplus, \preceq)$, where W is the set of (abstract) weights that can be assigned to edges with a special infinity weight $\phi \in W$ meaning that an edge/walk is not traversable, $\oplus$ is a composition operator for weights, and $\preceq$ is weight comparison.

Formally, the following properties are presumed.

1. $(W, \oplus)$ is a monoid (semigroup with identity) with zero element:
   - Closure: $w_1 \oplus w_2 \in W$ for all $w_1, w_2 \in W$.
   - Associativity: $(w_1 \oplus w_2) \oplus w_3 = w_1 \oplus (w_2 \oplus w_3)$ for all $w_1, w_2, w_3 \in W$.
   - Identity element: $\exists 0 \in W$ such $0 \oplus w = w \oplus 0 = w$ for every $w \in W$.
   - Zero element: $\exists \phi \in W$ such $\phi \oplus w = w \oplus \phi = \phi$ for every $w \in W$.
2. $\preceq$ is a total order on W with a maximal element:
   - Reflexivity: $w \preceq w$ for any $w \in W$.
   - Anti-symmetry: if $w_1 \preceq w_2$ and $w_2 \preceq w_1$, then $w_2 = w_1$ for any $w_1, w_2 \in W$.

- Transitivity: if $w_1 \preceq w_2$ and $w_2 \preceq w_3$, then $w_1 \preceq w_3$ for any $w_1, w_2, w_3 \in W$.
- Totality: for all $w_1, w_2 \in W$ either $w_1 \preceq w_2$ or $w_2 \preceq w_1$.
- Maximal element: $\exists \infty \in W$ such $w \preceq \infty$ for all $w \in W$.

3. $\preceq$ and $\oplus$ are consistent:
   - The zero element for $\oplus$ is the maximal element for $\preceq$: $\phi = \infty$.

We sometimes use the shorthand notation ab instead of $a \oplus b$.

Given a walk $q = (v_1, v_2, \ldots, v_k)$, we obtain the weight $w(q)$ of q by combining the weights of its constituent edges:

$$w(q) = \bigoplus_{i=1}^{k-1} w(v_i, v_{i+1}).$$

With this notation at hand, the preferred walk q^* in $\mathcal{A}$ between nodes s and t is simply the one with the smallest weight from the set of all $s - t$ walks $\mathcal{Q}_{st}$ over the relation $\preceq$. The path selection problem over $\mathcal{A}$ can take two alternative forms, based on whether we allow the output to be a walk or we require it to be strictly a path.

Definition 1. $Q_{\mathcal{A}}(G, s, t)$ *(Preferred walk computation problem): given a graph $G(V, E)$ with weight function $w : E \to W$ and a node pair $s, t \in V$, return an $s - t$ walk q^* so that*

$$w(q^*) \preceq w(q) \text{ for all } q \in \mathcal{Q}_{st} . \tag{1}$$

We further define the *preferred-path computation problem* $P_{\mathcal{A}}(G, s, t)$ similarly as above, whereas we also require the output to be a path. In addition, with a slight abuse of notation we define the "decision-form" of the problems $Q_{\mathcal{A}}(G, s, t, b)$ ($P_{\mathcal{A}}(G, s, t, b)$), where the task is to decide whether a walk q^* (path p^*) exists with weight $w(q^*) \preceq b$ (resp. $w(p^*) \preceq b$) for some given bound $b \in W$. Trivialy, $P_{\mathcal{A}}(G, s, t, b)$ is in NP but $Q_{\mathcal{A}}(G, s, t, b)$ is not necessarily, as the size of a preferred path is always polynomial as the function of the input but the size of the preferred walk is not.

The lexicographic product operator is a useful tool to compose complex routing algebras from simple ones [5]. Given two routing algebras $\mathcal{A} = (W_{\mathcal{A}}, \oplus_{\mathcal{A}}, \preceq_{\mathcal{A}})$ and $\mathcal{B} = (W_{\mathcal{B}}, \oplus_{\mathcal{B}}, \preceq_{\mathcal{B}})$, the *lexicographic product* of $\mathcal{A}$ and $\mathcal{B}$ is a routing algebra $\mathcal{A} \times \mathcal{B} = (W, \oplus, \preceq)$, where the weight composition operator is defined as $(w_1, v_1) \oplus (w_2, v_2) = (w_1 \oplus_{\mathcal{A}} w_2, v_1 \oplus_{\mathcal{B}} v_2)$ for all $w_1, w_2 \in W_{\mathcal{A}}$ and $v_1, v_2 \in W_{\mathcal{B}}$, and

$$(w_1, v_1) \preceq (w_2, v_2) = \begin{cases} v_1 \preceq_{\mathcal{B}} v_2 & \text{if } w_1 =_{\mathcal{A}} w_2 \\ w_1 \preceq_{\mathcal{A}} w_2 & \text{otherwise} \end{cases}$$

One easily checks that shortest path routing corresponds to the algebra $\mathcal{S} = (\mathbb{N}, \infty, +, \leq)$, while widest path routing, where preferred paths are those with the largest bottleneck capacity, is $\mathcal{W} = (\mathbb{N}, 0, \min, \geq)$ [14]. The lexicographic products of $\mathcal{S}$ and $\mathcal{W}$ also correspond to practically relevant routing policies: widest-shortest path routing $\mathcal{WS} = \mathcal{S} \times \mathcal{W}$ prefers from the set of shortest paths the one with the highest free capacity [1], and shortest-widest path $\mathcal{SW} = \mathcal{W} \times \mathcal{S}$, just contrarily, prefers the shortest from the set of widest paths [8, 16].

3   When Preferred Paths and Walks Coincide

Our aim in this paper is to study the computational complexity of the preferred-walk computation problem Q_A and the preferred-path computation problem P_A, in order to extend the traditional algebraic characterization to new routing architectures and policies. For this, first we have to make clear under which conditions we can at least hope for a solution. This is the goal in this section.

There are the following three cases: *(i)* there is no solution for Q_A but for P_A there is (e.g., if A is the shortest path algebra with negative cycles); *(ii)* both Q_A and P_A are solvable but the solutions differ (see Fig. 2); and *(iii)* both problems are solvable with equal result. Clearly, from a practical standpoint case *(iii)* is favorable, as in this case a simple preferred walk computation algorithm will readily deliver the preferred path as well (after removing cycles). Thus, in this section we give a sufficient and necessary condition for *(iii)* to hold.

Consider the following definitions:

- Non-Decreasing (ND): $w_1 \preceq w_1 \oplus w_2$ and $w_1 \preceq w_2 \oplus w_1$ for every $w_1, w_2 \in W$.
- Strongly Non-Decreasing (SND): non-decreasing with $w_1 \oplus w_3 \preceq w_1 \oplus w_2 \oplus w_3$ for every $w_1, w_2, w_3 \in W$.
- Monotone (M): $w_1 \preceq w_2$ implies $w_1 \oplus w_3 \preceq w_2 \oplus w_3$ and $w_3 \oplus w_1 \preceq w_3 \oplus w_2$ for every $w_1, w_2, w_3 \in W$.
- Commutative (C): $w_1 \oplus w_2 = w_2 \oplus w_1$ for every $w_1, w_2 \in W$.
- Polynomial Finite (PF): $f_A(n) = O(p(n))$ where $p()$ is a polynomial and

$$f_A(n) = \sup\{|B| : B \text{ is a subalgebra of } A \text{ generated by } n \text{ elements}\}.$$

The properties C, ND, and M are familiar from the literature [4,14]. In addition, we introduce two new properties.

First, PF formalizes the idea that the subalgebras generated by any small set of elements of an algebra are not "too large". In particular, let $A = (W, \oplus, \preceq)$ and let $W_G \subset W$ denote the set from which the links of a graph G take their weights from (easily, $|W_G| = O(n)$). Then, the number of weights that can be assigned to any walk of length n is at most $f_A(n)$, and the PF property simply requires that this quantity is polynomial in the size of the network (i.e., n). For example, in the case of the widest path routing algebra W the weight of a walk will be one of its constituting link weights, and if there are n different link weights then the size of their generated algebra is n, hence $f_W(n) = n$. Later, we shall see that this property is particularly useful to define fast path selection algorithms.

Second, our SND property extends ND to non-commutative algebras. The ND property in fact guarantees that, at least for commutative algebras, *(i)* every preferred path is a preferred walk and *(ii)* a preferred path can be obtained from a preferred walk by dropping all cycles[2]. For non-commutative algebras, however,

---

[2] Note that the known path selection algorithms (e.g. Dijkstra, Bellmann-Ford [12]) in fact search for a walk, but this walk is guaranteed to also be a path whenever the underlying routing algebra is SND, like e.g., the shortest-path algebra S.

we need SND for *(i)* and *(ii)* to hold, as shown below. (Note that SND $\Leftrightarrow$ ND over commutative algebras.)

Lemma 1. *For any graph $G(V, E)$ with weight function w, if $\mathcal{A}$ is SND then $Q_{\mathcal{A}}(G, s, t)$ is solvable for any $s, t \in V$.*

Proof. First, we introduce some notation. Let Σ be a finite alphabet, let S_{Σ} denote the set of finite words on Σ, and let $(S_{\Sigma}, \lhd)$ be a partially ordered set (poset) where $x \lhd y$ for some $x, y \in S_{\Sigma}$ if x can be obtained from y by deleting symbols. In addition, we define an antichain of $(S_{\Sigma}, \lhd)$ as a set $R \subseteq S_{\Sigma}$ so that neither $x \lhd y$ nor $y \lhd x$ holds for any $x, y \in R, x \neq y$. We use the following claim from [7, page 106–107]:

Proposition 1. *All antichains of $(S_{\Sigma}, \lhd)$ are finite.*

Now, suppose indirectly that there exists a SND algebra $\mathcal{A}$, a graph $G(V, E)$ with weight function w, and $s, t \in V$, such that there is no preferred walk from s to t. Hence, there is an infinite sequence of walks $s_i : i \in \mathbb{N}$ in G with $w(s_i) \succ w(s_{i+1})$ and obviously this has an infinite subsequence such that the length of s_i is strictly less than that of s_{i+1} for any $i \in \mathbb{N}$. By choosing $\Sigma = \{w(e) : e \in E\}$ and applying Proposition 1 to the poset $(s_n : n \in \mathbb{N}, \lhd)$, we find at least one pair of walks s_i and s_j with $i < j$ and $s_i \lhd s_j$. Observe that, by $i < j$ and transitivity of $\preceq$, we have $s_i \succ s_j$. On the other hand, by applying SND repeatedly we have $s_i \preceq s_j$, which contradicts $s_i \succ s_j$.

Theorem 1. *For any graph $G(V, E)$ with weight function w and any $s, t \in V$, (i) solution q^* to $Q_{\mathcal{A}}(G, s, t)$ and solution p^* to $P_{\mathcal{A}}(G, s, t)$ both exist and (ii) $w(q^*) = w(p^*)$, if and only if $\mathcal{A} \in$ SND.*

Proof. According to Lemma 1 if $\mathcal{A}$ is SND then a solution q^* to $Q_{\mathcal{A}}$ always exists. ($P_{\mathcal{A}}$ always has a solution, as the set of $s - t$ paths is finite and $\preceq$ is total.) From this the statement $w(q^*) = w(p^*)$ will follow, since SND guarantees that deleting a cycle from q^* to obtain p^* cannot increase the weight (see Fig. 2).

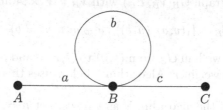

Fig. 2. Illustration of the SND property: SND guarantees that if we remove the cycle(s) from a preferred $A - C$ walk of weight abc then what we obtain is a preferred path since $ac \preceq abc$. On the other hand, if $\mathcal{A}$ is not SND then $abc \prec ac$ for some $a, b, c \in \mathcal{A}$ and on the above graph the preferred $A - C$ walk abc does not coincide with the preferred $A - C$ path ac.

To see the reverse direction, observe that if $\mathcal{A}$ is not SND then there are $a, b, c \in \mathcal{A}$ with $abc \prec ac$ and then one easily constructs a graph on which $q^* \neq p^*$ (see again Fig. 2).

Corollary 1. *If $\mathcal{A}$ algebra is* PF, *then $Q_{\mathcal{A}}(G, s, t, b)$ is in NP.*

We close this discussion by noting that $\mathbb{C} \wedge \text{ND} \Rightarrow \text{SND}$ and $\text{ND} \wedge \text{M} \Rightarrow \text{SND}$. The proofs are trivial and omitted here.

4   Polynomial Time Algorithms

Now, we are in the position to draw the algebraic silhouette of routing policies that admit a polynomial time path selection algorithm. This work was spearheaded by Sobrinho with the following claim [14]:

Proposition 2. *If $\mathcal{A} \in \text{ND} \cap \text{M}$, then $Q_{\mathcal{A}}$ and $P_{\mathcal{A}}$ can be solved in polynomial time by the generalized Dijksta algorithm.*

Note that Sobrinho's algebraic framework differs somewhat from ours, in that we do not require M neither minimality of 0. However, it is easy to see that ND implies the minimality of 0, and M and the minimality of 0 imply ND. Also note that the result holds only if the primitive operations $\oplus$ and $\preceq$ are $O(1)$. We shall use this assumption in the rest of the paper.

Sobrinho's result is important in that it guarantees a polynomial algorithm for many practically important policies (see Sect. 6). Unfortunately, it does not cover some crucial non-monotone cases (like the valley-free routing algebra of BGP [4]) and many exotic routing policies in SDN and service chaining (again, see Sect. 6). Our next result extends the family of routing policies for which polynomial time algorithm is warranted to the set of polynomial finite algebras.

Theorem 2. *If $\mathcal{A} \in$ PF then for any $G(V, E)$ with weight function w and $s, t \in V$, $Q_{\mathcal{A}}(G, s, t)$ can be solved in time polynomial in $|V|$.*

Proof. Let $\mathcal{B}$ denote the sub-algebra of $\mathcal{A}$ generated by $\{w(e) : e \in E\}$. Construct a new unweighted digraph $G_{\mathcal{B}}(V_{\mathcal{B}}, E_{\mathcal{B}})$ with $V_{\mathcal{B}} = V \times \mathcal{A}$ and

$$E_{\mathcal{B}} = \{((v, a), (u, b)) : a \oplus w(v, u) = b\} \ .$$

Clearly, there is a walk in $G_{\mathcal{B}}$ from $(s, 0)$ to (t, r) if and only if there is a walk in G from s to t with weight r. Algorithm 1 below uses this observation to solve $Q_{\mathcal{A}}(G, s, t)$.

The complexity of the algorithm is as follows. Let $n = |V|$ and let $m = |E|$. Since $\mathcal{A}$ is PF and $\mathcal{B}$ is generated by m elements, there is a polynomial $p(m)$ so that $|\mathcal{B}| = O(p(m))$. Easily, line 1 takes $|V_{\mathcal{B}}| = O(p(m)n)$ time, line 2 and line 3 run in $O(E_{\mathcal{B}}) = O((p(m)n)^2)$ time, and finally line 4 terminates in $O(\log(|\mathcal{B}|))$ time, so the total running time is a polynomial in n as $m = O(n^2)$.

Observe that the PF property guarantees only that we can compute the preferred *walk* in polynomial time using Algorithm 1. To actually obtain the

---

Algorithm 1. Preferred walk computation for $\mathbb{PF}$ algebras

---

1: Determine algebra $\mathcal{B}$.
2: Build graph $G_\mathcal{B}$.
3: Run a BFS traversal on $G_\mathcal{B}$ from $(s, 0)$ to every node in $\{(t, a) : a \in \mathcal{B}\}$.
4: Use binary search over $\preceq$ to find the least element of
$\quad \{a \in \mathcal{B} : \text{ there is a walk from } (s, 0) \text{ to } (t, a) \text{ in } G_\mathcal{B}\}$.

---

preferred *path*, we also need the $\mathbb{SND}$ property in addition to $\mathbb{PF}$, which, by Theorem 1, states that the latter can be obtained from the former in polynomial time by deleting cycles.

The question remains how to actually check whether a particular routing algebra is $\mathbb{PF}$. Easily, the naive approach will not work as the number of subalgebras of a routing algebra can be very large. As we shall see, the below algebraic properties are particularly useful to detect whether or not an algebra is $\mathbb{PF}$:

- Selective: $w_1 \oplus w_2 \in \{w_1, w_2\}$ for each $w_1, w_2 \in W$.
- Left-condensed: $w_1 \oplus w_2 = w_1 \oplus w_3$ for each $w_1, w_2, w_3 \in W$.

Lemma 2. *If $\mathcal{A}$ is a selective then $\mathcal{A}$ is $\mathbb{PF}$.*

Proof. If $\mathcal{A}$ is selective then every subset $\mathcal{B} \subseteq \mathcal{A}$ is closed under $\oplus$ and so $\mathcal{B}$ is a subalgebra. Thus, if $|\mathcal{B}| = n$ then the subalgebra generated by $\mathcal{B}$ is exactly $\mathcal{B}$, so it also holds n elements and hence $f_\mathcal{A}(n) = n$.

Lemma 3. *If $\mathcal{A}$ is a left-condensed then $\mathcal{A}$ is $\mathbb{PF}$.*

Proof. Suppose that $\mathcal{A}$ is left-condensed and let $\mathcal{B} \subseteq \mathcal{A}$ such that $|\mathcal{B}| = n$. Then, the subalgebra generated by $\mathcal{B}$ is $\{0, \infty\} \cup \mathcal{B} \cup \mathcal{B}^2$, it has at most $2n + 2$ elements, and thus $f_\mathcal{A}(n) = 2n + 2$ is again polynomial.

From Lemma 2 it immediately follows that widest path algebra $\mathcal{W}$ is $\mathbb{PF}$, due to it being selective [11].

5 NP-hardness Results

It seems that the family of routing policies for which a polynomial time path selection algorithm is available is reassuringly broad. Currently, it is an open question whether the algebraic characterization provided by Proposition 2 and Algorithm 1 can be broadened further (see Fig. 1). Below, we argue that this is non-trivial, because even as simple as commutative and non-decreasing algebras *can* already induce intractable path selection instances. Again, our characterization is algebraic, which allows us to sidestep piecemeal treatment for each new policy arising in practice. Instead, we identify entire "unsafe" algebraic regions where protocol designers may accidentally hit an NP-hard instance.

Theorem 3. *There is an algebra $\mathcal{A} \in \mathbb{M} \cap \mathbb{C}$, so that $P_\mathcal{A}(G, s, t, b)$ is NP-complete.*

Proof. The well-known NP hard longest path problem [12] can be trivialy formalized in this language. $\mathcal{L} = (\mathbb{N}, \infty, +, \geq)$.

Theorem 4. *There is an algebra* $\mathcal{A} \in \mathbb{SND} \cap \mathbb{C}$, *so that* $Q_{\mathcal{A}}(G, s, t, b)$ *and* $P_{\mathcal{A}}(G, s, t, b)$ *are NP-complete.*

Proof. We show an algebra, $\mathcal{SAT}$, and corresponding Karp-reductions 3"2DSAT $\propto Q_{\mathcal{SAT}}$ and 3"2DSAT $\propto P_{\mathcal{SAT}}$. Let a φ be a 3-CNF formula on some set of boolean variables X. Note that if $x \in X$ then $\neg x \in X$ and $\forall x \in X : \neg(\neg x) = x$. Let φ be a conjunction on n clauses $\varphi_1, ..., \varphi_n$ and $\varphi_i = \varphi_{i,a} \vee \varphi_{i,b} \vee \varphi_{i,c}$, where $\varphi_{i,a}, \varphi_{i,b}, \varphi_{i,c} \in X$ for every $i = 1, ..., n$.

We define $\mathcal{SAT}$ as follows. Let S be the power set of X endowed with an infinity element: $S = 2^X \cup \{\infty\}$, and let $\oplus$ be binary operation on S so that

$$\forall a, b \in S \setminus \{\infty\} : a \oplus b = \begin{cases} \infty & \text{if } \exists v \in a : \neg(v) \in b \\ a \cup b & \text{otherwise} \end{cases}$$

$$\forall a \in S : \infty \oplus a = a \oplus \infty = \infty .$$

Since $\mathcal{SAT}$ is $\mathbb{SND}$, it is enough to proove that $P_{\mathcal{A}}(G, s, t, b)$ is NP-hard.

We define a multi-graph $G(V, E)$ so that solving $Q_{\mathcal{SAT}}$ on G solves 3"2DSAT. Let $V = \{0, ..., n\}$, let $E = \{e_{1,a}, e_{1,b}, ..., e_{n,b}, e_{n,c}\}$, where $e_{i,j}$ is a directed edge from v_{i-1} to v_i and $j \in \{a, b, c\}$, and let $w : E \to \mathcal{SAT}$ be a weight function so that $w(e_{i,j}) = \varphi_{i,j}$ for all $i \in \{1, ..., n\}$ and $j \in \{a, b, c\}$. Clearly, G can be built in time polynomial in n. Now, one easily proves the following statement: the weight of the preferred $0 \to n$ path in G is less then ∞ if and only if φ is satisfiable. This completes the proof.

For convenience, we used a multigraph with parallel arcs in the proof, but it is trivial to rewrite it in terms of simple graphs by adding an artificial identity element to $\mathcal{SAT}$ and substituting every parallel arc with a two-hop path with one of the arcs having the identity element as weight. Note also that the NP-hard constrained shortest path problem ($\mathcal{CS}$), which is also in $\mathbb{C} \cap \mathbb{SND}$, [6] can also be posed as a path selection problem over a special algebra.

Our results indicate that each of the algebraic regimes $\mathbb{ND}$ (and $\mathbb{SND}$), $\mathbb{C}$, and $\mathbb{M}$ contain algebras with intractable path selection instances. Even the restrictions $\mathbb{SND} \cap \mathbb{C}$ and $\mathbb{M} \cap \mathbb{C}$ are unsafe from a practical standpoint, in that the related path selection problem might easily end up being prohibitive to solve in practice. This means that designing future routing policies requires extreme care [13].

As a corollary, we state the following.

Corollary 2. *If for a routing policy the preferred path computation problem over cannot be solved by the Dijkstra algorithm, then the existence of a polynomial time algorithm is not guaranteed.*

Table 1. Algebraic properties and computational complexity (of the preferred path selection problem) for some routing policies

Algebra	Notation/Definition	Properties	$f_\mathcal{A}(n)$	Complexity
Shortest path	$\mathcal{S} = (\mathbb{N}, \infty, +, \leq)$	ND, M, C, SND	–	Polynomial
Widest path	$\mathcal{W} = (\mathbb{N}, 0, \min, \geq)$	ND, M, C, PF, SND	n	Polynomial
Most reliable path	$\mathcal{R} = ((0,1], 0, *, \geq)$	ND, M, C, SND	–	Polynomial
Usable path	$\mathcal{U} = (\{0,1\}, 0, *, \geq)$	ND, M, C, PF, SND	2	Polynomial
Widest-shortest path	$WS = \mathcal{S} \times \mathcal{W}$	ND, M, C, SND	–	Polynomial
Shortest-widest path	$SW = \mathcal{W} \times \mathcal{S}$	ND, C, SND	–	Polynomial
SAT	$\mathcal{S}\mathcal{A}\mathcal{T}$	ND,C, SND	$2^{3n} + 1$	NP-complete
Constrained shortest path	CS	C	–	NP-complete
Longest path	$\mathcal{L} = (\mathbb{N}, \infty, +, \geq)$	M, C	–	NP-complete
Valley-free routing	$\mathcal{V}\mathcal{F}$	ND, PF, SND	6	Polynomial
Proxy	$\mathcal{X}$	ND,PF	–	Polynomial
Static Service-chaining	$\mathcal{S}\mathcal{C}$	PF	$n(n-1)/2$	Polynomial
Fixed Service-chaining	$\mathcal{F}_k$	PF, C	$k + 2$	Polynomial

6 Discussion

The implications of our results are summarized in Table 1, and Fig. 1 provides a comprehensive computational complexity classification. Here, $\mathcal{S}\mathcal{A}\mathcal{T}$ is defined as above, and $\mathcal{S}$, WS, $\mathcal{R}$, $\mathcal{U}$, and $\mathcal{W}$ are from the literature [14]. As the latter five are ND and M, the corresponding path-selection problems are polynomially tractable by Proposition 2.

An important example for a policy for which the generalized Dijkstra algorithm is not correct is valley-free routing, used extensively in the Internet inter-domain routing system [4]. Here, links are labeled according to the business relationship they represent as either *provider* (p), *customer* (c), or *peer* (r), and a preferred "valley-free" path is one that does not contain "economically unreasonable" portions (i.e., cp, cr, rp, or rr sub-paths). This is described by the algebra $\mathcal{V}\mathcal{F} = (W, \oplus, \preceq)$ (adopted from [4]), where $W = \{0, c, r, p, prc, \infty\}$ (prc is introduced to maintain associativity), $\oplus$ is defined by the Cayley table below, and the precedence is $0 \preceq c \preceq r \preceq p \preceq prc \preceq \infty$. Note that $\mathcal{V}\mathcal{F}$ is not M nor C, but it is PF so Algorithm 1 warrants the availability of a tractable path selection algorithm.

We wish to point out that the difference between ND and SND is, although subtle, not arbitrary. It is often the case in inter-domain routing, for instance, that some entity c rejects any packet received directly from a unless it has also been proxied through a third-party, say, b. In practice, such policy considerations are realized in the control plane, encoded by sophisticated BGP route filtering rules and BGP communities. The corresponding proxy algebra is $\mathcal{X} = (\{a, b, c\}, \oplus, \preceq)$, where $\oplus$ is the usual concatenation operator with the restriction that $a \oplus c = \infty$ and $\preceq$ is essentially arbitrary[3]. Then, $\mathcal{X}$ is ND but not SND, as $a \oplus b \oplus c \prec \infty = a \oplus c$, and hence solving $P_{\mathcal{X}}$ is far from trivial. However, it easy to convert $\mathcal{X}$ to PF, so again Algorithm 1 warrants polynomial tractability.

To demonstrate how new architectures bring up exotic new routing algebras, consider a simple service chaining example [10]. Here there are three functions, network address translation (n), deep packet inspection (d) and an virus scanning (v), and each flow must pass through each function exactly once and exactly in the order n, d, v. The corresponding algebra is $\mathcal{SC} = (\{0, n, d, v, nd, dv, ndv, \infty\},$ $\oplus, \preceq)$, where $\oplus$ is as

⊕	0	c	r	p	prc	∞
0	0	c	r	p	prc	∞
c	c	c	∞	∞	∞	∞
r	r	prc	∞	∞	∞	∞
p	p	prc	prc	p	prc	∞
prc	prc	prc	∞	∞	∞	∞
∞	∞	∞	∞	∞	∞	∞

⊕	0	n	d	v	nd	dv	ndv	∞
0	0	n	d	v	nd	dv	ndv	∞
n	n	∞	nd	∞	∞	ndv	∞	∞
d	d	∞	∞	dv	∞	∞	∞	∞
v	v	∞	∞	∞	∞	∞	∞	∞
nd	nd	∞	∞	ndv	∞	∞	∞	∞
dv	dv	∞	∞	∞	∞	∞	∞	∞
ndv	ndv	∞	∞	∞	∞	∞	∞	∞
∞	∞	∞	∞	∞	∞	∞	∞	∞

$\mathcal{SC}$ is not ND as $n \oplus d \oplus v \prec n \oplus d$, but it is PF so Algorithm 1 again gives a polynomial time complexity characterization.

In many upcoming service chaining deployments, the exact function realized by a particular middlebox is not fixed but instead freely configurable by the network operator or an SDN controller [9]. For instance, a service point may realize network address translation or deep packet inspection (but not both) at different points in time, and switching between the two can be done by downloading the adequate rules to the middlebox. In this dynamic service chaining architecture, the preferred-path computation problem $P_{\mathcal{A}}(G, s, t)$ involves both deciding which particular functionality to realize at a particular service point in G *and* to actually compute the preferred path itself between s and t. Thinking of the previous service chaining example, middleboxes are now wild cards, capable to realize network address translation (n), deep packet inspection (d), or virus scanning (v), and our task is to find route, from s to t, *through exactly* 3 *middleboxes*. Once we have the route, we can switch the traversed middleboxes to the required functionality.

This scenario perhaps best demonstrates how careful one must be when defining new routing policies. First, assume that the number of service points k a packet must traverse is not restricted. In this case, in an n node network we can easily require the packet to pass through exactly $n - 2$ service points, and hence our path selection problem boils down to a Hamiltonian path problem, a famous NP-hard problem. Or, if we require the packet to visit *at least* k middleboxes we arrive to the longest path problem $\mathcal{L}$. If, in addition, it is also a requirement to minimize the cost (or maximize the bandwidth) of the path, then the resultant

---

[3] Note that in our model link weights are assigned to links and not to nodes as would be needed in this and the subsequent scenarios, but it is easy to convert between the two cases.

algebra is equivalent to $\mathcal{L} \times \mathcal{S}$ ($\mathcal{L} \times \mathcal{W}$, resp.), problems that seem even more difficult.

Based on these considerations, it is plausible to impose a strict upper bound on the number of services a packet is required to visit. Let this bound be k. The difference from the above setting is that now k is a fixed constant and it is not allowed to vary with the input, and hence the above simple reductions to NP-hard problems, where k is part of the input, do not apply. Suppose now that the task is to route a packet through at most k middleboxes[4]. Then, we arrive to the algebra $\mathcal{F}_k = (W, \oplus, \preceq)$, where $W = [0, k] \cup \infty$ and

$$a \oplus b = \begin{cases} a + b & \text{if } a + b \leq k \\ \infty & \text{otherwise} \end{cases}$$

$$\infty \oplus a = a \oplus \infty = \infty .$$

The ordering is $k \preceq k - 1 \preceq \ldots 1 \preceq 0$. Easily, $\mathcal{F}_k$ is $\mathbb{C}$, and since it is also $\mathbb{PF}$ the path selection problem in this case can be solved with Algorithm 1. Moreover, the related lexicographic products $\mathcal{F}_k \times \mathcal{S}$ and $\mathcal{F}_k \times \mathcal{W}$ can also be solved in polynomial time.

Finally, we note that there are some practically important routing policies which fall outside our characterization. For instance, $\mathcal{SW}$ is not $\mathbb{M}$ therefore the Dijkstra algorithm does not work, neither it is $\mathbb{PF}$ so Algorithm 1 does apply either. For this particular case a special algorithm guarantees polynomial time path selection [16], but further extending the algebraic classification presented in this paper to the general case (if at all possible) is currently an open problem.

7   Conclusion

Routing theory is often counted as a "cold" research area [3], suggesting that we can sit back and relax knowing that the major questions that can be raised in connection with routing are more or less well answered. However, it turns our that the latest developments concerning the core philisophy of networking (data centers, SDN, service chaining, etc.) pose considerable challenge for today's routing theory. We have shown that new routing policies are emerging at the near horizon, which may for instance embrace routing loops to facilitate meeting strict policy considerations, whereas in today's routing theory loops count as heresy.

The main message of this paper is to point out that there is still much to do out there and it is time to rehash routing theory to cope with the upcoming challenges. We have taken the first steps towards realizing this ambitious goal. We have extended the algebraic policy routing theory with a sufficient and necessary characterization for the preferred-walk and preferred-path selection problems to be both solvable with the same output and we have provided a comprehensive classification of routing policies based on the computational complexity of

---

[4] The settings when we require the packet to meat *at least* k middleboxes or *exactly* k middleboxes are handled similarly.

the corresponding path selection problem. Our findings indicate that defining routing policies in these upcoming routing architectures requires extreme forethought [13], as seemingly simple routing policies, even as simple as commutative, non-decreasing, and monotone ones, can easily give rise to intractable routing problems.

Acknowledgments. Gábor Rétvári was supported by the OTKA/PD-104939 grant. This work was partially supported by the European Union and the European Social Fund through project FuturICT.hu (grant no.: TAMOP-4.2.2.C-11/1/KONV-2012-0013) and the High Speed Networks Laboratory.

References

1. Apostolopoulos, G., Guerin, R., Kamat, S., Tripathi, S.K.: Quality of service based routing: a performance perspective. In: SIGCOMM, pp. 17–28 (1998)
2. Caesar, M., Rexford, J.: BGP routing policies in ISP networks. Technical report UCB/CSD-05-1377, EECS Department, University of California, Berkeley (2005)
3. Crowcroft, J.: Cold topics in networking. SIGCOMM Comput. Commun. Rev. **38**(1), 45–47 (2008)
4. Griffin, T., Sobrinho, J.: Metarouting. In: SIGCOMM '05, pp. 1–12 (2005)
5. Gurney, A., Griffin, T.: Lexicographic products in metarouting. In: IEEE International Conference on Network Protocols, pp. 113–122 (2007)
6. Handler, G.Y., Zang, I.: A dual algorithm for the constrained shortest path problem. Networks **10**(4), 293–309 (1980)
7. Lothaire, M.: Combinatorics on Words. Cambridge Mathematical Library, Cambridge (1997)
8. Ma, Q., Steenkiste, P.: On path selection for traffic with bandwidth guarantees. In: Proceedings of the 1997 International Conference on Network Protocols (ICNP '97), p. 191 (1997)
9. Qazi, Z.A., Tu, C.C., Chiang, L., Miao, R., Sekar, V., Yu, M.: SIMPLE-fying middlebox policy enforcement using SDN. In: Proceedings of the ACM SIGCOMM 2013 Conference on SIGCOMM, SIGCOMM '13, pp. 27–38 (2013)
10. Quinn, P.: Network service chaining problem statement. Internet draft (2013)
11. Rétvári, G., Gulyás, A., Heszberger, Z., Csernai, M., Bíró, J.J.: Compact policy routing. In: Proceedings of the 30th Annual ACM SIGACT-SIGOPS Symposium on Principles of Distributed Computing, PODC '11, pp. 149–158 (2011)
12. Sedgewick, R., Wayne, K.: Algorithms. Pearson Education (2011). http://books.google.hu/books?id=idUdqdDXqnAC
13. Seehra, A., Naous, J., Walfish, M., Mazieres, D., Nicolosi, A., Shenker, S.: A policy framework for the future Internet. In: HotNets-VIII (2009)
14. Sobrinho, J.: Algebra and algorithms for QoS path computation and hop-by-hop routing in the Internet. IEEE/ACM Trans. Netw. **10**, 541–550 (2002)
15. Sobrinho, J.: Network routing with path vector protocols: theory and applications. In: SIGCOMM '03, pp. 49–60 (2003)
16. Wang, Z., Crowcroft, J.: Quality-of-service routing for supporting multimedia applications. IEEE J. Sel. A. Commun. **14**(7), 1228–1234 (2006)
17. Younis, O., Fahmy, S.: Constraint-based routing in the internet: basic principles and recent research. IEEE Commun. Surv. Tutorials **5**(1), 2–13 (2003)

Detection of DNS Traffic Anomalies in Large Networks

Milan Čermák[✉], Pavel Čeleda, and Jan Vykopal

Institute of Computer Science, Masaryk University, Brno, Czech Republic
{cermak,celeda,vykopal}@ics.muni.cz

Abstract. Almost every Internet communication is preceded by a translation of a DNS name to an IP address. Therefore monitoring of DNS traffic can effectively extend capabilities of current methods for network traffic anomaly detection. In order to effectively monitor this traffic, we propose a new flow metering algorithm that saves resources of a flow exporter. Next, to show benefits of the DNS traffic monitoring for anomaly detection, we introduce novel detection methods using DNS extended flows. The evaluation of these methods shows that our approach not only reveals DNS anomalies but also scales well in a campus network.

Keywords: Domain name system · DNS · IP flow monitoring · IPFIX · Traffic anomaly detection · Internet measurements

1 Introduction

The Domain Name System (DNS) provides fundamental functions in directing Internet traffic today. Despite the fact that DNS concepts (RFC 1034, RFC 1035) are more than three decades old, DNS remains of the utmost importance for recent network technologies. Due to the wide use of DNS we can detect not only attacks based on DNS protocol security flaws but also other attacks reflected in the DNS traffic. Since the Internet has no borders, cyber-attacks which rely on DNS or are reflected in DNS traffic may come from anywhere and at any time.

Our research is mainly motivated by valuable information carried by a DNS protocol; there is high potential to use this information for network security monitoring. In order to successfully use DNS information, it is important to find out effective ways how to gather DNS data from monitored networks. In this paper, we attempt to answer the following research questions: (i) How can DNS traffic be effectively analysed in large networks? (ii) What are the differences in the analysis of DNS traffic using standard and extended flow records? (iii) What are the advantages of combining DNS traffic information with flow records for network anomaly detection?

The contribution of our work is twofold: (i) We proposed and evaluated new algorithm to process flows with DNS information that can significantly reduce the number of DNS flow cache entries in current flow exporters. (ii) We

© Springer International Publishing Switzerland 2014
Y. Kermarrec (Ed.): EUNICE 2014, LNCS 8846, pp. 215–226, 2014.
DOI: 10.1007/978-3-319-13488-8_20

introduced novel anomaly detection methods which use extended DNS flows to enhance the detection of network threats.

The paper is organized in five sections. Section 2 describes related work. Section 3 contains a description of approaches used for flow-based DNS traffic monitoring in large networks. Section 4 proposes new DNS traffic anomaly detection methods using standard and extended flows. Finally, Sect. 5 concludes the paper.

2   Related Work

To detect DNS traffic anomalies, it is important to determine where and how the data are gathered. A query logging on DNS servers represents the simplest way how to monitor DNS traffic without additional monitoring infrastructure. The analysis of server logs was presented in [2,16] including the optimization of this process for a large amount of logs. The main disadvantage of this approach is its inability to monitor traffic that does not pass through the monitored servers. To avoid this problem it is necessary to use network-based monitoring approaches [3,11,20] with probes installed in the network.

Methods for analysing DNS traffic collected from networks differ from the purpose of this analysis. One of these purposes is the collection of domain characteristics and their history. This information may be used for reverse lookups with IP addresses for which no reverse DNS records exists [18], for malicious domains detection [1,3,13,20] based on time-based features, answer-based features, or abnormal TTL values. The disadvantage of this approach for large network monitoring is its focus only on domains and not for the whole DNS traffic.

Network traffic statistics may be used to get general information about a DNS network's behaviour. These statistics can be created by tools such as dnstop [19], dnsgraph [14], or DSCng [9] which aggregates DNS data from packets and represents them as tables or charts. With these statistics, it is possible to detect misconfigured network devices or anomalies in traffic volume but the main drawback is the focus on the whole network and the inability to analyse the DNS traffic of one specific device or domain.

To analyse behaviour of specific device, flow-based approach could be used. Although flow records provide limited information about DNS traffic, some of the DNS anomalies can be still detected. For example, [5] suggests a method for DNS tunnelling detection using statistic tests or [7] presents the detection of cache poisoning attacks.

To obtain more specific information about DNS traffic it is necessary to store all important DNS packet fields such as source and destination addresses, queried domain name, or response data. This approach is used by [4,10,11] for the detection of botnets based on the same DNS behaviour of devices, abnormal DNS traffic or malicious domain usage. This type of data can be also used for an intrusion detection system based on DNS traffic monitoring which was introduced in [15]. The drawback of monitoring only DNS traffic is that we have no information about the other network communication of a device such as information about visiting the queried domain.

Another approach to detection is an analysis and correlation of DNS traffic with other network data. This approach transforms captured packets and whole traffic into events which are then processed by network anomaly detection methods. Such methods may be implemented, for instance, using The Bro Network Security Monitor [12].

3 Flow-Based DNS Traffic Monitoring

3.1 Standard Flow Monitoring

There are two basic requirements for monitoring large and high-speed networks such as campuses or ISPs. First, monitoring tools must provide near real-time data analysis and, second, the tools must not demand large storage space. To fulfil these requirements, the concept of *network flow* is used. A flow is defined in RFC 7011 as "a set of IP packets passing an observation point in the network during a certain time interval, such that all packets belonging to a particular flow have a set of common properties". The standard flow record is a vector:

$$F = (IP_{src},\ IP_{dst},\ P_{src},\ P_{dst},\ Prot,\ T_{start},\ T_{dur},\ Pckts,\ Octs,\ Flags),$$

where the flow is defined by the source and destination IP addresses IP_{src} and IP_{dst}, source and destination ports P_{src} and P_{dst}, protocol $Prot$ and the start time T_{start} with duration T_{dur}. The fields $Pckts$ and $Octs$ represent the number of transferred packets and octets, and $Flags$ TCP flags.

The flow exporter aggregates packets with common properties into one flow until the flow is terminated. This termination can be caused by the expiration of flow cache entry (active time-out, idle time-out or resource constraints), natural expiration based on packet flags indicating connection end, emergency expiration or cache flush [6]. In networks with a large volume of traffic, it is necessary to have sufficiently large and free flow cache to avoid emergency expiration or cache flush, which may cause unwanted flow records split.

Flow acquisition can be done by common network devices that support flow record export, such as routers, or by specialized network probes [6] which provides greater data accuracy and are able to effectively process a large volume of traffic. Figure 1 depicts a monitored network with the probes installed at the local network uplink and also inside the network. The probe aggregates packets and export them as flow records to the flow collector that provides tools for basic flow processing and analysis.

Although flow records do not contain information about application protocols, it is still possible to use them for monitoring DNS traffic. A DNS flow can be distinguished from others by port-based protocol identification that relies on the fact that the TCP and UDP port number 53 is assigned to the DNS protocol by IANA. This port number is by default used by DNS resolvers which listen to this port. DNS monitoring using standard flow records can reveal anomalies

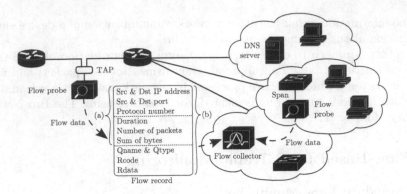

Fig. 1. Flow monitoring architecture with probes exporting (a) standard flow and (b) extended DNS flow record.

that affect the volume characteristics of transferred data. However, anomalies connected to DNS application data remain undetected. Another disadvantage is that the port 53 can also be used by other applications or protocols which may cause false positives. But this traffic usually forms only a small portion of the whole network traffic on this port.

3.2 Flows Extended by Information from a DNS Traffic

To answer the question *how can DNS traffic be effectively analysed in a large networks?*; we performed several measurements in the campus network of Masaryk University and in the Czech national research and education network, CESNET, which connects 27 Czech universities.

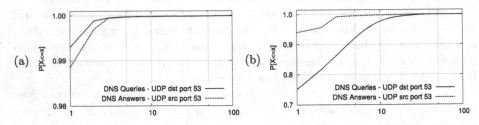

Fig. 2. CDF of DNS packets per flow observed in (a) the network of Masaryk University and (b) the Czech national research and education network, CESNET.

At first, we examined whether the flow monitoring concept is suitable for DNS traffic. Figure 2 shows the cumulative distribution function (CDF) of packets per flows which were collected in both networks over one day. Figure 2a shows that approximately 99 % of flows with the source or destination port 53 contain only one packet. This indicates that aggregation is not used. The rest of the flows carry DNS zone files, DNS tunnelling or other protocols. Through manual packet analysis, we found that one of these protocols is the BitTorrent protocol which exploits fact, that the traffic of port 53 is not restricted by network firewalls. To verify our results, we compute the same statistics depicted in Fig. 2b for CESNET. This network is primarily a transport network, therefore the traffic associated with port 53 contains a greater portion of other protocols than DNS. We also observed that a large amount of flows containing more than one packet with the destination port 53 are caused by attempted DNS amplification attacks which were performed almost constantly. To sum up, we observed that a typical DNS conversation consists of one packet carrying the DNS query and one packet carrying the DNS response.

Since the both DNS query and response are each represented by one flow record, it is possible to extend the standard flow record by DNS application data, such as queried domain name and type. This information does not disrupt the flow record and also does not excessively increase the flow record size. As a result, we could analyse DNS traffic together with other flows that can reveal traffic anomalies which otherwise would only have been detectable by deep packet inspection.

We identified that only four DNS packet fields are useful for most of the DNS traffic analysing methods: queried domain name $Qname$, queried record type $Qtype$, response return code $Rcode$ and response itself $Rdata$. The others may unnecessarily increase the size of the flow record. Therefore, a DNS flow record contains the selected four fields:

$$F_{DNS} = (Qname,\ Qtype,\ Rcode,\ Rdata)$$

Because the DNS response may contain more than one answer, we recommend storing only the first answer with the same record type as a query or authoritative nameserver. For instance, in the event of a DNS query for the A record type, the flow record with DNS response will contain the address of the queried domain in the $Rdata$ field.

3.3   Flow Cache Optimization Using DNS Extended Flows

For efficient flow-based DNS traffic monitoring, we modified the standard algorithm of flow metering and export to fit the characteristics of DNS traffic. The flow cache plays a vital role in flow monitoring, but the performance of current implementations is constrained by its limited size. The translation of domain name precedes most of the network connections so we believe that DNS traffic represents a significant part of all collected flows. Storing DNS flow records in the flow cache leads to its rapid exhaustion in a very short time so we propose a modified algorithm that saves storage space in the flow cache by exporting extended DNS flow records immediately after the packet is parsed.

The algorithm checks if the packet is coming to/from the port 53 and protocol UDP. If these conditions are fulfilled, it is necessary to decide if the packet really carries a DNS payload which could be distinguished by DNS header analysis. If the packet carries a DNS payload then F_{DNS} is obtained and concatenated with a standard flow record F generated at the beginning of the algorithm.

The resulting flow $F_{ext} = F \cdot F_{DNS}$ is immediately exported as an extended DNS flow record to the collector. Otherwise, the standard flow records are stored in the flow cache.

In order to investigate the impact of the algorithm, we measured, in the network of Masaryk University and CESNET, the portion of flows using port 53 in the whole traffic. We observed that approximately 20 % and 15 % of all flows are flows possibly containing DNS traffic. In the proposed algorithm the DNS flows are not stored in the flow cache, so the algorithm saves up to 20 % of cache storage space. It can significantly help to prevent forced cache flush which causes that flow records which were originally split are now in an one record. Another advantage is that the flows extended by DNS data can be analysed in real-time because there is no need to wait for exporting timeouts. This means it is possible to detect some suspicious DNS traffic at the beginning and prevent potential damage.

4   DNS Traffic Anomaly Detection

In this section, we present several methods for the detection of DNS traffic anomalies. We first briefly discuss detection based on standard flows and then provide more details about novel methods which employ DNS extended flows. The methods were implemented as Perl scripts for an IPFIX collector and are available at [17]. In our implementation was used DNS flow data acquired by [8].

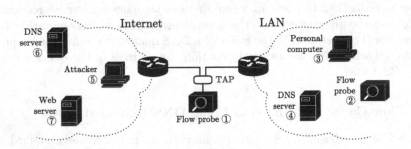

Fig. 3. General network schema with device roles.

For a clear description of the proposed methods we will refer to Fig. 3 which represents the general schema of our monitoring architecture, including the roles of individual devices.

4.1   Anomaly Detection Using Standard Flows

Although standard flow records do not contain DNS application data, it is still possible to detect some attacks targeting DNS infrastructure. The DNS amplification DDoS attack represents one of the most used network attacks involving DNS infrastructure. This attack is characterised by a large amount of same queries with spoofed IP address coming from attacker ⑤ passing to a rogue open DNS resolver. This open resolver is a misconfigured DNS server ④ or device infected by malware ③ that acts as a rogue DNS resolver. It responds to all queries by an abnormally large packet payload that contains answers. Thus, an increasing count of flows, with high bytes-per-packet ratio and the source port 53, may indicate this type of attack.

In well-maintained networks, we can use detection techniques based on access control lists reflecting network security policy. Based on this knowledge, it is possible to use flow-based methods which report every communication from or to a DNS server out of the list. This communication may be caused by a malware-infected device ③ which operates as a rogue DNS resolver. Another example is a malicious change of device settings which causes a local DNS resolver ④ to be replaced by another ⑤ which returns incorrect answers referring to fraudulent websites.

Since flows identified only by the usage of port 53 may contain different application data than DNS, it is necessary to specify a threshold indicating when suspicious traffic could be identified as anomaly to avoid false positives. This may cause stealth DNS amplification DDoS attacks to not be detected. In Masaryk university's network we observed 8 examples of this kind of attack during three months of testing. Detection using standard flows is difficult in large and not well-maintained networks where it is hard to distinguish DNS servers from clients. In such networks, the DNS server may be incorrectly identified as open DNS resolver even if the server only correctly responds to the DNS query that contains the local domain.

4.2   Anomaly Detection Using Extended Flows

Flow records extended by DNS information can be analysed as standard flows using basic Top-N statistics of the entire local network or individual hosts. Statistics related to DNS traffic may include queried record types, return codes or, for example, most queried domain names. Any major change in these statistics may indicate abnormal behaviour. For instance, an increasing number of DNS error return codes can be caused by malfunctioning devices, or a large number of MX record queries not originating from a local e-mail server can even indicate malware-infected device that attempts to send spam.

The main advantage of using extended flow records for DNS monitoring is that these data can be analysed together with other flow records. We can search the corresponding communication in standard flows based on a returned IP address in a DNS response and confirm the visitation of a queried domain.

The combination of DNS extended flows with standard flows can be also used for tracing the originator of a query even though the DNS flow exporter ① is used only at the network edge, i.e. all DNS queries have the same source address. It is possible to use DNS responses containing the IP address of a queried domain and check if a device started communication with this address. It is very likely that it is the same device which performed the query. The disadvantage of the presented method is that device must visit the queried domain, otherwise, it is still impossible to trace the originator of the query.

Using DNS extended flows does not enable only detection of a visit to the queried domain or trace the device performing a query. DNS extended flows also enable detection of advanced network attacks and anomalies which are hardly, or not, detectable by standard flows. To show advanced examples and the *advantages of combination DNS traffic information with flow records for network anomaly detection*, we proposed several novel detection methods focusing on open resolvers, non-local DNS resolver usage, or malware domains queries. These methods are independent of the version of the IP protocol and thus it is possible to deploy them easy in IPv6 networks.

Method 1: Open DNS Resolvers Detection

Amplification DDoS attacks using open DNS resolvers are currently widely used by attackers because they can generate small packets and easily make a service inaccessible. The detection of this attack using standard flow requires a high threshold to avoid false positives. We are able to reduce the threshold by detecting the same queried domains using DNS extended flows but a threshold is still required.

The detection of an open DNS resolver can be easily done in small and documented networks by observing traffic of recognised DNS servers. In large or not well-maintained networks a list of recognised DNS servers may not exist. For this purpose, we propose a new detection method based on DNS extended flows. The method is described in the Algorithm 1. The main challenge is to distinguish an open DNS resolver ③ from a regular DNS server ④ which responds to a query containing a local domain. For this purpose, the method analyses all DNS responses observed at the network edge ① and checks if the domain is assigned to the monitored network. This check is done by requesting the local DNS resolver ④ for ANY record type of this domain. If the result does not contain at least one record with an IP address from the monitored network then the DNS server is reported as an open DNS resolver, otherwise the domain is added to the local domains list.

The advantage of the presented method is that we are able to detect an open DNS resolver by observing only one response. Over three months of testing in the campus network of Masaryk university, we observed 207 IP addresses operating as open DNS resolvers. In the same period, the Open Resolver Scanning Project[1] reported 76 addresses for this network. The different amount of addresses is caused by the fact that Open Resolver Scanning Project performs scans only once per day. An interesting side effect of the method is that we discovered all domains that are hosted in the campus network.

---

[1] https://dnsscan.shadowserver.org/.

Algorithm 1. *Open DNS Resolver Detection*

1: **function** GETOPENDNSRESOLVER (W : local domains, L : local network, F_{ext} : analysed flows)
2: **end function**
3: $F_{responses} = \{F_{ext} \mid F_{ext}.IP_{src} = L \wedge F_{ext}.IP_{dst} \neq L \wedge F_{ext}.P_{src} = 53 \wedge F_{ext}.P_{dst} \neq 53 \wedge$
$\qquad F_{ext}.Qname \neq W_1 \wedge \cdots \wedge F_{ext}.Qname \neq W_n \wedge F_{ext}.Rcode = 0\}$;
4: aggregate $F_{responses}$ by IP_{src} and $Qname$ to $F_{resolvers}$;
5: **for each** $F_{resolver}$ in $F_{resolvers}$ **do**
6:     request all information about domain $F_{resolver}.Qname$ by ANY query type;
7:     **if** domain information contain IP address from L **then**
8:         add $F_{resolver}.Qname$ to W ;
9:     **else**
10:         **return** "$F_{resolver}.IP_{src}$ is open DNS resolver" ;
11:     **end if**
12: **end for**

Method 2: External DNS Resolver Usage Detection

The use of an external DNS resolver ⑥ instead of the local network DNS resolver ④ may cause delay and also presents a security risk if the external DNS resolver responds with fraudulent IP addresses. In large, not well-maintained networks, it is necessary to distinguish between a client device ③ and a local DNS resolver ④, which tries to resolve a queried domain. The proposed Algorithm 2 utilizes the fact that the DNS resolver performs only queries and the client visits the queried domain. The visit is checked by finding standard flows with communication between the client and the queried domain ⑦, which starts within approximately two seconds of the query. If the client did not visit first N selected domains then it is marked as a possible DNS server.

Algorithm 2. *External Resolver Usage Detection*

1: **function** GETCLIENTSUSINGEXTERNALDNS (N : number of checked domains, L : local network,
$\qquad F_{ext}$: analysed flows)
2: **end function**
3: $F_{responses} = \{F_{ext} \mid F_{ext}.IP_{src} \neq L \wedge F_{ext}.IP_{dst} = L \wedge F_{ext}.P_{src} = 53 \wedge F_{ext}.P_{dst} \neq 53 \wedge$
$\qquad F_{ext}.Rcode = 0 \wedge (F_{ext}.Qtype = A \vee F_{ext}.Qtype = AAAA)\}$;
4: sort $F_{responses}$ by IP_{dst} to $F_{responses_{sorted}}$;
5: **for each** $F_{response}$ in $F_{responses_{sorted}}$ **do**
6:     $F_{com} = \{F_{response} \mid F_{ext}.IP_{src} = F_{response}.IP_{dst} \wedge F_{ext}.IP_{dst} = F_{response}.Rdata \wedge$
$\qquad F_{ext}.T_{start} \geq F_{response}.T_{start} \wedge F_{ext}.T_{start} \leq (F_{response}.T_{start} + 2 \ sec)\}$
    ;
7:     **if** number of flows F_{com} ¿ 0 **then**
8:         **return** "$F_{response}.IP_{dst}$ uses external resolver $F_{response}.IP_{src}$" ;
9:     **end if**
10:     **if** $F_{response}.IP_{dst}$ was seen N times **then**
11:         go to the next $F_{response}.IP_{dst}$;
12:     **end if**
13: **end for**

During the evaluation of the method in Masaryk university's network, we found that the most used DNS resolvers are public DNS resolvers operated by Google or OpenDNS. The rest were DNS resolvers of local network providers or antivirus solutions, which offer DNS resolvers as a part of user protection. We also found several malicious DNS resolvers which returned forged IP addresses of popular web pages.

Method 3: Malware Domains Query Detection

The detection of malware domains is one of the most used detection techniques based on information from DNS traffic. The detection is based on testing whether the queried domain is contained in a blacklist of known malware domains. Such inspection may be very time consuming in networks with a large amount of traffic. For these type of networks, we suggest shrinking number of checked domains only to domains queried after a device starts up. We suppose that most malware is launched automatically at the device start and attempt to immediately contact its command and control centres or download more malware.

Algorithm 3. *Malware Domains Queries Detection*

1: **function** GETMALWAREAFFECTEDDEVICES (N : number of checked domains, F_{ext} : analysed flows)
2: **end function**
3: $F_{queries} = \{F_{ext} \mid F_{ext}.P_{src} \neq 53 \wedge F_{ext}.P_{dst} = 53 \wedge F_{ext}.Qname = dns.msftncsi.com \wedge$
      $(F_{ext}.Qtype = $ A $\vee F_{ext}.Qtype = $ AAAA$)\}$;
4: aggregate $F_{queries}$ by IP_{src} to F_{starts} ;
5: **for each** F_{start} in F_{starts} **do**
6:      $F_{domains} = \{F_{start} \mid F_{ext}.IP_{src} = F_{start}.IP_{src} \wedge F_{ext}.P_{src} \neq 53 \wedge F_{ext}.P_{dst} = 53 \wedge$
         $F_{ext}.T_{start} \geq F_{start}.T_{start} \wedge F_{ext}.T_{start} \leq (F_{ext}.T_{start} + 5 \; minutes) \wedge$
         $F_{ext}.Qname \neq *windowsupdate.com \wedge F_{ext}.Qname \neq *msftncsi.com \wedge$
         $F_{ext}.Qname \neq *microsoft.com$;
7:      select first N queried domains D from $F_{domains}$;
8:      **for all** queried domains D **do**
9:          exclude $D.Qname$ contained in the Alexa top domains list ;
10:         check if domain $D.Qname$ is reported as malware domain ;
11:         **if** $D.Qname$ is marked as malware domain **then**
12:             **return** "$F_{start}.IP_{src}$ queried malware domain $D.Qname$" ;
13:         **end if**
14:     **end for**
15: **end for**

The device start can not be easily detected using standard flows, but with the DNS extended flows we discovered that the Windows operating systems ③ immediately query the domain dns.msftncsi.com to check if the configured DNS resolver ④ works. The proposed method of testing domains queried after the device startup is described in the Algorithm 3. To avoid unnecessary checks, we suggest excluding domains which are associated with Microsoft services and also the most used domains from the *Alexa Top Domains List*[2]. The rest of the domains are checked in our implementation whether they are listed on several blacklists by the *VirusTotal*[3] service.

The evaluation of the method showed that the checked domain must occur almost in 4 blacklists used by VirusTotal to avoid false positives because there were several blacklists marked by users, which are unreliable. In our campus network, we detected one device which was reported as infected by malware and also operated as an open DNS resolver.

---

[2] http://www.alexa.com/topsites.
[3] https://www.virustotal.com/#url.

5   Conclusion

We have presented an effective technique for DNS traffic monitoring in large networks based on the extension of standard flows. For these DNS extended flows we introduced examples of new anomaly detection techniques able to detect anomalies that were previously hard to detect using standard flows. To conclude our paper, we shall now summarize our research questions and answers to them.

As an answer to the research question *how can DNS traffic be effectively analysed in a large networks?*, we propose using a flow based monitoring approach. We suggest extending standard flow by four new fields from DNS application data. To gather these data we proposed a new flow exporting algorithm respecting DNS traffic to be able to effectively save space in the flow cache which plays vital role in the flow metering process. Our algorithm enables the analysis of DNS data in real-time in contrast to standard flows.

To show *differences in the analysis of DNS traffic using standard and extended flow records*, which was our second research question, we introduced novel methods of DNS traffic anomaly detection using standard and DNS extended flows. The methods using standard flows are limited by the port identification and allows only the analysis of basic flow characteristics. On the other hand, DNS extended flows enable us to clearly identify DNS traffic and use DNS application data as a basis for detections.

The DNS extended flows can be analysed together with standard flows which allows us to make detection methods more accurate. To demonstrate the *advantages of combining DNS traffic information with flow records for network anomaly detection*, we introduced new detection methods utilizing the fact that DNS query can be combined with flows containing communication with queried domains. Thus, it is, for example, possible to check if a device really visited the queried domain.

The presented paper shows that DNS extended flows are a suitable extension of standard flows that may help in the detection of network traffic anomalies. In future work, we plan to use DNS extended flows for detecting other DNS traffic anomalies such as DNS tunnelling, or for advanced malware infected devices detection. We also plan to examine drawbacks and potential backdoors of proposed methods and provide appropriate solutions to them.

Acknowledgments. This material is based upon work supported by Cybernetic Proving Ground project (VG20132015103) funded by the Ministry of the Interior of the Czech Republic.

References

1. Antonakakis, M., Perdisci, R., Dagon, D., Lee, W., Feamster, N.: Building a dynamic reputation system for DNS. In: USENIX Security Symposium, pp. 273–290 (2010)
2. Begleiter, R., Elovici, Y., Hollander, Y., Mendelson, O., Rokach, L., Saltzman, R.: A fast and scalable method for threat detection in large-scale DNS logs. In: 2013 IEEE International Conference on Big Data, pp. 738–741 (Oct 2013)

3. Bilge, L., Sen, S., Balzarotti, D., Kirda, E., Kruegel, C.: Exposure: a passive DNS analysis service to detect and report malicious domains. ACM Trans. Inf. Syst. Secur. **16**(4), 14:1–14:28 (2014). http://doi.acm.org/10.1145/2584679

4. Choi, H., Lee, H.: Identifying botnets by capturing group activities in dns traffic. Comput. Netw. **56**(1), 20–33 (2012)

5. Ellens, W., Żuraniewski, P., Sperotto, A., Schotanus, H., Mandjes, M., Meeuwissen, E.: Flow-based detection of DNS tunnels. In: Emerging Management Mechanisms for the Future Internet, pp. 124–135. Springer (2013)

6. Hofstede, R., Čeleda, P., Trammell, B., Drago, I., Sadre, R., Sperotto, A., Pras, A.: Flow monitoring explained: from packet capture to data analysis with netFlow and IPFIX. IEEE Communications Surveys & Tutorials (2014). doi:10.1109/COMST. 2014.2321898

7. Karasaridis, A., Meier-Hellstern, K., Hoeflin, D.: Detection of DNS anomalies using flow data analysis. In: Global Telecommunications Conference, 2006. GLOBE-COM'06. IEEE. pp. 1–6. IEEE (2006)

8. Kováčik, M.: DNS plugin (2014). https://www.liberouter.org/technologies/dns-plugin/

9. Košata, B., Čermák, J., Surý, O., Filip, O.: DSCng: DNS server monitoring program (2013). http://www.dscng.cz/

10. Manasrah, A.M., Hasan, A., Abouabdalla, O.A., Ramadass, S.: Detecting botnet activities based on abnormal DNS traffic. Int. J. Comput. Sci. Inf. Secur. **6**(1), 97–104 (2009)

11. Marchal, S., Francois, J., Wagner, C., State, R., Dulaunoy, A., Engel, T., Festor, O.: DNSSM: a large scale passive DNS security monitoring framework. In: Network Operations and Management Symposium (NOMS), 2012 IEEE, pp. 988–993 (Apr 2012)

12. Paxson, V.: Bro: a system for detecting network intruders in real-time. Comput. Netw. **31**(23–24), 2435–2463 (1999)

13. Perdisci, R., Corona, I., Giacinto, G.: Early detection of malicious flux networks via large-scale passive DNS traffic analysis. IEEE Trans. Depend. Secur. Comput. **9**(5), 714–726 (2012)

14. Qu, J., Sztoch, P.: Dnsgraph (2003). http://dnsgraph.sourceforge.net/

15. Schonewille, A., van Helmond, D.J.: The domain name service as an IDS. Research Project for the Master System-and Network Engineering at the University of Amsterdam (2006)

16. Snyder, M., Sundaram, R., Thakur, M.: Preprocessing DNS log data for effective data mining. In: IEEE International Conference on Communications, 2009. ICC '09, pp. 1–5 (June 2009)

17. Čermák, M.: DNSAnomDet (2014). https://is.muni.cz/publication/1131184

18. Weimer, F.: Passive dns replication. In: FIRST Conference on Computer Security Incident (2005)

19. Wessels, D.: Dnstop: Stay on top of your DNS traffic (2013). http://dns.measurement-factory.com/tools/dnstop/

20. Zdrnja, B., Brownlee, N., Wessels, D.: Passive monitoring of DNS anomalies. In: Hämmerli, B.M., Sommer, R. (eds.) DIMVA 2007. LNCS, vol. 4579, pp. 129–139. Springer, Heidelberg (2007)

Author Index

Printed in the United States
By Bookmasters